When the Bullet Hits Your Funny Bone

The Essence of a U.S. Navy SEAL

By Billy Allmon

Twilight Times Books
Kingsport Tennessee

When the Bullet Hits Your Funny Bone: The Essence of a U.S. Navy SEAL

Paladin Timeless Books, an imprint of
Twilight Times Books
P O Box 3340
Kingsport TN 37664
http://twilighttimesbooks.com/

First Edition, January 2012

Library of Congress Control Number: 2011945646

ISBN: 978-1-60619-066-1

Cover art by Damon Shackelford

Printed in the United States of America.

Dedication

To my wife and good friend, Alice: thank you for standing by me for better and for worse, and we both know that I gave you much worse than better.

To my children (two daughters and two sons), throughout all the years of my deployments, trials, and tribulations, though I may not have been there for you, I want you to know that all of you were the source of my strength and greatest joy.

To my brother Norm, I have no words that could ever describe the admiration, loyalty, and love that I feel for both Marilyn and you.

To all the Frogmen and SEALs out there, I thank you. Without your humor, this book would not have been possible, and let me also say, "Thank you all for your unwavering dedication and service to our country."

Preface

Like anyone who is or was in the military, you are always asked what you did in the service. Ask any SEAL (SEAL is an acronym which stands for — Sea, Air, Land — the three elements in which U.S. Navy SEALs are trained to perform their missions) and he will tell you that he was/is a sailor, a medical corpsman, or even a Marine. Most SEALs try to dodge the "I was/am a SEAL" response. Why do most SEALs NOT go around saying, "I am/was a SEAL?" Call it being secretive, carrying a strange sense of guilt, or just being humble (for the most part, it is the latter). Besides, when you think about all the classified missions that SEALs are required to do and have done, why in Gods name would any U.S. Navy SEAL go around telling everyone "I was/am a SEAL, and this is what we did!" However, there is no dodging the question when certain people, who know your background, introduce you, "I want you to meet my friend, he is/was a U.S. Navy SEAL."

I decided to write this book after I had attended a formal party, where I was asked to share a story about an experience that I had in the SEALs. So, I chose a story that I thought would be funny. To my surprise, all the people who were listening to my story thought that my "funny story" was horrifying, and I was the only one laughing about the story.

I was later informed by my gracious host that some people who knew nothing of the SEALs and their sense of humor would never enjoy such "funny stories." I thought to myself, now that was an odd statement to make. It might be true that only SEALs, Special Operations personnel, Police Officers, Firefighters, and emergency personnel will/would understand a SEAL's sense of humor and the feelings of brotherhood toward each other. However, after the urges of my wife, daughter and a few of my friends (as they felt strongly that this "type" of book needed to be written), I thought that I would try to give the average person out there a better understanding of why SEALs use their warped sense of humor on anyone, especially other SEALs, and to try and describe our sense of brotherhood toward each other.

Simply put (and there is nothing simple in the career of a U.S. Navy SEAL), it is because of all the tragedies that SEALs see or experience in their operational careers that a Navy SEAL would much rather seek out ways to laugh and enjoy life, than to sulk or cry. Even so, in reality, there is so much more to it than this "simple" explanation.

I do not personally feel that it is paramount for everyone out there to understand that the men who serve in the U.S. Navy SEAL teams have a unique sense of humor and a deep sense of loyalty to our country, and to other brother SEALs. However, I do feel and for the purposes of this book, and for all the people who are on the "outside" trying to look in, the general public might just think, from all the NEWS reports and from overheard conversations, U.S. Navy SEALs are nothing more than a group of well trained professional killers, and the general public would never know that Navy SEALs have a unique" sense of humor, and they use their unique sense of humor as a defense mechanism to escape all the harsh realities of their chosen profession.

I also feel the general public, who know nothing of the Navy SEALs, may not understand that what SEALs find humorous and the pranks that they play on people to include themselves, when viewed afterward, borders on insanity. Additionally, the general public might be curious as to why SEALs use their humor to make certain tragic events, funny. If one is to try to understand a Navy SEAL's sense of humor, and their sense of brotherhood, then one must try to understand all their shared tragic, horrific sights and actions, which Navy SEALs are exposed to throughout their professional lives, and carry with them for the rest of their lives.

You must also try (if you can) to understand what every U.S. Navy SEAL knows, and that is — Whenever a Navy SEAL goes out on a training mission or into actual combat, there is always the strong possibly for a Navy SEAL to break a bone, lose some bodily appendage, be wounded or get killed. It is because of those reasons that many of the SEALs I know/knew, take/took a lighter approach to the seriousness of their job, and to life in general. Because, after experiencing being shot at by a bunch of bad guys hell bent on trying to kill you, what could be SO bad in your life after that?

Many of the events that I have disclosed within this book took place several years ago, and during those times the Navy SEAL teams were a bit different than they are today, and in general, so were the people within the Navy. Many years ago, we were given lots of autonomy; in large part this was due to the high-risk and secretive nature of our missions. Because every time SEALs went on a combat mission, it was highly probable that a few of them would not be coming back. So we lived life to the fullest, in the event that we were severely wounded, or we did not come back from one of our missions. As anyone who serves on the front lines as a warrior knows, life can be brief.

I make no apologies for the past actions of myself, or for those who perpetrated the somewhat comical events that you are about to read within this book. For everyone's protection (except my own), I have changed all of the names of the perpetrators and victims in this book, to include many of the locations where the events had taken place. The stories that I have written about are true, and I mean NO disrespect to anyone in the SEAL community. In fact, many of the SEALs that were involved in these stories wanted me to use their names, but I felt it better not to, as I know my SEAL brothers very well, and payback for some of the jokes would never end!

The public only sees or hears about the serious side of the Navy SEALs and the results of our violent acts, those who have actually served and are serving in the SEAL teams know our way of life, and our humor. So, I had to say no disrespect intended for all those non-SEALs out there who do not understand a Navy SEAL's sense of humor or the life that we share/shared together. As "they" might think that I am being disrespectful in my writings about you, my brother SEALs, when nothing could be further from the truth.

If you are not a special operations person, or you have never been in combat, then you might find some of the humor in this book a bit odd, warped, uncouth, raw, or gross to say the least. So for all you lucky "average" people out there who are reading this book, it is my hope that after you have read "When the bullet hits your funny bone," you will possibly develop an understanding and an appreciation for the man who wears the Navy SEAL trident (the gold emblem portrayed on the cover of this book, which is worn on the uniform of all U.S. Navy SEALs). Because, in the performance of a U.S. Navy SEAL's professional duty, a U.S. Navy SEAL will face death so often that he will come to know Death by its first name, and if it were possible, a Navy SEAL would even invite Death for a beer.

Chapter 1

Underwater Demolition and SEAL Team History

By the end of the 1950s, there were very few Special Operations Forces. The Army had the Green Berets, and the Navy had their Underwater Demolition Teams (UDT). These elite units were trained to fight and operate behind the enemy lines of a conventional war, specifically in the event of a Russian drive through Europe.

The Navy entered the Vietnam conflict in 1960, when the UDTs delivered small watercraft far up the Mekong River into Laos. In 1961, Naval Advisers started training the Vietnamese UDTs. These men were called the Lien Doc Nguoi Nhia (LDNN), roughly translated as the "soldiers that fight under the sea."

President Kennedy, aware of the situations in Southeast Asia, recognized the need for a new type of military unit for this type of unconventional warfare and the need to utilize Special Operations units as a measure to combat guerrilla activity. In a speech to Congress in May 1961, Kennedy shared his deep respect of the Green Berets. He also announced the government's plan to put a man on the moon, and, in that same speech, he allocated over one hundred million dollars toward the strengthening of the Special Forces units in order to expand the strength of the American conventional forces.

Realizing the administration's favor of the Army's Green Berets, the Navy needed to determine its role within the Special Forces arena. In March of 1961, the Chief of Naval Operations recommended the establishment of guerrilla and counter-guerrilla units within the Navy. These units would be able to operate from sea, air, or land. This was the beginning of the official Navy SEALs. Many SEAL members came from the Navy's UDT units, who had already gained experience in commando warfare in Korea; however, the UDTs were still necessary to the Navy's amphibious force.

In 1962, President Kennedy established SEAL Team ONE, and SEAL Team TWO from the existing UDT Teams to develop a Navy Unconventional Warfare capability. The Navy SEAL Teams were designed as the maritime counterpart to the Army Special Forces "Green Berets." They deployed immediately to Vietnam to operate in the deltas and thousands of rivers and canals in Vietnam, and effectively disrupted the enemy's maritime lines of communication.

The first two teams were on opposite coasts: SEAL Team Two in Little Creek, Virginia, and SEAL Team ONE in Coronado, California. The men of the newly formed SEAL Teams were educated in such unconventional areas as hand-to-hand combat, high altitude parachuting, safecracking, demolition with explosives, advanced combat medicine, and foreign languages. Among the varied tools and weapons required by the SEAL Teams was the AR-15 assault rifle, a new design that evolved into today's M-16.

The SEALs attended UDT Replacement training and they spent some time cutting their teeth with a UDT Team. Upon making it to a SEAL Team, they would undergo a three-month SEAL Basic Indoctrination (SBI) training class at Camp Kerry in the Cuyamaca Mountains. After SBI training class, they would enter a platoon and train in platoon tactics (specifically for the conflict in Vietnam) in the swampy and muddy areas of the Alamo River in southern California.

The Pacific Command recognized Vietnam as a potential hot spot for conventional forces. In the beginning of 1962, the UDT started hydrographic surveys, and Military Assistance Command Vietnam (MACV) was formed. In March of 1962, SEALs were deployed to Vietnam for the purpose of training South Vietnamese commandos in the same methods that they themselves were trained.

The SEAL Teams' mission was to conduct counter guerrilla warfare and clandestine maritime operations. Initially, SEALs advised and trained Vietnamese forces, such as the LDNN (Vietnamese SEALs). Later in the war, SEALs conducted reconnaissance missions, and nighttime Direct Action missions such as ambushes and raids to capture prisoners of high intelligence value.

In February 1963, operating from USS Weiss, a Naval Hydrographic recon unit from UDT 12 started surveying just south of Da Nang. From the beginning, they encountered sniper fire and on 25 March, they were attacked. The unit managed to escape without any injuries. The survey was considered complete and the USS Weiss returned to Subic Bay in the Philippines where the UDTs had their forward deployed base.

The CIA utilized Navy SEALs for covert operations in early 1963. At the outset of the war, operations consisted of ambushing resupply movements, and locating and capturing North Vietnamese officers. However, due to poor intelligence information, these operations were not very successful. When the SEALs were given the resources to develop their own intelligence network, the information became much more timely and reliable. The SEALs were so effective that the enemy named them, "the men with the green faces." At the war's height, and primarily in the Mekong Delta area, eight SEAL platoons were in Vietnam on a continuing rotational basis. The last SEAL platoon departed Vietnam in 1971 and the last SEAL advisor in 1973.

On 28 October 1965, Robert J. Fay was the first SEAL killed in Vietnam by a mortar round. The first SEAL killed while engaged in active combat was Radarman second-class Billy Machen who was killed in a firefight on 16 August 1966. Machen's body was retrieved with the help of fire support from two helicopters, after the team was ambushed during a daylight patrol. Machen's death was a hard reality for the SEAL teams, and a sign of what was yet to come. Between 1965 and 1972, there were 46 SEALs killed in Vietnam.

The SEAL teams experienced the Vietnam War like no others. Because of the thick jungle environment, combat with the VC was very close and personal. Unlike the conventional warfare methods of firing artillery into a designated location, or dropping bombs from thirty thousand feet, the SEALs operated within inches of their enemy targets. SEALs had to kill at short range and respond without hesitation or be killed. Into the early 70s, the SEALs made great headway with this new style of warfare. Their method of fighting comprised the most effective counter-guerrilla and guerrilla actions of the war. The SEALs in general showed an immense success rate. The U.S. Navy SEALs earned numerous awards and citations, and they became one of the most highly decorated units of the Vietnam War.

On May 1, 1983, all U.S. Navy UDTs were re-designated as U.S. Navy SEAL Teams or Swimmer Delivery Vehicle Teams (SDVT). SDVTs have since been re-designated SEAL Delivery Vehicle Teams.

The U.S. Navy SEAL teams are split into two groups, Group ONE is based on the West Coast near San Diego, CA under the Pacific Command, while Group TWO resides on the East Coast at Virginia Beach, VA under the Atlantic Command.

The current U.S. Navy SEAL teams include teams 1, 2, 3, 4, 5, 7, 8 and 10 with SEAL Team 6 being renamed U.S. Navy Development Group or DEVGRU. There are two SEAL Submersible Diving Vehicle units – SDV team 1, and SDV team 2.

I do not have the statistics of all those who have fallen in WWII;. my best efforts start with the Korean War. The Naval Special Warfare community lost two frogmen during the Korean War, 49 Frogmen and

SEALs combined during the Vietnam War, 4 SEALs during the Grenada conflict, and 4 SEALs during the Panama conflict. Sadly, as of this writing, a total of 41 SEAL have fallen in Afghanistan and Iraq.

There have been other SEALs and Frogmen who have fallen both in training and in actual operations. As a testament to the degree of realism and operational tempo that all U.S. Navy SEALs must train, the number of Navy SEAL deaths due to non-combat and training accidents outnumber SEAL combat deaths more than two to one.

End of the history lesson... Well, at least for now.

Chapter 2

Some Background Information

To all of you younger SEALs out there that do not know me, I guess I need to establish my credentials. You, the reader, might be unfamiliar with the U.S. Navy SEALs, and you should know that there are many people out there claiming to be Navy SEALs (especially after the killing of Bin Laden), who are, in fact, not Navy SEALs or Frogmen at all. Recent estimates from the FBI place the reported number of phony SEALs at about 300 phony SEALs for every real Navy SEAL, and with the fame of the U.S. Navy SEALs in the news, the numbers of phony SEALs keeps growing.

Should you ever want to find out if someone who is claiming to be a Navy SEAL is indeed (and you really should check) a Navy SEAL or a Frogman (a Frogman is the name given to the men who were in the U.S. Navy or served as scout raiders in WWII and later called the Underwater Demolition Teams. They existed long before the Navy SEALs, and they are the cornerstone from which the birth of today's Navy SEALs came), just ask them for their full name, and their class number (no one ever forgets their class number. That is a BIG clue that they are a phony if they say that they do not remember it).

Once you have gleaned the proper information, go to an official SEAL website, or you can YouTube "Phony Navy Seals" by Don Shipley or Steve Robinson, on any computer. Submit the name of the person in question (the Naval Special Warfare center has the name of EVERY person who was a member of the World War Two Scouts and Raiders, NCDUs, UDTs, and they also have the names of every U.S. Navy SEAL since their establishment in 1962), include the person's class number in which they claim to have graduated (it's ok if you do not have it or if they said, "I don't remember it."), and you will soon have your answer.

In addition, there is NO truth to the phrase, "What I did in the SEAL teams was so secret that there is no record of me." Or "My records are sealed or were destroyed to protect me from foreign government agencies." Or "I did not go through the BUD/S training, because I was recruited directly into the SEAL teams." People who say that stuff are full of 100% pure USDA BS!

As to what exactly is a U.S. Navy SEAL? Well, in my humble opinion, a Navy SEAL comes from a common family brought up on the traditional beliefs of God, family, and country. He is a dedicated professional who loves his family, his country, his teammates, and the flag under which he so proudly serves/served. It is for those core principals that he is willing to sacrifice all in the name of honor and freedom for which he so strongly believes.

As I had said earlier, I had graduated in UDTRA class 58. UDTRA means Underwater Demolition Training; this was before BUD/S, which means Basic Underwater Demolition/SEAL training. I was a "West Coast puke," or a "Hollywood Frogman," which are harassing terms of endearment given by East Coast SEALs, for the SEALs that went through training in sunny southern California or who are/were stationed on the West Coast).

I spent almost 15 years at SEAL Team One before transferring to the East Coast. What was the reason for my transfer? Well, I decided to go to DLI (Defense Language Institute) to learn how to speak, read, and write Spanish; as Mexico was close to our base in San Diego, I thought that this was a logical thing for me to do.

Before graduating from DLI, I was informed that the Department of the Navy was putting together a few new SEAL teams to deal with the various threats around the world, and I was going to be sent to SEAL Team 4. SEAL Team 4 was going to need Spanish speakers to deal with the possible threats in Central and South America, and this was going to be SEAL Team Four's new operational area. Therefore, after graduating from DLI, I was transferred to the East Coast for my new assignment at SEAL Team Four (so much for my logic about Mexico).

Not that SEAL Team 2 (which is stationed/located on the East Coast) could not handle going anywhere in the world to meet a threat or challenge. They already had members of their SEAL team in Central and South America, and they are/were extremely professional at what they did, and they were doing an outstanding job down there.

The basic reason for the change was because SEALs were/are in high demand, and it was the sign of the times, because the operational tempo of the SEAL teams was increasing dramatically. SEALs were spending more time overseas on operational missions than they were at home with their families. It was not unusual for certain members of a SEAL Team to spend a year or more deployed to a contested area of the world.

In order to fill this huge and immediate requirement for new SEAL Teams, the higher-ups solved the manning problem by converting all Underwater Demolition Teams into SEAL teams. I guess this was a logical segue, because, by and large, beach reconnaissance for amphibious landings was becoming outdated. Many of us within the SEAL Teams found this idea to be similar to any small corporation that is bought out by a larger corporation; as they are absorbed into "the Borg" of the larger corporation, "Resistance is futile!"

The downside of this is that your unit/organization becomes less the general practitioners in the art of unconventional warfare, and more of an expensive surgical unit with specific operational skill sets to a certain theater of operation. Your unit has become less likely to adapt and deploy to any new threats around the globe, and less elite (in my opinion), which is also why there are so many different SEAL Teams, as each SEAL Team has their own designated area of expertise for a certain area of the world.

While I was assigned to SEAL Team One, I deployed numerous times. I also became an instructor within the "training cell" at SEAL Team One, life on the West Coast was great, and I never wanted to go to the East Coast. I mean come on, who would want to leave the hot babes, beaches, mountains, and deserts? Well, the West Coast babes were hot until you pissed them off, then you realized that babe is not a babe at all, but someone with a cold heart. As Will Greer said in the movie Jeremiah Johnson, "A woman's heart is the coldest stone on earth, and I can find no man's mark on it."

But mostly, guys stay on a certain coast because they develop a "comfort zone" with the team to which they are assigned. However, let me say here that I preferred being stationed on the East Coast more than I did being stationed on the West Coast. The reason for me was a simple one; people on the East Coast seemed to be more apt at looking out for a SEAL's family while he was deployed overseas (at least back in my day this was true). Because, when you are deployed or in a combat zone, you have enough "things" going on in your life to worry about without the added burden of not being there to help your family should something happen to them.

Many SEALs brag to other SEALs about going through training in a winter class, because it was supposedly colder and more difficult. There is no doubt that this WAS true for all the trainees who went through training (many years ago) on the East Coast. For all you West Coast SEALs that have never been to Little Creek, VA in the wintertime for an ocean swim, picture busting the shore ice in a snowstorm just so you can get out in deep enough seawater to do your two-mile morning swim every week. I went through a summertime training class on the West Coast, so sue me!

Upon my completion of DLI (Defense Language Institute) for Spanish, and being assigned to UDT-21/SEAL Team 4 on the East Coast (remember that this was during the time that all UDTs became SEAL teams), and after I had settled into my new team assignments at SEAL Team Four, I was asked by a few of the East Coast SEALs, who have never been to the West Coast, what my training was like. So I told them that it was so hot during my training on the West Coast that we were all given glasses of ice water to drink by the instructors. The instructors would also turn on huge fans to cool us down during our ten-minute workouts before they made us get into the air-conditioned trucks to transport us over to the dining hall where we were served lobster and steak dinners by the instructors.

It always amazed me that one or two East Coast guys would believe that crap.

For me, UDT training was a real revelation. I never knew that people in our military that are responsible for training men to be the best in the world in unconventional warfare, could make you feel as if they themselves were the enemy. Our instructors were looking for intelligent men who could take pain, endure suffering, and who would never quit under any kind of pressure. Every student who went through UDTRA or BUD/S training would come to realize that this was a testament to how seriously the instructors took their jobs, and they took it personally to put only the very best individuals into the SEAL teams.

Because, as it was before my time in the teams, when I was in the teams, and as it is to this very day, lives depend on it.

Chapter 3

The Beginning of the Brotherhood

A long time ago on a warm summer day, I was walking down Main
Street in my hometown. I looked into the window of the Navy recruit-
ing office and saw three members of my high school swim team standing
inside, so I walked in. I asked them what they were doing, and of course
they said, "We are joining the Navy."

I then asked, "What are you going to do in the Navy?"

The recruiter spoke up and said, "They are going to be Frogmen in the
Underwater Demolition Teams."

"That sounds cool," I said. "I want to do that too!" So, to the astonishment of my parents and a few friends, I tossed aside my full college
scholarship, which I got for swimming, to Princeton University, and I
enlisted in the United States Navy.

After I had completed Navy boot camp, I was sent to Jet Engine
Repair School in the state of Tennessee. As you had to have a military
rating/job description when you are in the Navy, working on jet engines,
I thought, would be cool. However, later in my career, the only jets I saw
were the ones flying over my head on their way to blow the crap out of
whoever the designated bad guys were. Upon completion of Jet engine
"A" school at Millington, Tennessee, I departed for Coronado, California
to begin my UDT training.

When I arrived at the UDT training command/compound in
Coronado, California, my class (number 58) was not to start training
until the following week. After I had completed checking into the UDT
training command (UDTRA), I was assigned guard duty.

The instructors told me that I was now a tadpole (the embryo of a
frog/frogman), and I was to stand guard duty on the armory door until
I was relieved by someone (the armory is where the instructors kept
some weapons and pyrotechnics that they would use during our training), which I did.

There I was, 18 years old and standing guard duty on a locked steel
door in my dress blue Navy uniform thinking about what type of training I was going to be subjected to, when out of one of the Quonset huts
(a barracks for trainees) ran a trainee. An instructor spotted him, and the
instructor yelled, "Freeze, you maggot!" The trainee did as the instructor

requested, and stood at attention while facing the instructor who told the trainee to freeze.

I watched this instructor (who looked like the Hulk) as he walked up to the trainee, putting his face to within 6 inches of the trainee's face, and he began yelling all kinds of obscenities at the trainee for not wearing his helmet while he was outside of his training barracks.

The yelling of obscenities ended with the instructor saying, "Drop down you dummy, and start doing pushups until "I" get tired!" The student started counting out his pushups and after about 100 pushups; the student was starting to struggle. The instructor began to yell more obscenities at the trainee for being so appallingly weak. As I stood there guarding the steel door of the armory, I was astonished as I watched this instructor kicking the trainee in the ribs with the side of his foot.

The sight of this instructor kicking the trainee troubled me, and I thought that the instructor had obviously lost his mind. So, I left my guard post at the armory door, and went into the office where the medical corpsmen were. I said to the corpsmen, "There is an instructor outside that is kicking one of the students in his ribs."

One of the corpsmen looked at me and said "Really? Well, we have got to see this for ourselves! Lead the way, my good little tadpole!"

Both corpsmen got up from their desks and walked back outside with me; one of the corpsmen looked at me and said, "By God, you're right, tadpole, just look at that instructor." The other corpsmen yelled out to the instructor, "Hey Big Lou! You got a new tadpole here, and he left his guard post on the armory door just to squeal on you!"

Do you know that feeling you get when you think that you are in trouble? Well, this feeling was much worse. Now, this instructor, "Big Lou" (so named because he is 6'8" tall and 220 pounds), turned away from the trainee who was lying on the ground, and slowly walked towards me.

As "Big Lou" approached me, I could feel my heart pounding with fear. When Big Lou was standing inches from me, he leaned down and whispered in my face with a tone of meanness that would have scared the hell out of Satan himself. "Who the F--k do you think you are, tadpole? I am going to send you through hell on earth you little F--king, snitching, piece-of-shit, want-a-be maggot, and when I am done with your sorry little tadpole ass, you will either quit or you will DIE!"

As "Big Lou" turned to walk away from me, I saw the word "God" embroidered on the back of his instructor's ball cap. I thought to myself, what the hell kind of training did I volunteer for? I never knew real fear until that day, and until that day, I never imagined the physical and mental torture to which I was going to be subjected by all the instructors, and in particular, Big Lou. Big Lou was on a mission, and I was going to be his daily target of opportunity.

During our class training, Big Lou was always quick to offer up many obscene words of encouragement to me, especially while standing on my stomach as I laid on my back and did flutter kicks. I was physically exhausted and hurting. However, for me, quitting was out of the question, and if I could help it, so was dying.

Every day of our basic training, our entire training class was mentally and physically tested. Once, while our training class was on a three-mile run, Big Lou would smoke a cigar and blow the smoke from his cigar into my face as we all ran down the beach. I felt like puking my guts out from breathing in that cigar smoke, but if I did puke, I was sure that Big Lou would have made me pick it up and eat it, or he would somehow torture me with it.

Whatever Big Lou's sick mind would come up with, I knew that I would have to suffer through evil he devised to make me want to quit UDT training. Big Lou always singled me out as a "volunteer" for his sick little mind games, like the volcano. This is where all the trainees sit in a circle facing out, with me in the center. One day, before our class started our three-mile run down the beach. I was told to get wet in the surf zone, and after I was wet, I was told to dive into the center of the volcano. Big Lou would yell out, "Eruption!" and every trainee would start throwing sand over their heads to bury me in the center, after which we would all go for our run down the beach covered in sand.

The real God must have been upset at Big Lou for having his instructor hat embroidered with the name "GOD" on the back of it, and possibly (though doubtful), he felt some sympathy for me. Because as luck, or divine intervention, would have it, on my fourth week of training before "Hell Week" was to begin (this is one week of extreme physical and mental training without any sleep), Big Lou retired! I thank you God, both of you!

In truth, during my time in UDT training or BUD/S (Basic Underwater Demolition/SEAL training), our entire training class (including our officers) was always badgered, mentally and physically, by all the instructors. One comment stuck with us, and that comment was made by one of our instructors, which was, "For some of you, if you aren't cheating, you aren't trying. However, if anyone or all of your stupid cheating asses ever gets caught, you will wish that you never did cheat."

As was customary in UDT training, the instructors would form all the trainees into boat crews of seven men per boat/IBS (Inflatable Boat Small), and as a boat crew you would always carry your 260-pound rubber IBS on top of your heads, everywhere you went on land. As you can well imagine that at 260 pounds, the IBS is not a light rubber boat, and as you ran along in a group with the boat on top of your heads, the heavy rubber boat would pound your heads down into your shoulders, and it would also remove what little hair you had left on top of your heads.

On one of our weekends off, our boat crew got together and agreed that we would all cheat by making the weight of our IBS lighter. Our plan as to how we would lighten our 260-pound rubber boat was a simple one; we would use helium.We all chipped in and purchased a large tank of helium gas. We waited until dark, and while out of sight of any instructors, we filled our IBS with enough helium mixed with air so that our rubber boat did not float away, and in the event a strong breeze came up, the mixture was just heavy enough that it would stay on the ground wherever we put it.

Monday was Rock Portage. Not all the beaches along a coastline are made of sand; some are very rocky with cliffs. Rock portage was a training exercise where we had to paddle our rubber boats out through the surf zone, and then paddle back in through the surf zone, catch a wave in our rubber boats, ride that wave all the way onto the rocks, and then drag our boats out of the water and over the large rock boulders and keep repeating the exercise until the instructors felt that we were all doing the rock portage exercise properly.

When Monday came, the instructors told us that our class was going to conduct a rock portage exercise with our rubber boats, into and onto the rocks, which were located about a mile down the beach. Depending on the size of the waves (say 6 feet or more), this could result in the breaking of IBS paddles, arms, ankles, or legs. We lifted up our boat and put it on our heads. What a huge difference! It was so light! There was little weight at all on our heads. The instructors ordered our class to run a mile down the beach, with our IBS on our heads, to the location where we were all going to conduct the surf passage through the rocks.

As we were running down the beach, our boat crew was passing all the other boat crews with ease; primarily because we were not hindered by any weight from our rubber boat (gotta love that helium). It was hard to keep from laughing at how easy it was running with our rubber boat on top of our heads, and we were all thinking that this was almost fun.

When our boat crew arrived at the designated position near the rocks, we were ordered to put our boat down. When all the other boat crews finally arrived, the instructors told the rest of our class to keep their boats on top of their heads. Because our boat crew came in first we got a break, as the instructors said, "It pays to be a winner, people!" (Or, as in our case, a bunch of cheaters).

When the instructors had completed their long explanation about how the surf passage and rock portage maneuver was to be conducted by our training class, the instructors ordered the rest of the boat crews to put down their rubber boats. As soon as this was done, we were all told to hit the surf (get wet); we all ran into the ocean without our boats to roll around in the surf zone to get completely wet. As we were coming back out of the surf zone, and slowly making our way towards the beach, we observed one of the instructors as he walked up to our IBS and for no apparent reason, he kicked our rubber boat. When the instructor did this, our IBS went skidding across the sand for about 20 feet.

All instructors' mouths opened in total disbelief at what they had just seen (how could a 260 pound rubber boat skid 20 feet across the sand?). We watched from the surf zone as all the other instructors who were standing there looked astonished at what they had just seen. They then all turned and looked at our boat crew (all seven of us with that "oh shit, we're screwed" look on our faces).

We watched from the surf zone as all the instructors walked over to our rubber boat. One instructor bent over to pick up the front of our IBS, while the other instructor bent over to pick up the rear of the IBS, as both instructors lifted our IBS up, they both tossed what should have been a 260-pound rubber boat, high into the air above their heads. With that effort, all the instructors turned their anger towards our boat crew.

While we were standing there in the surf zone, waiting for the instructors to give their next command, our officer looked at us and said, "Men, may God have mercy on us, because these instructors are not going to!"

Do you know that feeling that you get when you think that you are in trouble? Well, this feeling was much worse. All the instructors told us to come in and drop down in the pushup position, which we did. The lead instructor came over to our officer and asked him if he knew anything about the lack of weight to our boat. Our officer snapped out a reply that I thought was brilliant, "No instructor, perhaps it is the heat from the sun that is making it so light, like hot air inside a balloon." The instructor was not amused, and the instructor told our officer that he was the one full of hot air.

Then one of the instructors told a member of our boat crew to suck some of the air out of our IBS (we knew then, that we were all totally busted), as our boat crew member did what the instructor had asked, the instructor asked our boat crew member to yell out his name, and of course out came that squeaky duck voice from inhaling helium. The instructors were totally pissed off at us, and for our punishment, they told us to fill up our IBS with sand.

For the rest of the training exercise, we had sand filled up inside of our rubber boat. Going through the surf was not too bad with all that sand as it stabilized our rubber boat and kept us from flipping over whenever a wave would hit us. What the killer for us was, when we had to shoulder carry our IBS back to the training area. Because of all that additional weight from the wet sand, we came in last, and because we came in last we got extra time in the surf zone, rolling in the sand on the beach, doing pushups, and as a point of total torture, we were ordered to take our boat (deflated and rolled up) through the entire obstacle course.

We never filled our IBS with helium again, and the instructors were always kicking everyone's IBS before every evolution to make sure that everyone's IBS was not filled with helium.

For everyone who goes through it, BUD/S training is both physically and mentally demanding, but thank God, we had the weekends to ourselves. Some of you older SEALs and Frogmen out there might remember back in the day (prior to 1974), if you wanted to go off any military base on "liberty" (a term meaning that you were free to leave the military base and go out into the local town) you had to have a liberty pass. If your command did not issue you one, you could not leave the military base. Being in UDT training made it even worse, because only the lead boat crew (the winners of that week's training events), would be awarded the coveted liberty passes for the weekends. So, what were the rest of us to do if we wanted to go out on the town for a good time?

Well, getting off the military base was a simple matter. I mean, all we needed to do was to put our clothes and shoes into plastic bags, swim across the bay, get dressed, and go out into the town for a good time. The Coronado Bridge was a good rest stop before swimming on into the city of San Diego. One night, we got the idea to spray paint our class number

(58) on the main concrete support of the bridge before continuing with our swim into San Diego, and a few good times.

Painting our class number on the side of the Coronado Bridge was a vane and senseless move, and it proved to be our undoing. Because when a few of us, without liberty passes, were all swimming out to our favorite main bridge support one night, we were intercepted by two instructors in a PBR (Patrol Boat River), and they illuminated our position in the water with the boat's searchlight. There we all were, illuminated like four turds in a punch bowl.

Remember that feeling you got when you thought you are in trouble? Well, this feeling was much worse. It sucks to get caught, but hey, we were trainees (tadpoles) and far from being Navy SEALs. We would learn much later in our training that you never take the same route in and out of your operational area while conducting a mission, and NOT to mark (spray paint) your rally position for others to know where you are or have been.

The instructors told all of us to get into their boat, and of course, we all did. We were told that because we felt as if we were not getting adequate swim time during our normal training hours, they were going to help us out with our desire for more training. (Of course, this was NOT what we had in mind!)

So, off we went into the night with our instructors on the PBR. We cruised out of the San Diego bay, and out into the Pacific Ocean. The four of us were huddled in the back of the boat soaking wet with nothing on but our swim trunks and flippers. The night air was cold, and so was the water, to include the hearts of our instructors. The instructors ripped open all of our plastic bags and took out our dry clothes. They removed our wallets from our pants and from our wallets, they took our military ID cards, to include all of our money that we had for beer. The instructors told us that the money was payment for the extra training; they then tossed all of our clothes into the ocean.

When we got next to the jetty by North Island, we were told to swim to the Coronado Bridge where we would be picked up, and to rest assured that the instructors would be there waiting for us. They kept our military ID cards and told us that we would get them back when we all arrived at the Coronado Bridge.

We all jumped into the water by the North Island Naval Air Station jetty, and started swimming back into the San Diego bay towards the Coronado Bridge. Funny that the water felt colder now than before we got caught. The instructors were in the PBR and followed along for about the first mile, and then they sped off in their boat into the night ahead us.

As we did not see or hear the PBR anymore, we figured that they could not see any of us either. We all decided to swim into shore and make our way around the North Island shoreline to the Coronado Bridge and then swim out to where the instructors would be in their PBR. After all, we were already in trouble, and we all thought, just how much worse could it get?

Well, that question was soon to be answered. Being the stupid tadpole trainees whom we were, we did not count on being caught by these same instructors. It seems that they had figured we would do what we were doing. So, they had the PBR beach them on the shoreline where they could wait for us to run by in the event that we would try to cheat.

As far as spotting us out there swimming in the water, the elements were in their favor. Because if we swam by, they would have seen us from the light reflecting off the water caused by the perimeter security lights on the nearby military base, and they would have followed us along the shoreline. Nevertheless, we cheated, and now we were totally screwed, and the instructors were going to show us just how screwed we were going to be.

Needless to say, our instructors were very pissed-off at us. They took away all of our fins, and told us to get our asses back to our barracks training area on the base as fast as we could. When we finally got back to our base, we saw our entire training class standing there with their rubber boats on top of their heads, while the instructors were hosing them down with a fire hose.

When we announced to the instructors that we had arrived, our entire training class was dropped into the pushup position, and the instructors told our class about what we had done, and that we disregarded our punishment, which was given to us by our instructors. It was because of our lack of respect to our instructors that the rest of our training class was going to suffer dearly for what we had done.

The instructors told us to go to our barracks and put on our training uniforms and report to where the rest of our training class was standing. When we came back, our training class was still in the pushup position being hosed down by the instructors. The instructors told us to stand at attention, which we did. The instructors then informed our training class that we were special, and because we were special, we did not have to do anything except watch while the rest of our training class suffered at the hands of our instructors for what we had done.

This was a difficult thing for us to watch, and it did not sit well with us. We yelled to the instructors that it was not fair to punish our entire training class for what we had done. The instructors fired back and said that it was not right what we had done, and it was not right to disregard the punishment given to us by the instructors. So, if we did not care about the punishment that we were given by the instructors, our entire training class was to suffer for what we had done, and for the punishment that we had rejected.

We told the instructors that we would carry out our punishment if they would stop punishing our entire training class for what we had done. The instructors told us to go to hell, shut up, and that for the entire night, we were to finish watching our training class being punished for our actions, and for our total disregard of the instructor's punishment for us.

We stood there at attention watching the instructors use a fire hose to spray down our classmates as they did pushups and duck walked with the rubber boats on top of their heads. We all felt like spiders' asses (the lowest thing to the ground that actually does not touch the ground that I am aware of).

When morning finally came, our training class was dismissed, and the instructors came over to us and asked us how we felt. We all replied, "Shitty."

The lead instructor said, "Good, perhaps last night you assholes learned something about respect and honor."

We did. We learned that we should take our punishment like men, and not let others suffer through a punishment for what we are responsible for doing. The lead instructor looked hard at us and said, "If you assholes cannot embrace honor, then there will never be a place for you in the SEAL teams." He then gave us back our money that he said was payment for the extra training, turned his back on us and yelled, "Return to your class you maggots!"

Chapter 4

We Got New Guys Checking In;

Get Them Measured For Their Body Bags!

After graduating from our BUD/S training, we all received our orders to report to our new prospective commands, mine was SEAL Team One. We were all eager to go and fight in a war, any war. It is after all, what we had trained so long and hard for, is it not? When part of our training class, 19 of us (the other members of our graduating class reported to UDT 11, 12, and 13), arrived at SEAL Team One, we all got our collective welcome aboard greetings from the Command Master Chief. The Command Master Chief of SEAL Team One was a wise man of great stature, and he was well respected by all Navy SEALs.

Because we were the "new guys," all the other SEALs with combat experience were looking down on us and making remarks like, "Stupid FNGs," "Look at them in their brand new uniforms, thinking that they are SEALs," and "Those guys are just pieces of shit." We were all standing at attention, in our brand new starched green uniforms feeling; well, "new." As we were all standing there at attention, the Command Master Chief dismissed all the other SEALs, and told us to "stand by." Once the other SEALs were dismissed, the Command Master Chief imparted several encouraging words to all of us. They were momentous and heart warming words that made you feel like you belonged to a great family, words like; "The commanding officer did not come out here to greet you assholes today because he would rather piss in his toilet than to waste his time speaking to you worthless F--king New Guys (FNGs); You don't know shit from lips on your asses, you're just a bunch of stupid assholes with shit for brains, nothing but worthless peons that we can't use yet; My God what the hell is going on at the training command to produce such poor excuses for want-a-be SEALs," and so on.

You have to understand that back in the day, and in the eyes of SEAL Team One, as new guys, we *were* worthless peons until we had completed SEAL Basic Indoctrination training (SBI), and Basic Airborne (parachute training). It was ONLY after completing SBI training and Airborne training that you had received enough training in order to be placed into a SEAL platoon, and then you could be deployed overseas.

After our "welcome aboard" greeting by our Command Master Chief, we were then introduced to the Chief Master at Arms. The Chief Master at Arms was responsible for assigning SEALs to their daily duty assignments within the SEAL command. As we all had to wait until training slots opened for SBI and basic airborne training, the Chief Master at Arms briefed all of us on our assigned janitorial duties. After the Chief Master at Arms had completed giving his briefing to all of us FNGs, he directed all of us to go over to the medical office to get measured for our body bags. When we all started walking over to the medical office, the Chief Master at Arms yelled out to us, "You don't want to get the wrong sizes do you? If you get the wrong size, they will have to cut off your heads, or saw off your legs to fit you inside your f--king body bags, you worthless pieces of shit." I thought to myself, nothing like giving the new guys a supportive and colorful mental picture of things yet to come.

So, we (the FNGs) all started walking toward the medical office, and once we had arrived there we told the corpsmen there that we are all here to get measured for our body bags. The corpsmen said, "Ok, strip down and form a line!" Why we all had to strip down to get measured for our body bags made no sense to me, but hey, we are the FNGs, and as the Command Master Chief said, "We don't know shit from lips on our asses."

We all took off our clothes as the corpsmen had asked, and the corpsmen started measuring each of us, and he yelled out our measurements to another corpsman that was writing them down on a clipboard that he had with him.

As we were all standing there in line, naked (this was long before female support types were allowed to be assigned to the SEAL teams), things appeared to be moving along rather slowly. The corpsmen were measuring all of our arms, legs, torsos, and heads, until the operations officer came waking over to us. The operations officer cocked his head in a perplexed manner while looking at the 19 naked new guys standing in a line outside the medical office. The operations officer then went inside the medical office and asked, "What the F--k is going on here?"

The corpsmen replied, "We are measuring these FNGs for their body bags' sir."

The operations officer said, "What? That's enough screwing around with these idiots! You worthless new guys get your f--king clothes back on and finish checking in!" It would seem that when it comes to body bags, one size fits all. Even if the body bags did not fit, I am sure that there were few complaints, if any at all, about them.

After we had all completed the "checking in" process, we were all assigned to X-ray platoon. This is a platoon where they assign all the "FNGs" for any and all crappy jobs that are needed in and around the SEAL compound while you, as a FNG, are waiting to be assigned to Basic Airborne school and SEAL Basic Indoctrination (SBI), and finally, every new SEAL's dream of dreams, to be placed into a SEAL platoon and then to be deployed overseas.

Stan and I were assigned to clean up the SEAL team community restroom. Every day it was our job to clean the 6 mirrors, 6 sinks, 6 toilets, 6 urinals, the walls, and floors. Just the kind of job every new SEAL team member dreams about having after graduating from UDT/BUDS training, and arriving at his newly assigned command.

I mean come on, after all that basic training that we went through, you arrive at an operational SEAL command, and the only thing a new SEAL is qualified to do is to clean a restroom. Well, it is true! (At least back in the 1970s it was).

After a month of cleaning the common SEAL team restroom, I had had enough. I told Stan, who was working with me every day, that I had had enough of this crappy job. I went to the chief Master at Arms office and said, "Chief, I am sick of the job that you gave me. I didn't go through UDT/SEAL training to clean mirrors, toilets, sinks, and urinals. I want something more than this."

The Chief Master at Arms looked at me and said, "You want something more? Well, you know what, shit for brains, I think you are right; a man with your many talents who is still shitting BUD/S chow deserves something more. Come on, follow me."

I started to feel good inside myself about what I had said to the Chief Master at Arms, and I was thinking that I should have said something sooner. I thought, finally, perhaps he will assign me to the Armory to work on weapons or to the Parachute loft to work on parachutes or something worthwhile, which would prepare me for combat.

As we were leaving the chief Master at Arms office, to my dismay, we went right back into the SEAL team community restroom. The chief Master at Arms looked at Stan and said, "Stan, because you did not complain about your assignment like Mrs. Allmon's little boy Billy here, you are relieved! Mrs. Allmon's little boy Billy, you are now in charge of the entire restroom. How's that for something more, your highness? And your highness, should you want something even more after this, please feel free to come and see me anytime, because your needs are my top priority, and I will do whatever I can to make sure that your stay with us is better than anyone else's."

Note to self, must learn to keep my big mouth shut, and choose my words more carefully. I did that crappy job for another 30 days before being sent to SBI and after completing jump school, I finally got into a platoon. However, to this day, I still struggle to think before I speak.

Chapter 5

US Army Jump School, Polishing Our Brotherhood Skills

Back in the early days of the SEAL teams, all UDT and SEAL team members went through the US Army basic parachute training school at Fort Benning, Georgia. When we all arrived at Fort Benning, Georgia (there were about 40 of us, both UDT and SEAL team members from our respective commands), we all checked into an open bay barracks (an open bay barracks is a building with no rooms, common toilets, sinks, showers, and 20 bunk beds, hence the term "open bay"). After storing all our gear, we all received our briefing on how to act on an Army base. I guess because we were Navy, the Army thought that we were not a "real" military unit and we all needed a briefing on proper military conduct.

Who knows why the Army, or for that matter, any military unit, do the administrative things that they do? Nevertheless, the important thing to the Army, about our arrival on their military base, was that we were all going to be assigned to KP (Kitchen Patrol) duties, aka dishwashers and food servers, during our off duty training time (breakfast, lunch, and dinner) while assigned to the US Army and parachute training command.

We were no strangers to getting up early for training. However, the Army gets this wild hair up their asses about getting up at 3am to jump out of an airplane by 8am, and mind you, we lived only 15 –minutes' walking distance from the airfield where we had to board the aircraft that we were all going to jump out of for training.

This 3am lunacy warranted some sort of evaluation by us, and after careful reasoning, we figured out that it was all because of the so-called "Cover your ass factor" that every Army officer cranks into their training schedule to cover their asses, and to ensure that the "trainees" get to the airfield on time, so they never have to explain to their higher ranking officer why the troops were late for training.

So, after giving the Army training schedule some thought, we figured it went something like this: The General tells the Colonel that all trainees must jump by 0800 every morning. So the General says to the Colonel, "Colonel, tell all the trainees to be ready to jump by 0730."

To cover his ass, the Colonel calls the Major, and tells the Major to have the trainees ready to jump by 0700.

To cover his ass, the Major tells the Captain to have the trainees ready to jump by 0630.

To cover his ass, the Captain tells the Lieutenant to have the trainees ready to jump by 0600.

To cover his ass, the Lieutenant tells the Sergeant Major to have all the trainees ready to jump by 0530.

To cover his ass, the Sergeant Major tells the Top Sergeant to have all the trainees ready to jump by 0500.

The Top Sergeant schedules the dining hall to be open for breakfast at 0330 to 0400, to ensure that all the trainees will be finished with their breakfast, and the trainees will be picking up their parachutes at the parachute loft by 0430.

Reveille (a military term meaning to wake up the troops) will be held at 0300 hours. Everyone's asses are covered, and all are happy (except for the trainees that have to get up at 3am for an 8am parachute jump!).

One good thing about training with the Army was that the weekends were ours, and of course, we had to get out of the Army barracks in order to have a good time. Our "good time" consisted of consuming mass quantities of any and all alcoholic beverages, and let the night provide us with whatever entertainment that would unfold, or what we could find that would be amusing to us.

Once, it was turning out to be a boring night, and it did not take long for a few of us to consume enough mind altering booze to come up with an idea that would unknowingly bring down the wrath of the US Army upon us.

While in town, we went to the local hardware store and purchased a few cans of bright green spray paint; we also went to another store to purchase a diver's face mask and fins. After we had all our "goodies," we caught a ride back to the Army base, where we put our diabolical plan into action.

There is this bronze statue on the Army base of an Airborne trooper called "Iron Mike." I guess he was a representation of a WWII paratrooper. However, in our drunken stupor, we all felt that he could use a little "dressing up." Our plan was simple and innocent, we would spray paint the bronze statue of Iron Mike "frogman green," and secure a diver's face mask on his head, and we tied a pair of fins looped through his right arm so that he looked like a Navy Frogman with a Thompson submachine gun. After our handy work, Iron Mike looked SO cool!

We all got a great laugh about our, what we thought was a harmless, joke. Little did we know how harmless this joke was NOT going to be with the US Army when they discovered our little prank. (To hear them tell it, you would have thought that we all pissed on the American flag!)

When Monday morning came, our entire training unit (Navy only) was standing in formation waiting for a certain Colonel to address all of us on a "very serious issue" that he had with all of us. When the Colonel arrived in his chauffeured military vehicle, we all snapped to attention as he stepped out of his vehicle.

The Colonel walked up to our officer in charge (every enlisted man can attest that it truly sucks to be an officer in charge around us when we have done something that affects everybody). The Colonel asked our officer if he knew anything about who the idiots were that defaced their coveted statue of Iron Mike, by making Iron Mike look like a Navy frogman.

Our officer turned to all of us and asked, "Ok, who were the idiots that spray-painted the statue of Iron Mike, and put fins and a face-mask on him?"

Tommy stepped up first and said, "Sir, I am that idiot." Then, the rest of us who were involved with this reprehensible deed stepped up and admitted to being the idiots of the defacing, and then we were followed by our entire group (guys who were not even there) admitting to this dastardly deed, and being the idiots who defaced the statue of Iron Mike.

Our officer turned to the Colonel and said, "Sir, I present you with the idiots of the defacing of Iron Mike and sir, I was the head idiot in charge of the defacing operation." (In truth, our officer was not even there).

The Colonel turned to the Sergeant Major and said, "Sergeant Major, I do not care what you do with these idiots, but by noon today Sergeant Major, that statue had better look as it was before those idiots touched it, if not better!"

"Yes sir! I will see to it personally sir!" barked at the Sergeant Major.

The Colonel got back into his chauffeured vehicle, and left us at the mercy of the Sergeant Major. The Sergeant Major looked at all of us and said, "Ok you idiots, you heard the Colonel, make it happen, and be back here in one hour!"

We all gathered up every bit of cleaning supplies we could find, to include wire brushes, and we all went to the bronze/green statue of Iron Mike. Upon our arrival, we all commenced to wire brushing off the green paint, to include removing the fins and the face mask. When we were all done, we returned to our barracks where the Sergeant Major would be waiting for us.

When we arrived back at our barracks, to our bewilderment, the Sergeant Major was there with a couple of boxes of white "T" shirts and a can of green spray paint. The Sergeant Major told all of us to put the white "T" shirts on over our green uniforms. Once we all had our white "T" shirts on, the Sergeant Major walked up to each of us, and with the can of green spray paint, he spray painted a green "I" on the front and back of our white "T" shirts.

When the Sergeant Major had finished spray-painting each of us, he said, "You are all idiots, and you will wear your idiot white shirts all day today, and when anyone asks you what that "I" on your shirt means, you will respond: I am an idiot!"

We did exactly as the Sergeant Major instructed us to do, and the Sergeant Major thought it was hilarious. It was reported to us that the Sergeant Major was saying, "It is always good to know who and where the idiots are!"

He did have a point; too bad there is not a law today that would require idiots to be so identified!

Chapter 6

A Basic Breakdown of a SEAL Platoon:

Some Duties are Better than Others

In my day, when you were assigned to a SEAL team, and after you had acquired a few operational skills, you were placed into a platoon for advanced SEAL training, and finally, your platoon was deployed overseas. Each man has key responsibilities and duties within your operational platoon. Deploying overseas is always exciting; it gives you a chance to come together as a platoon, and to deepen your bond with your SEAL teammates.

During my time in the teams, at a minimum, every SEAL platoon would have two officers. These officers are the poor brave souls that are responsible for every one of us and tasked with leading all of us on our assigned missions to hunt down and destroy the bad guys. When we all were not on a mission, it would seem that they are tasked with protecting, and defending our sorry enlisted asses whenever we got into trouble.

There was one all knowing and wise chief petty officer whose duties included, but were not limited to, advising and looking out for the platoon officers, the enlisted men, and at times when a few enlisted men would get out of control, the chief petty officer would try and prevent the platoon officers from choking their enlisted men out. Depending on the personalities of the platoon, the chief might also serve as an intermediary between platoon members, and if needed, a disciplinarian.

Two radiomen have the duties of maintaining all the electronic and radio equipment assigned to the platoon, insuring that the platoon can communicate with the rest of the world while out on a mission. God help the radioman if he cannot make communications with the SEAL platoon's support elements. Because there is nothing more threatening than an armed SEAL platoon looking at you, the radioman, when they all need to get the hell out of a hot area.

There are a few designated machine gunners strategically positioned within the SEAL platoon. These machine gunners are responsible for the total destruction of all enemy forces, and to provide cover fire for the SEAL platoon, allowing them to run like hell should the SEAL platoon be engaged by a battalion, or any force with superior numbers and firepower.

Last, but never least, is the platoon corpsman. His duties include giving us all sorts of shots, meds, killing the enemy, and stitching up our wounded asses all at the same time.

There are other duties, responsibilities, and assignments within a SEAL platoon, but the aforementioned are pretty much the essence of an old SEAL platoon.

It is not often that you envy the abilities of another person in your platoon, as you are all valued for your professional abilities and the schools or advanced training that each of you has gone through. Nevertheless, Doc Oscar was one man that our entire SEAL platoon envied.

Doc is the term of endearment given to any platoon corpsman or medical person in a SEAL platoon; these corpsmen are extremely well trained in emergency field medicine for combat. However, Doc (as good as he is) is NOT a doctor.

As an operational SEAL platoon, we were all stationed together in a foreign country. During our time off, a lot of us went into the local town to mingle with the flavor of the week (or night depending on your hunger). Our Doc, however, took an entirely different, yet professional, approach to his allotted time off.

Being a bit of an entrepreneur, Doc Oscar established himself as a local gynecologist. Doc went into all the bars and hotels that were outside the gates of our base (of which there were hundreds) and gave a quick blurb about who he was (a gynecologist) to the head madam, and offered his "services" to the "ladies of the night." Doc even had business cards printed up in town (where they would professionally print up anything you wanted).

50% OFF YOUR FIRST TWO VISITS
Dr. J. Oscar - Obstretrics & Gynecology

I will handle your problem areas with care and compassion.
Hours of operation 11 am-1300 and 1700-1900 daily

Location -- 2nd floor barracks 24B room 213

50% OFF YOUR FIRST TWO VISITS

Doc would hand these fake business cards out to the managers and owners of all the local establishments where the "ladies of the night" would be working. His business cards offered 50% off their first two gynecologist visits! I ask you, the reader, is this idea pure genius or what?

Not only were these ladies of the night beating a path to his barracks' room (and that should have been a clue that he was not a real doctor. However, there is no reasoning with a woman when it comes to a sale), but they were paying him! In truth, Doc was doing everyone a service of sorts, our thoughtful corpsman did give these women shots for syphilis or pills for gonorrhea, so in that regard, he was helping these ladies of the night, and their prospective customers.

When these ladies of the night would set up an appointment to visit our Doc, he would welcome them into his room, and after a quick exam, he would respond with, "Ok everything looks great," or (if they were infected) he would tell them, "I want you to take these pills and see me next week." Doc's treatment of these ladies of the night must have been really good, because he never got any complaints, and they would always come back!

I once asked Doc about his examination procedures for the ladies, and he told me that his examination process for these ladies of the night was hilarious. Doc looked at me grinning and said, "It goes something like this, 'Come on in and step on the scale, let me take your temperature and blood pressure.' and after I did that I asked them to pee in this fruit jar."

"Fruit jar?" I asked.

Doc said, "Yeah, fruit jar. Don't interrupt.

"After all of that, I would interview them like this, 'Ok, I have a few questions to ask so please answer truthfully to the following yes or no questions, Are you having sex? Do you practice safe sex? Do you think about sex? Do you prefer one location to another? Do you accept money for sex? Do you wash after having sex? Do you perform oral sex?'"

Doc would ask other questions that were not relevant (well, not relevant from a true doctor's point of view) such as, "Did you have sex before you came to my office? How often are you having sex? How many partners do you have sex with each day? On an average, how many partners do you have sex with each week? Do you prefer to have sex in the morning, afternoon, or evening? Do you have sex with women? Do you have sex with animals?"

I am reasonably sure those are not the types of questions that a real gynecologist would ask. However, I was a radioman in a SEAL platoon, and as I am not a female, what the hell would I know about it?

Doc would also have them strip completely naked, and he would give them a full physical exam. Doc was so busy with these ladies of the night that he was booked every day of the week, and he was getting referral service too!

Whenever we were tasked with a mission that was going to take us out of the area for a while, Doc would let all the ladies of the night know that he was going to a conference in Geneva or some other medical event, and these women would have to reschedule their appointments with him so that when he came back, they could continue their visits. Doc made good money from his practice, and from time to time, he would treat us all to drinks and dinners from his profits.

The best part of all this (for Doc anyway) was that when they could not afford to pay him for their medical visit, they gave him sex as a form of payment! Again, I ask you, the reader, is this brilliance or what? Doc Oscar's whole gynecologist plan was (for Doc anyway) one of the most well thought out plans ever!

Oh yeah, for the all women reading this – Doc was a real jerk! Imagine his nerve, taking advantage of those poor prostitutes, where were his moral principles? I mean really, shame on him!

Chapter 7

In Combat, You Might Get Killed Twice

For what it is worth, I think that it is nice to know when you die, those who are left alive will place your dead ass in whatever container that you fit in, and you are laid to rest for all eternity (Ahhh peace at last). That is, unless there is a war going on in some part of the world where they bury you above ground, because the water table there is so high, like it is in New Orleans or Key West, Florida. Even so, really, what difference does that make? I mean, you are dead right? It is not as if you can feel anything, or that you are going to say, "Hey! I am getting wet inside my casket! Can somebody call a plumber?"

Another thought here, why do those who are left alive buy those huge headstones? Are all the other dead people going to say, "Wow, look at that headstone, I wish I had one like that!" Life is for the living, when you are dead the party is over, and it is time to answer up for what you have done, big headstone or not!

That is why most SEALs feel that you must live your life to the fullest and not worry about all the small details, such as where they are are going to stick your dead ass after you die. I mean, do you really care? Is there a five star graveyard out there with phenomenal coffin service? Ok, I think that is enough of the preparatory talks about this subject.

In a far-off war zone, a SEAL squad was bravely engaging the enemy. As it happens sometimes, the intelligence reports about the enemy size and activity in their area of operation was not quite as accurate as it could have been. Because of the bad intelligence, this particular SEAL squad of seven men came under heavy enemy fire. At first, the SEALs were really putting the hurt on the enemy, and then certain events during this ongoing deadly assault were starting to go very badly for the SEAL squad. Despite the enemy losses, it seemed that the enemy was trying to encircle the entire SEAL squad, as the enemy fire was becoming more intense and many SEALs within the squad were reporting enemy fire coming from more than one location in the jungle.

The SEAL squad officer was the first to realize that his squad had engaged the point element of an enemy battalion (a battalion is a military unit of around 300 to 1200 soldiers), and that the enemy was looking forward to putting an end to all of his men. The SEAL squad started to throw out smoke grenades to obscure their position from the enemy;

the squad then tried to break contact away from the enemy. The SEALs placed claymore mines with one-minute time fuses to kill any advancing enemy soldiers in hopes of slowing their advance on the evading SEAL squad (Claymore mines are small explosive charges, which when detonated, would hurl 1000 ball bearings at the enemy).

It was becoming very clear to the entire SEAL squad that they were all going to be in deep trouble if they did not get out of the area, and soon. The SEAL squad was heading in the direction of a small river, and the SEAL officer told his radioman to call for a patrol gunboat to extract them out of the area. However, the enemy was trying their best to make sure that did not happen by attempting to encircle the SEAL squad, preventing them from reaching the river. During the battle, several of the enemy rushed at the SEALs' position. John, seeing the danger to his fellow teammates, stood up with his M60 machine gun and opened fire on the advancing enemy with a hail of bullets, killing seven of the advancing enemy soldiers. But in doing so, John was the first to be wounded in the ensuing firefight. Buck quickly ran to pick up his wounded teammate and carry him out of the enemies' line of fire as his fellow teammates provided covering fire.

Buck quickly checked John's condition, and he saw that John had been severely wounded. The SEAL squad was still evading the enemy, throwing smoke grenades, and placing claymore mines to slow the enemies' advance on them, and there was no time for the corpsman to treat John's wounds. To make matters worse, the SEAL squad was getting low on ammunition and grenades. Luckily, they had all arrived at their extraction point on the riverbank where the PBR (Patrol Boat River) was waiting for them; the entire SEAL squad boarded the patrol boat as quickly as possible. Once all the SEALs were onboard, the PBR sped out of the hostile area, spraying the entire extraction point down with bullets from the rear minimum (a Gatling gun that fires about 1000 bullets a minute).

On the deck of the patrol boat, John's wounds were quickly being tended by the platoon corpsman. The platoon corpsman was doing everything that he could to save John's life, but it was too late. John had received six bullet wounds during their firefight with the enemy, he had severe internal damage, and he had lost an excessive amount of blood. It was a somber moment for the SEAL squad as they watched John breathe his last breath on the deck of the patrol boat. The platoon corpsman held John in his arms while each member of the SEAL platoon knelt before John, and said goodbye to their SEAL brother.

When the SEALs arrived at their base, John's body was taken away, and the rest of the SEAL platoon was debriefed about their mission. John's remains were transported back to the rear operational area for processing back to the States, where his family and friends would lay him to rest.

The next day, the entire SEAL platoon was sitting around inside their quonset hut, feeling bad about the loss of their brother SEAL. As the platoon chief was going through John's personal effects to send back to John's family, the rest of the SEAL platoon looked on. A few solemn moments had passed when the platoon chief spoke up and said that he had found an envelope from John that was addressed, "To the entire platoon in the event of my death." The chief opened the envelope and inside the envelope there was $100.00 in cash, and a short letter from John saying, "In the event of my death, this $100.00 is for you guys to celebrate my time with you. So raise your glasses to me, you assholes, and don't feel bad! One day, we will all meet again on the other side, and we will have a good laugh about our times together." After reading Johns' note to the platoon, the platoon chief said, "Well, I guess John doesn't want all of us to sit around on our asses feeling sorry about him being gone, so let's go carry out John's last request." The SEAL platoon decided that they would all go into the nearby town and celebrate the life of their departed brother SEAL, by drinking and toasting to all of his humorous memories.

Everyone was having a great time drinking heavily, and recanting funny stories about John. However, before everyone got too drunk to drive (it wasn't as if they would be pulled over by a cop in a combat zone), they all decided to return to their base. So, everyone got into the 5-ton truck, Buck and Stan got into the front, and Buck said that he would drive. Buck was speeding back to their base camp with everyone hanging onto whatever they could that was attached to the truck.

What is the reason for speeding in your vehicle? Well, going fast makes you a harder target to hit should the enemy decide to shoot at you, and as the enemy did not always wear their uniforms, one would never know if the person walking down the street was a common civilian or the enemy.

As bad luck would have it, it was the monsoon season, and they were all caught in a tropical downpour. The thunder sounded as if bombs were exploding and when the lighting flashed it looked similar to an explosion at night. Because Buck had been drinking as much as he had, the alcohol impaired his judgment. For a brief moment when the lighting flashed, Buck thought they were under attack, and he sped off the side of the road.

Because Buck was driving the truck so fast, he could not stop the truck in time, and he crashed the truck right through a concrete wall. The truck came to a stop in a muddy field several yards on the other side of the concrete wall.

Both Stan and Buck fell out of the truck and checked themselves for any injuries, and the rest of the SEALs that were in the back of the truck were yelling obscenities at Buck for driving like an idiot. All was well, but their truck was indeed stuck in the mud, and there was a lot of debris piled up under the front end of their truck, making it difficult to move the truck at all.

They knew that they could not leave their truck, and as Buck was driving with Stan in the front, the rest of the SEAL platoon decided it was Buck and Stan's fault for driving and poor navigating. So the rest of the SEAL platoon stayed in the back of the truck to supervise. Buck and Stan started to collect some wood planks from a nearby fence. They used the planks to dig out enough mud and debris to get their truck unstuck from the mud.

Things were looking good until Stan noticed something terribly wrong under the front of the truck and yelled out to Buck, "Hey, Buck! You got a big problem here! You better come over here and take a look at this!" Buck made his way through the mud to the front end of their truck, and there before his eyes were three bodies.

Looking at the three bodies, Buck said, "Oh my God! They're all dead!"

Stan looked at Buck and said, "Shit Buck, you must have killed them when you drove through the wall. They look pretty torn up; I bet that they were all sleeping on the other side of that wall when you crashed through it."

The rest of the SEAL platoon climbed down from the truck to see the bodies jammed under the front of the truck, and they began calling Buck a murderer and saying, "You are so screwed Buck, what are you going to do now?"

Buck fell to his knees in the pouring rain shaking his head, looking closely at the three dead bodies under the front end of their truck. Buck slowly started to look around at where he was, then Buck looked up at everyone and said, "You sons of bitches. This is a graveyard. They are ALL dead in here!"

Everyone began to laugh and Stan said, "Yeah, but you're the only guy that I know that can have a traffic accident with dead people!"

Buck laughed and said, "Well, at least I didn't kill them, they must have been Zombies! Let's get the hell out of here before more show up!"

With the truck unstuck, they all drove back to the base camp, muddy, smelling from dead bodies that they reburied, missing John, and laughing about another good time that was shared among SEAL brothers.

Chapter 8

Think that You Might be Going Bald?

Well, If You are in a SEAL Platoon, You Are!

In the SEAL teams, it is a fact of life that the longer you serve in the SEAL teams, the more deployments you will make, and the more time you will spend with your team-mates overseas on missions, training, or attending special schools. In fact, you will spend more time with your teammates than with your girlfriends or your spouses, and you will get to know your teammates' deepest thoughts and concerns.

Every SEAL platoon has at least one guy who makes you say, "Hmmm, how did he get here?" While this might be the case for a few SEAL team members who are assigned to a SEAL platoon, I know that there are several, and more serious weirdo types in civilian life, and they do not make you say hmmm, they make you say, "Damn, **WHY** is he here?"

Our SEAL squad was assigned as a mobile training team in a country somewhere in beautiful Central America where we were training commandos. As a few of us volunteered to extend our deployment time for an additional year, to continue training the commandos for combat, we welcomed a brand new SEAL team member named "Zack," who was assigned to our training team to assist us in the training of the commandos. Zack was a bit of an odd fellow and he was starting to go bald. Zack was extremely upset about the prospect that he was going to lose all of his hair, and he was always complaining to us that he was too young to lose his hair. (Really, I do not get what the big deal is about losing all of your hair. Does it change who you are? Are you less of a man because you do not have any hair on top of your head?)

To prevent the loss of all of his hair, Zack decided to purchase four bottles of hair grow tonic. Have you EVER known anyone (not an actor) that said, "Hey, this hair grow tonic really works!"

I would tell Zack, "You know Zack, when the enemy is shooting at you, I don't think that they really care if you have any hair or not." Zack would just raise his middle finger in response to my statement.

The instructions on the bottles of the hair grow shampoo, which Zack had purchased, instructed the user to apply the hair grow shampoo at least twice a day. Before going to sleep at night, the user was also to massage a small dab of this shampoo into their scalp, and leave it over-night until the next day when the user took their morning shower, and they could then rinse it out.

As I was thinking about how vain Zack was, and all that hair grow tonic he had purchased, I thought to myself that Zack's situation would be an excellent stress reliever for a few of us who were dealing with the occasional loss of life from the daily combat on the side of the com-mandos that we were all training, and it would be a great opportunity to have some fun, at Zacks' expense. To cover my actions, I told everyone that I had a meeting up at the command post. I went into town and purchased a couple of bottles of the hair remover. The next day, while Zack was out training the commandos, I filled Zacks' hair grow tonic with the bottles of the hair remover I had purchased (oh come on, this is funny). I shook the bottles of hair grow tonic to ensure that my secret sauce was mixed thoroughly. I told a few of the guys about my plan so that they could share in the enjoyment of this prank of mine. After all, no practical joke is worth playing, unless it is played well and totally enjoyed by all!

The next morning, Zack came into my room all upset; he stood there in my room with his hands full of his hair and said, "Look, I am losing all of my hair! I don't know what's happening to me! What the hell could be causing this to happen!?!"

I was thinking to myself, "Yes, what indeed!" Looking at all that hair in his hands, I also thought, "Now that's a lot of damn hair, man that Nair stuff really works better than I thought it would."

Feeling bad for Zack (well, not really) I said, "You know what I think is causing you to lose that much hair, Zack? It is your nerves. You need to go see the doctor and ask him for some tranquilizers to help you get a nice, deep, and relaxing sleep at night. I am sure that will help you to stop losing all of your hair."

Zack looked at me and said, "Really? I think you might be right! I will go see the doctor right after I eat my breakfast."

Feeling that there was a good chance that I could be busted for my joke if Zack saw the doctor before I'd did, I lied to Zack and said, "Zack, I will see you later, I got a meeting right now with the base commander about some training issues that I really need to brief him on. So I'll catch up with you in a few."

I took off as fast as I could to go see our doctor before Zack did. I needed to tell the doctor what I had done before Zack came in there to see him. When I walked into the doctor's office, I told the doctor that I had a "special problem" that I needed him to keep quiet about. In fact, I said, "I want your word that you will not repeat what I am going to tell you to anyone!"

The doctor looked at me and said, "You're not pregnant are you?"

"Very funny," I said, "Now give me your word, because I do not have much time, and I really need to tell you what I have done."

The doctor gave me his word, and I proceeded to tell the doctor what I had done to Zack. We both had a good laugh about the whole thing, and the doctor told me that he would give Zack some placebos to take every night for his "nerves." To my amazement (and amusement), Zack kept using the "hair grow tonic," with my secret sauce in it. By the time he was on his second bottle of hair grow tonic, Zack had lost all of his hair.

The house cleaners whom we hired to come into our compound to do the daily washing, laundry and room cleaning, refused to go into Zack's room to clean it or to even touch any of his clothes. With all his hair falling off his head, the house cleaners felt that he had contracted some sort of contagious disease. So, every day Zack had to clean his own room, and he had to wash his own laundry.

I never told Zack what I had done to him, as I saw no logic in being shot over the loss of his hair. Besides, I felt that his newfound and permanent baldness was an improvement.

Hey Zack, if you are reading this, it was a joke! Ok? Are we cool? Are you still bald?

Chapter 9

The Naked Warrior

Some SEALs, and Special Operations types, are over the top when it comes to being paranoid about the bad guys coming after them. I have known a few SEALs that had pistols under their pillows, in their shower, in their refrigerator, and in their cars. Some of these guys would "clank" when they walked with all the guns, knives and throwing stars that they would carry on themselves to protect themselves from any would-be bad guy.

I have always felt that in combat, if it is your time to go, there is not too much that you can do to prevent it, because a well placed bullet or explosive charge could care less about all the special or advanced training that you may have had or gone through. I have known some very well-trained people who were killed by lesser-trained people. It is always sad to lose a brother, but the way many of us who live by the sword try to look at it is that it was just their time.

When a small group of us were deployed to a hostile area, we had a team house (a team house is a place where we would sleep and eat together at the end of every day) that was well fortified with individual fighting positions on the perimeter and inside our courtyard area. If we were ever attacked, we could retreat from our primary fighting positions to several fighting pits. In the event of a large-scale enemy attack, these fighting positions were to be our last stand positions where we would make the enemy pay dearly for their assault on us. If it looked like we were going to lose, we would then all escape through a thirty-two inch wide sewer drainage pipe that went from our team house area underground, to where it emptied our daily sewage, 500 feet out into the bay.

One day, I went into Marty's room, and I asked him what he was doing with all the sandbags inside his room. Marty looked at me and said that he was building a bunker. Marty, who was a young SEAL and a member of our Mobile Training Team (MTT), said that if we were ever under an enemy attack, not to run by his window where he was building his bunker. Looking at Marty, I asked him, "Why not?"

Marty said, "I might shoot you!" Marty further informed me that should we come under an enemy attack at night, that he was going to shoot anything that moved past his window. This meant me, as I had to run past his window from my room in order to get to my designated fighting position.

I looked at Marty, as if he had lost his mind, and I said, "Are you serious?"

Marty said, "Well, no. Even so, remember that I warned you, just in case you get shot." As there was no other exit for me except to run past Marty's window to get to my fighting position, and I did not know if Marty was serious or not, I got the idea to test Marty's totally absurd statement (my other idea was to throw a grenade through his window; lucky for him, I went with the following).

On a weekend that we were not too busy with the daily training of the commandos, I went into our team room (an area where we would relax and listen to a few tunes, watch the local TV, or play a movie over a few beers). I took a speaker out of our stereo system, and with about 80 feet of speaker wire, I climbed on top of our team house roof. I removed a couple of the Spanish style stone shingles to make sure that I was right above Marty's bed. Seeing that I had the correct position, I replaced the roof tiles. I placed the speaker on top of the roof tiles above Marty's bed, and I covered it with a few palm branches. I then ran the speaker wires back down to the stereo tape player that was inside our team room.

When all of my manual labor "pre-staging" work had been completed, I invited a few commandos that we had been working with to play the parts of the bad guys. We made a tape recording, which sounded something like this (only in Spanish): "Help me up.... Ok, I'm up, now throw up the explosives... Ok, wait here, and I will lower down the rope for the rest of us to climb up after the bomb explodes. Let me find where the stupid gringo is, I see the stupid gringo, and he is sleeping... Ok, I am arming the explosives. Death to all Gringos! Ha HA! Ok, let's get out of here... quickly... quickly before the bomb explodes... DIE GRINGO, DIE!"

With that recording completed, and the speaker in place on top of Marty's roof, I was ready for the next phase of my operation. I informed the base guards about what I was going to do, and at the designated time that I was going to play the tape, so if they heard anything, like yelling or screaming, they should ignore it. The guards thought that I was crazy, but they liked the joke that I was going to play on Marty. I told the guards not to run into our courtyard no matter what they heard, unless they first spoke with me out in front of our iron gate, and they all agreed with me on this. I was glad that they agreed with me, because I was not sure what Marty would do when I played the tape.

After I was assured that the base guards would not react, I briefed the other MTT guys, including the base commander, on what Marty had told me about shooting anything that moved in front of his window. I also told them the reason for my joke, and that I was planning to test his statement tonight at one o'clock in the morning, to see if he was indeed serious about shooting anyone that moved past his window.

After my briefing, I invited all of them, including the commando personnel that helped to make the tape, into our team room. That night, when we were all safely inside the team room where I had the tape recorder, I told all of them that no one was to leave once I started playing the tape, to which everyone agreed.

At one in the morning, while we were all drinking a few beers, I started to play the tape. We were all giggling like a bunch of school kids at what we were hearing. When we all heard the part on the audiotape, "Die gringo, die," the night erupted with the sound of a submachine gun being fired (thank God, I told the guards about my joke), followed by Marty screaming, "They're coming over my roof!" This was followed by more submachine gun fire. Then, everything got very quiet, and none of us dared to go outside the door, as we did not want to be shot by Marty.

A few more moments passed; we all waited and watched as our team room door slowly opened. There standing in the dim moonlit night was a naked man, holding an UZI submachine gun in one hand, and a grenade in the other. What a sight! We all burst out laughing, that is, all of us except the naked warrior. Marty stood there looking pissed off about my joke. He called me a F--king asshole, and returned to his room with the big hole that he put in his Spanish roof tiles above his bed where he had emptied two magazines of about 60 bullets. I told Marty that he might want to re-think his bunker in the room plan, as I had a lot more jokes like this one planned for him, if he did not.

On the positive side, Marty now had a great view of all the stars through that hole in his roof. Well, that is except when it was raining.

Chapter 10

Shark Prevention

When a SEAL is serving in a platoon, advanced training is always a major part of every SEAL member's life, and when it comes to advanced SEAL training, this type of training is usually conducted in or at remote areas where we can use a lot of explosives and shoot an assortment of weapons anywhere that we wish.

Upon arrival at our advanced training site on an island somewhere in the Pacific Ocean, our SEAL platoon was preparing and staging all of our platoon equipment for advanced training exercises on this remote island. On the day that we were to begin our advanced training, I observed that there was a large fishing vessel anchored in the cove of the island where we were going to conduct night diving operations. The crew of this fishing vessel was cleaning their daily catch, and throwing all the fish guts into the water for the sharks and other sea creatures to feed on.

As our platoon was going to be conducting night diving operations in that very cove, I did not like the idea that these fishermen were threatening the lives of my brother SEALs by attracting all the sharks with the fish guts that they were all throwing into the water.

With that thought in mind, I got into one of our rubber boats and went out to the fishing vessel to speak with the captain and crew of the fishing vessel. When I got onboard the fishing vessel, I told the captain and crew that this was a restricted training area, and that we were going to be conducting night diving operations in this cove and that they would have to leave our training area. I was given a few choice words by the captain and the crew, and I was told that they will fish wherever they please. I was then told to get the "F--K" off their boat, and not to come back.

As I was heading back towards the beach, I started to get pissed off about my encounter on the fishing vessel between myself, and the captain and crew. I did not favor the prospect of anyone in my platoon, or myself for that matter, being devoured by a shark all because of these assholes, who were chumming the water with all of the fish guts that they were throwing over the sides of their vessel.

By the time I got to shore, I was in full pissed-off mode. I got out of the boat, and I went into our weapons armory. I took out an M79 grenade launcher, and several 40mm explosive training rounds (these training rounds make a loud bang, a little bit stronger than an M80 firecracker. However, unlike the real 40mm explosive rounds, when one would fire these training rounds, no one gets hurt. 40mm means 40 millimeters, the size of the explosive round). I took my M79 grenade launcher with all of my 40mm explosive training rounds, and started up a small path to a cliff that overlooked the cove where the fishing boat was anchored, and I sat down.

It was a beautiful summer's day, I watched all the seagulls circling over and around the fishing vessel as they dove for the fish guts that the fishermen were still throwing over the sides of their large fishing vessel. I drew in a slow deep breath as I loaded my first 40mm explosive round, took aim, and I fired the M79 grenade launcher. I watched the 40mm explosive round as it traveled through the air towards the fishing vessel, impacting short of the fishing vessel. The 40mm training round made a loud boom as it exploded on the water about 50 yards away from the fishing vessel.

When the 40 mm training round exploded, it was so cool to watch all the seagulls screaming as they scattered in all directions flying erratically away from the fishing vessel. Even more humorous was watching all of the fishermen running around their boat deck trying to see where the incoming explosive round had come from, as they yelled out obscenities. I smiled as I recalled their words, "We will fish anywhere we like, so get the f--k off our boat!"

I thought aloud, "I will shoot my grenades wherever I like, so get the f--k out of our cove!"

I fired my next 40mm training round, and the wind had picked up a bit. I noticed that my 40mm grenade was going to hit close to their fishing vessel. "BAM!" It hit the water about 10 feet off their bow. By this time, my entire platoon was watching the action from the beach, and they looked up at me on the cliff whenever I fired a 40mm round in the direction of the fishing vessel. The SEALs in my platoon would cheer whenever a 40mm training round would explode near the fishing vessel.

I fired my next round, and it exploded behind their fishing vessel. Now, I guess that they must have figured that I was trying to kill them, because they cut their anchor line and hauled ass out of there. As I watched them speeding away out to sea, I was hoping that they would take all of the sharks with them. Once they started to fade from my view, I started back down the cliff path to return my weapon and the few explosive training rounds that I had left into the armory.

As I was heading towards the armory, my platoon officer came up to me and asked, "What the hell was that all about?"

I simply said, "Shark prevention, sir."

He looked away from me and in the direction of the fishing boat that had sped away and said, "You could have hit them, you know."

Looking in the direction of the fishing vessel, I said, "I know sir, but I wasn't trying to. Besides sir, these are only training rounds, but should they decide to come back, I will show them the difference between training rounds and the real ones."

My platoon officer said, "Let's hope they are not that stupid, Billy, I don't need the damn paperwork!"

"Yes sir," I replied. Thinking to myself, I hoped that they would not be that stupid either.

Chapter 11

The Ugliest Woman Contest

To all who participate in them, military training exercises are extremely challenging. It is for this reason that it is not uncommon for most participants to work 12 to 16 hours each day to get their assigned jobs completed. This does not include those military forces that are in the field being evaluated that might get little, if any, sleep at all. So, any free time that you can have to yourselves is a big bonus, even if it is just a chance to catch up on some sleep, or to have a good time together as a SEAL platoon out in the local nearby town or city.

As with any SEAL platoon that is away on an exercise or a deployment, the SEAL team guys collectively seek out all the fun things that you can do together as a platoon in order to release the stress of being in combat or under the microscope while on high visibility training missions. On a large military exercise, every platoon is evaluated for their professional performance. Because the higher-ups are comparing your field performance against all the other military units out there on the field of mock combat. So as you might imagine, there is a lot of pressure on any SEAL platoon to do their very best, and never fail.

It is for that reason that whenever you get a chance to break away, and head into town for a drink or two with your brother SEALs or to have some fun, you jump at it. (What did you think a bunch of SEALs trained in the art of unconventional warfare would do in their time off? Go to an art museum? Take in a ballet or an opera?)

While our SEAL platoon was deployed for this high tempo military exercise in the USA, a few of us got together in our tent during a break between one of our several military exercises for SEAL platoon evaluations, and we discussed the possibilities of having an ugliest woman contest. This was just for our amusement, and there was certainly NO disrespect intended to any of the beauty challenged women out there that we were going to try and find.

The rules for the contest are simple, all participants must agree to take their "dinner date" to the same restaurant at the designated time, and the guy with the ugliest woman (agreed by all those who are present) wins a night out on the town with all his food and drinks paid for by all the losers.

As you can well imagine (or not, depending on whether you have done this before), the hunt for the ugliest woman is truly no simple task; I mean she has to be the ugliest woman that you have ever seen in your life, and sometimes (in your hunt) the older she is the better. Otherwise, what is the point of having an ugliest woman contest?

Walking around a town looking for the ugliest woman that you have ever seen in your life to take to a nice restaurant for dinner is harder than one might imagine. You try lines like, "Hey baby, are you busy tonight? I would love to take you to dinner!" The woman would look at you as if you had lost your mind, and send you to hell.

Some guys tried lines like; "Are you hungry? I'm buying, no strings attached, just a meal, so what do you say? You want to come with me to this restaurant?"

The common response to their requests was, "Get lost you psycho!" or "Get the hell away from me, or I will call the cops!" Let me say here that to be rejected by a pretty woman is one thing, but to be rejected by the ugliest woman that you have ever seen in your life for a dinner date is truly a huge blow to your ego.

This rejection is compounded, because if you do not bring an ugly woman to the restaurant, you automatically lose, and all the SEALs in your platoon will know that not even the ugliest woman alive would want to be with you. So the pressure is really on all of the participants to find the ugliest woman that they have ever seen, and bring her to the restaurant at the designated time.

When the designated time had arrived, most of us were already at the restaurant and waiting for the last few SEALs to come in with their dinner dates. Steve came in carrying a female bulldog, and he was disqualified (nice try Steve). Larry found his "winner" sleeping under a highway overpass. Not only did she look like a homeless crack head suffering from leprosy, but she also smelled as if he dug her up from a graveyard that was from a swamp in Louisiana!

She was a revolting sight to watch as she loudly slurped on her food like some hungry swamp creature gnawing on its fresh kill. Her old torn clothes smelled like urine, and she had open sores on her face and hands. It was, however, somewhat amusing to watch this woman as she put everything that she did not finish eating into one of her plastic bags, to include the table napkin, fork, spoon, and the salt and pepper shakers.

Well, I guess there is truth to that old saying, "To the victor go the spoils." She smelled like old spoiled garbage, and the image of her eating still makes me wince. As Larry sat there with her, he just smiled at the rest of us losers with our "dates," knowing that he had won with his "homeless queen."

However, the truth came out when our SEAL platoon was on a mission and patrolling through the field. Larry confessed to all of us that he had given his homeless queen 100.00 dollars to accompany him to the restaurant. NOW, who do you think was the real winner?

Chapter 12

Numb Nuts

Even when SEAL platoons are on an operational deployment, the training within that SEAL platoon will never end. The reason for this is because each SEAL must maintain his skill level (if you don't use it, you lose it). When SEALs are deployed, and when not in a combat zone, SEAL platoons are sent on training missions or exercises that can last from several days to several weeks. A lot of us who are assigned to a SEAL platoon think that the higher ups do this so that SEALs cannot get into any trouble. Because if you are keeping all the SEALs in the field, then they are out of any cities or towns, and in particular, out of all the local bars or pubs. However, the true reality of this is, a SEAL platoon is a sophisticated weapons system, and like any sophisticated weapons system, if it is not maintained and cared for, it will not function properly when it is needed the most. When the time came for our platoon to be sent on a training mission, we all suited up with all of our necessary combat gear to complete a direct-action training mission against a fictitious enemy.

For this particular direct action training mission/evaluation, our mission tasking was to ambush the common bad guys, whoever they are. In short, the intelligence report that we received stated that six insidious bad guys were going to be patrolling down a jungle trail at night on their way to blow up a vital military communications station. The purpose of our ambush was to intercept and kill these six bad guys that were going to blow up the vital military communications station.

In reality, this was a simple training operation, which was set up to evaluate our stealth and concealment as a seven-man squad moving undetected through the jungle at night, to an ambush position and to evaluate our command and control abilities in an ambush (mainly our ability to communicate with each other, to control our fire on the enemy, and to dispense with the bodies afterwards).

Trying to patrol as quietly as possible through the jungle at night is a difficult task, as there is always a possibility that you can scare up a few animals that will give away your position. As I had said earlier, you have to move slowly and quietly by looking where you are walking, and you must take care as to where you step with your feet, or what you grab with your hands (e.g., bamboo vipers aka small poisonous snakes that live in or on bamboo). As you are patrolling through the jungle, you must also look through the jungle for any signs of movement and listen for any noise made by any possible bad guys.

When we all got close to our pre-designated ambush site, we slowly crept up and moved into our respective firing positions near the trail that the bad guys would be patrolling. We all camouflaged ourselves so that the bad guys could not see us when they entered our kill zone. We prepared ourselves for our long wait for the bad guys to come down the trail, and into our ambush position so that we could kill them.

Everyone knew their assigned tasks and the basic idea of our mission. We were to shoot all the bad guys with blanks, grab any intelligence papers that they might have, hide their bodies, and then patrol to our extraction point and board our patrol boat for a long ride back to our military base. There, we would get our debriefing on how well, or badly, we had all done on our assigned training mission.

After about two hours of waiting, which is not a long time, as most of us have waited quietly in one spot for 8 to 10 hours to ambush the bad guys, one of the guys in our squad jumped up and started slapping his crotch area. This action really pissed me off, because if the bad guys were close to us, then they could surely hear this activity, and they would know where we were. By knowing our location, it would give the bad guys a chance to either ambush us, or turn away from our position and take another route to the military communications station.

I went over to the position where I heard the noise and saw one of my guys standing in the middle of the foot trail slapping his crotch and asked him, "What the hell is wrong with you, you moron! You want ALL the bad guys to hear where we are?"

Paul dropped his pants, took out his flashlight, and with his flashlight turned on, we all saw the huge red welt left by a centipede as it made its way up his left leg to his nuts, and there on his nuts were the remains of the crushed centipede's body parts where it had been squashed.

Looking at all of us, Paul said, "I took the pain until it reached my nuts, and that was it, I just couldn't take it anymore, and this IS a training exercise you know!"

I said, "Well done you crybaby, now let's all get the hell out of here before the bad guys get us!"

We failed that part of the mission exercise because we did not ambush the bad guys, but Paul got a new name... "Numb Nuts," as he lost all feeling in his nuts from the poisonous centipede.

Chapter 13

Claymore Truck

In any war, there are always new and innovative ideas that are researched, and then developed into "widgets." These widgets are then tested to see if, in fact, it can counter whatever the threat is that is taking friendly lives.

During the war in Vietnam, there was always the threat of a US military supply truck being ambushed on the sides of the road, and in some areas of the country, certain roads were called B-40 alley (B-40 is an anti-tank rocket),because of all the B-40 rockets that the enemy would shoulder fire at any US trucks that would drive by. To combat this threat, someone came up with the idea to make mini claymore mines, and mount them on the sides of the military trucks.

For those of you out there who are unfamiliar with claymore mines, regular claymores contain one pound of C4 plastic explosive, and about one thousand ball bearings. When the claymore is exploded, it would send all 1000 ball bearings in the direction of the enemy. What was funny about these things was the warning on the outside of the container, "Do not eat contents," and they were marked, "Front towards enemy." Just how dumb do you have to be not to figure out which end of this thing is the front, or that you should not eat explosives?

I guess it is good to put the wording on them in the event that the enemy finds one of these things, then he will know how to set them up, or if he gets hungry, he won't open it up and start eating the explosive filler.

The mini claymores were about one quarter of the size of the regular claymores. By comparison, the mini claymore was about the size of a soap dish, filled with hundreds of tiny steel ball bearings/BBs, and about ¼ pound of C4 explosive.

As I stated earlier, these new mini claymores were designed to be used on the sides of large trucks for countering ambushes that were set up by the enemy on the sides of the roads, which in some areas were a common occurrence. Some enemy ambush areas were so common that US soldiers gave them names, such as B-40 alley (the B-40 would explode on contact with its' intended target). The truck driver had a switch panel mounted inside his truck with firing switches for the left and right side of his truck (depending on what side the enemy was firing from), so the driver could then select what side from which he wanted to fire.

To ensure that the mini claymores did not damage the truck when they were fired/exploded, the mini claymores were mounted on 1-inch thick steel plates that were welded to the steel frame on the sides of the trucks. This was done so that when the mini claymores were detonated during an ambush, the mini claymores would propel all the steel BBs at the enemy, and there was little or no damage to the steel frame on the truck.

As it turned out, the mini claymores were not too effective against the enemy, and towards the end of the war, the mini claymores were no longer used or produced. Ahh, once again Washington spends copious amounts of money on a poor idea to solve a problem that people were over-reacting to. Because as it turned out, trucks with armed soldiers were better at deterring the enemy from accurately firing at the trucks as they sped down the road. However, at the time I guess that these mini claymores were better than nothing for the military truck drivers.

Some Army guys got word about this new tactic of using claymores mounted to the sides of a truck to counter an enemy ambush, and thought that they would employ this idea on one of their own military trucks. So, they got a 5-ton truck, and they taped on six regular claymore mines to each side of their truck (Remember, a regular claymore has 1 pound of C4 plastic explosive, and about 1000 ball bearings in them).

Thank God they had enough smarts to test it first without a driver inside the truck, because when they set off the 12 pounds of C4 (this is the total explosive weight of all the claymores taped to the side of their truck), little was left of the 5-ton truck to drive. Picture in your mind a huge explosion, and when the smoke cleared, the only thing you saw was the front end of the twisted cab of the truck, and a few smoldering tires.

I would have loved to hear the explanation given to their Captain or Colonel for cause of damage to a 5-ton truck by claymores. Oops!

Chapter 14

Something for His Efforts

In the military, it would seem that as you mature, and after you have spent awhile in combat, there are times when each individual that has endured combat will question what is right or wrong about the war or "conflict," which they as front line soldiers, or a U.S. Navy SEALS, are involved in. While our platoon was back at our base camp and sitting around a campfire, the question came up about whether what we were fighting for was right or wrong. Our platoon officer looked at all of us and said, "It is a great question to ask. Consider this, the enemy is fighting for what he believes is right and just, and so are we. Can you tell me who is wrong?"

I replied, "No sir, I cannot."

Our officer said, "That is why, as a warrior, you never try to rationalize war. The enemy soldier, for the most part, is someone's son, brother, cousin, uncle, or a father, just like any of us. All you owe any enemy soldier is to kill him quickly, before he does the same to you, or to someone that you or a family member cares about."

This book is not just about the blood, guts, and daily suffering that all U.S. Navy SEALs have to see and endure in combat. It is also an attempt to give you, the reader, an overall picture of what a Navy SEAL is and how SEALs use their humor to escape the tragedies of their chosen profession, and all the horrors of war during the battle, even long after they have returned.

One early afternoon in a far-off combat zone, a SEAL platoon received an intelligence report about an enemy sampan (which is a small dugout canoe) that would have three high level VC in it (VC or Viet Cong), were also called the People's Liberation Armed Forces (PLAF). The VC were created by the North Vietnamese communists to escalate the armed struggle in South Vietnam. These three high level VC soldiers were going to come down the river for a meeting with several other enemy VCs. To prevent the VC from exchanging or passing on any tactical intelligence, a squad of SEALs (seven men) was tasked with ambushing these three high level VC to prevent them from meeting the other VC that would possibly be coordinating some future attack on American troops.

Acting on their intelligence reports, the SEAL squad quickly formulated a plan to interdict the three VCs in their sampan. The SEALs patrolled to their ambush site, and they set up their ambush position on the muddy riverbank that would afford them a good view of the approaching sampan. Once all the SEALs were in their fighting positions, they waited quietly to take out (execute) all three of the enemy soldiers who were coming down the river on their way to their designated meeting point.

As the enemy soldiers entered the "kill zone" in their sampan, the SEALs opened fire with four M60 machine guns and three Stoner machine guns. The massive amounts of bullets being fired at the enemy created a huge water spray from all the bullets hitting the water. This huge spray from the water concealed the enemies' location. The SEALs had to stop shooting to see where their targets were. When the SEALs stopped firing, the SEALs saw that two of the three VC were dead and floating face down in the river, and the third was frantically swimming to the other side of the river, away from the SEAL squad.

The SEAL squad opened fire again with massive amounts of bullets, aimed at the enemy swimmer. The SEALs would stop firing to see where the enemy swimmer was so that they could resume firing again. The SEALs repeated this until the enemy soldier made it to the other side of the riverbank, at which time the officer of the SEAL squad yelled, "Cease fire!"

When the enemy swimmer crawled out of the water, and onto the muddy bank of the river, he was clearly exhausted. The enemy soldier stood there, knee deep in the mud on the other side of the river; he then slowly turned around and looked at the SEAL squad. The enemy soldier began yelling at the SEAL squad and pounding his chest. When the enemy soldier finished yelling, he then stretched out his arms, waiting to be shot by the SEAL squad. Instead of being shot, all the SEALs began to applaud him. For a moment, the enemy soldier just stood there with his mouth open, looking at all the SEALs applauding him; he then turned around and ran into the jungle where he disappeared from sight.

Bravery, even between enemies, can sometimes be respected. Besides, when it is not your time to go, it is not your time. At least he was applauded for his efforts.

Chapter 15

Adapt, Overcome, and Improvise

At camp Pendleton in California, there is a large military base where thousands of Marines are stationed. Our platoon was sent there to participate in a few war games against various units of the US Marines. Our platoon was tasked with playing the role of the bad guys. The Marines were always happy to have us go against them. As one Marine Major put it, "If my men can prevent a SEAL element or platoon from achieving their objective, then my men can beat any enemy unit out there." It was flattering to hear, but it also creates a very competitive spirit between both the US Marines and U.S. Navy SEALs, and sometimes it can get personal.

No one ever wants to fail a mission (training or real), so when we simulated blowing up a large electric power sub station that was defended by 25 Marines, the Marines said that we never made it into our target to blow it up. The Marines stated to the referee that they never saw or heard any of us, and there were no shots fired. Our officer was pissed off at this statement and said that we had indeed hit our target, and that we could prove it. The Marine referee told our officer to produce his proof, and our officer went to the electric power sub station in the daylight with the referee. When they all arrived at the power substation, our officer showed the Marine referee two timing clocks that were attached to fake explosive charges, which were mounted on the oil tanks of two very large electric power transformers.

When the Marine referee saw where the explosive charges had been placed, the Marine referee was amazed and said that we were fools to risk our lives placing the fake charges where we had because we could have been electrocuted. Our officer said, "We will do anything to accomplish our mission, but we would never say that we did something which we had not!" The Marine referee gave us the win, and the Marines, who were defending the electric power sub station also showed that they were men of honor, as they had not seen or heard us; they apologized to us for their false accusation and shook our hands for a well-executed mission. We all smiled and our officer said that the reason we placed our fake explosive charges where we had was because of the tight security the Marines had around the electric power sub station, and that was the only place where we could get in. We were hoping not to be electrocuted in the process, as it was a very dangerous path to travel in order to place the fake explosive charges.

It was after that mission that a few of us decided to take a break and go into town to drink a few beers, and check out the local attractions. (Navy guys in a Marine town, what were we thinking).

We went into a local bar and sat down for a few brews. Three girls came in that caught our attention (actually, anything female would catch our attention). We invited them over to our table to join us for a few drinks. We were all having a great time until in came several members of the US Marine Corps. When they asked us where we were from (as our hair was longer than a Marines' haircut), we said the Navy. This got us the usual chuckles and the snide "Swabby" and "Squidly didly" remarks.

One of the Marines walked up to our table and informed us that this was a Marine bar, open to only men. "You Navy ladies will have to leave, and these sweet ladies sitting here with you, they will be joining us men."

As you can imagine our blood began to boil a bit. As four SEALs against seventeen Marines is not the ideal win ratio, and it takes a lot to keep from fighting when you are being challenged, because numbers mean nothing to a SEAL when he is challenged, as most SEALs figure, even if a SEAL should lose the fight, the aggressors will not be bragging about it.

However, before there was any exchange of fists, our platoon corpsman (Chuck) spoke up, saying, "Gentleman, how about letting me act as your waitress tonight? I will serve you 'men' free beers on us if you let us stay here and drink."

To which the Marines replied, "That sounds great sweetheart!" The ladies who were sitting with us got up and left with the Marines, and we all sat back down. Chuck gave us a wink, and then he went up to the bar and ordered four pitchers of beer for the Marines.

While Chuck was at the bar, we watched him as he removed a small brown bottle that he took from his pocket, and he poured a small amount of liquid from the bottle into each pitcher of beer, Chuck then returned that small brown bottle back to his pocket. Chuck delivered the pitchers of beer to the tables of the waiting Marines, and to the women who were once sitting with us. The Marines thanked him for the beers, and for being so sweet. After dropping off their beers, Chuck rejoined us at our table.

Once we were all again sitting together, I asked Chuck what it was that he had poured into their pitchers of beer. Chuck looked at me grinning and said, "Ipecac." (Ipecac is a colorless vomit inducing liquid). Chuck said, "Just sit back and wait a few minutes for the drug to take effect." After about 10 minutes, we all bore witness to the funniest and most impressive puke festival on the planet. Marines were projectile vomiting all over the place. The Marines were puking on the floor, on the tables, on each other, and they were also puking on the women that left us for the Marines! It was by far the funniest sight that we all had ever seen. As all the Marines were displaying their manhood to the ladies, we got up from our table and left them all puking. Poor bartender sure had a big mess to clean up.

So remember guys, when you are outnumbered, take a page from the Marines and adapt, overcome, and improvise — use ipecac. Semper Fidelis!

Chapter 16

God Must Have a Soft Spot for SEALs

I do not know how to explain what happens to some SEALs that have near death experiences. Some SEALs that I know, and have seen doing whatever it was at the time that they put their lives in danger, should have clearly died, or have been killed. It is my belief that God has a soft spot for U.S. Navy SEALs, or he is so amused by SEALs that he cannot wait to see what they will get into next.

During one of our demolition training exercises at a remote base out in the Southern California desert, three instructors hauled an old mobile home out onto the bombing range for us to blow up. When the instructors had finished positioning the trailer, they all left to go into town for lunch and a few beers. While they were away, we were left under the supervision of the remaining instructor to continue with our explosive training.

Our platoon was instructed to attach what would total out to be about 20 pounds of TNT to the old mobile home at various positions. We also did a test burn on some time fuse, and we all decided on 60 minutes for a safe burn time for the fuse that we would use to set off the explosives. We measured and cut the proper length of time fuse and attached it to the explosive charges; we then started the time fuse burning (time fuse is like the wick on a firecracker). Sixty minutes of time fuse would give our platoon plenty of time to get away, and observe the explosion from a safe distance.

When we all got back to the safe area at our training camp, our platoon went up on top of the sand berm to sit down and watch the old trailer while waiting for the explosive charges to go off. As we were all waiting for the explosion, to our utter astonishment, we watched as a jeep with three instructors in it, who were returning from lunch, drove up to the mobile home trailer with the 20 pounds of TNT attached to it.

We all began yelling and waving our arms trying to get their attention and warn them, but they were too far away to hear us. They pulled up right in front of the mobile home, and the moment that they all got out of the jeep, the whole trailer exploded!

We all ran down from our observation point to get into our vehicles, thinking that the three instructors were probably all dead from the explosive blast and the flying debris. Knowing that we were all going to out there to recover their bodies, our corpsman grabbed his medical bag and yelled to another platoon member to go and get some body bags.

When we got to where the jeep was positioned in front of where the mobile home use to be, we all saw that the trailer was completely obliterated and the three instructors who got out of the jeep fifteen feet from the position of the mobile home were now lying on the desert floor. Our corpsman walked over to where one of the instructors was lying face down on the desert floor and rolled him over. After checking for a pulse, the corpsman yelled, "He's alive!" We checked the other two, and they were both alive as well.

Except for being knocked out cold from the concussion of the blast that was caused by the explosion, they had a few cuts and scratches from flying debris. Nonetheless all three instructors were alive. A few of us were looking at our corpsman as he started grinning.

Our corpsman told us to put the instructors inside the body bags. Our officer asked, "What do you want to do that for?"

"It is going to be a learning experience sir," the corpsman replied. We put the unconscious instructors inside the body bags as the corpsman had requested, and we transported them back to camp. We laid the instructors on the floor inside the huge walk in food freezer, and we unzipped the body bags just enough to allow air inside it. We left one platoon member to keep a watch on the unconscious instructors. Should any of the instructors regain consciousness, the platoon member was to call for the corpsman immediately.

It was not long before the guard heard the screams, "I'm alive, I'm alive, get me the f--k out of this body bag!"

The corpsman came running into the freezer and unzipped the body bag to check over the instructor. The corpsman told the instructor that when he had checked him after the explosion, he was dead just like the other two instructors next to him, and that he was he was getting ready to cut them all open to perform an autopsy on each of them.

When our corpsman finished saying that, the other two instructors in their body bags started yelling, "We're alive, you asshole, don't f--king cut us open!"

The corpsman said, "What a damn shame. I could have used the autopsy training!"

Chapter 17

If You are an Anti-Military Protester, and Stopped at a Traffic Light...

When the Light Turns Green You Had Better Go!

I will never understand why some war protesters protest against the men and women who serve in our military. The people in the military are always under orders to carry out their assigned duties as it pertains to the rules of engagement set down by the policy makers of our government. The lunacy of this is that most of these policy makers have never even served in combat. So why take your hatred of a war or conflict out on those who are ordered to serve on the front lines? The men and women who serve on the front lines are the ones being wounded or killed, because they are ordered to carry out the policies of our government. If you want to protest a war or a conflict, go to Washington DC and do it, and leave the rest of us who serve our country with honor, out of your anger.

One of my brother SEALs must have felt the same way. Berry had just returned from a deployment in a combat zone, and he was driving a 5-ton truck over to the main base to pick up some supplies. On this particular day, while Berry was stopped at a traffic light outside of the SEAL base on the Silver Strand in Coronado, California, there, stopped in front of him at the same traffic light, was a woman in a white Buick.

When the traffic light turned green, the woman in the white Buick did not move. Thinking that the woman was daydreaming, Berry laid on his horn to wake her up. The woman responded by sticking her hand out of her window, and giving Berry her middle finger. Even though the light was green, she still did not move her car. Thinking something must be wrong with this woman, Berry got out of his truck to check to see what might be the matter with her.

When Berry walked up to the driver's side of her car, he noticed that her car was full of all kinds of anti-military paraphernalia. When the woman sitting in the car saw Berry, she began to cuss at him and call him all kinds of names. Berry interrupted her and said, "The light is green lady, why don't you go?"

To which she replied, "Screw you asshole, this is a free country. I will go when I am ready to, and not when you tell me to, or are you going to kill me like all the other innocent people that you have killed?"

Berry replied, "You know what, honey buns, you're right, this is a free country."

Berry walked back to his 5-ton truck, got in, and when the light turned *red*, Berry put his truck into six-wheel drive and proceeded to push her, inside her white Buick, out into the oncoming traffic.

The woman was laying on her car horn and standing on her brakes, but it wasn't helping her as Berry was in a 5-ton truck. Berry slowly pushed her car into the center lane of all the oncoming traffic. Of course, this blocked all of the oncoming traffic on the road with her vehicle and his 5-ton truck. It was quite a sight to see with all the stopped traffic blocked by a military truck, and a hysterical woman screaming inside her car.

The woman was screaming so loudly that it was rumored her screaming could be heard out in Arizona. Berry backed his truck up and out of the intersection; he watched this hysterical women rant and rave outside of her car to anyone who would listen about the SEAL that was trying to kill her. There was no real risk of that happening, but Berry stood there outside his truck, and waited calmly for the Coronado police to arrive.

When the police finally arrived, they listened to the hysterical woman explain to them how this murderous trained killer had tried to kill her. After they had listened to her entire explanation, the Coronado police asked Berry for his side of the story. Berry explained the whole event to the police officers, and after he had completed his explanation, Berry was charged with reckless endangerment. However, Berry argued with the police officers, saying that it was not reckless, it was very precise. The officers agreed based on the skid marks from her tires, but the officers felt that this was a lesser charge, as Berry was clearly a victim of an insane war protester that hated all military personnel.

The officers thanked Berry for his service to our country and for fighting for their freedom. Berry smiled, and while looking at the woman whom he had pushed out into the traffic, he said to the officers, "Freedom is not just for the sane people, it is for everyone, even people like her."

Berry did get his ass chewed by our commanding officer, and he had to pay for all the damages to the back of her vehicle. Hopefully, she found a different place to hold her protesting of the military, as not every SEAL is as compassionate or understanding as Berry was with her.

Chapter 18

Lack of Training Funds

Depending on who is in the political office, funds for the military will be either feast or famine. If it is famine, all the people serving in the US military will suffer because any extra training that you might need or want will most likely be canceled, as it was deemed too expensive. However, if you really want to attend the specialized training or school, it will come out of your own pockets. It is a true statement that when the government wants to save money, the first place that the government will make any cuts to the budget is in security or defense.

As an example, our SEAL platoon was sent on a military training exercise in Alaska. This was during the time when many financial cutbacks in the military were occurring due to the promises made by the political parties that were running for office and were now in office because of those promises.

It was because of all the campaign promises, made by the elected president, that all of our per diem (funds for lodging and food) was suspended for one year. This meant that all of us who could afford to live off base, had to spend extra money for food and lodging that we did not have. So, when our platoon was deployed to Alaska to attend a joint military training exercise with the US Army without any per diem, a few of us soon ran out of our own money. Several of us did receive a small monthly allowance to live off base, but we could not eat at the base mess hall because we would have to pay for the food, as per military regulations. The point was moot, because we did not have any more money to purchase food for ourselves.

As several of us were all out of money, and we could not eat our "C" rations, because they were for the field exercise, a few of us went into town and sat around inside a McDonald's restaurant. When the people got up to throw out the food that they were not going to finish eating, we would ask if we could have it, and then we would take it from them and eat their leftovers.

This worked great, but only for a while. Because the manager felt that we were nothing more than a blight on his business, he threw us all out and told us not to come back. We said, "Hey were not homeless, we're just hungry!" However, back in the 1970s very few people cared about anyone that was in the military, so we left McDonald's to find other sources of food.

We all sat down in our barracks and we conducted a mission profile for finding food. As our good fortune and planning would have it, we attacked the only logical target on the military base, the base dining hall. Late at night we picked the lock on the base dining hall door and acquired from the freezer and pantry all the food that we would need before the start of our field exercise. Too bad that we did not think of this sooner, because we acquired three large hams, six loaves of bread, two large bricks of Swiss cheese, and six dozen eggs to feast on. That was truly a great mission, as we did not destroy anything, we did not get caught, and we were no longer hungry.

There was another time, during military financial cutbacks, when two of us went to the Army Marksmanship Instructor School at Fort Bragg, NC, again without funds. Whenever we got hungry, Sambo and I would wait until dark and hang out in the back of the officers' mess where they would throw out all the food that was not eaten during dinner, and sometimes we were lucky enough to eat steak!

As it would happen, all good things must come to an end. While Sambo and I were dumpster diving for food, the base MPs (military police) rolled up on us. We were taken inside the officers' club dining room to meet a two star general who was informed about two members of the military eating out of the dumpster every night. The general asked us if we knew who he was, and Sambo said, "No sir general, do you not know who you are?"

The general was not amused, and he said, "Gentlemen, I am in command of this entire base. That means I am also in command of you two clowns, so if you would be so kind, I would like to know who you two garbage eaters are."

We snapped to attention and said, "We are U.S. Navy SEALs sir." He then asked why we were going into the officers' club dumpster and eating the food that was thrown into it every night.

We told the general that the food inside the dumpster behind this officers' club was better than the dumpster food behind the enlisted chow hall. The general said, "Gentleman, I find nothing humorous in your actions, you both got ten seconds to explain yourselves, or you will both see a very dark side of me." We told the general about the funding situation at SEAL Team One, including the standing order from our commanding officer that SEALs who wanted to go to school for any advanced training would have to pay out of their own pockets for the training they wanted. "So we paid for our training on your base sir, because our commanding officer seems to be about saving the SEAL command's money. We don't have anymore money for food, so we came here to eat out of the dumpster sir.

"Really," said the general. "So, you are telling me that you men are paying for your training on my base with your own money, and because of that you are now without funds for food?"

We both looked at the general and said, "Yes sir, what we have told you is indeed the truth sir, and that's why we do not have any money to buy food sir."

The general said, "I want you two gentlemen to order whatever you want from the menu at this club every day that you are here, and I want the both of you to see me tomorrow morning at 1000 AM sharp in my office, is that clear gentlemen?"

We both replied, "Yes sir." The general gave us each 50.00, which we both tried to refuse, but to no avail. The general said it was an order that we take his money, and that no soldier should have to resort to eating garbage while on his base.

The next day, at 1000 AM, Sambo and I were both standing tall before the two star general. After our exchange of formal salutes and greetings, the general asked if we had eaten at the officers' club last night and this morning as requested. We both replied that we had, and the general asked us both again to explain what the hell we were doing eating out of a garbage dumpster, and to explain in detail the standing order given by our commanding officer that individuals are to use their personal funds for any advanced training that they wanted to attend.

When we were both done with our explanations, the general asked both of us if what we had told him was indeed the truth. We both replied that it was, and then the general became clearly pissed off saying that, "No commanding officer should have so little regard for his troops that his own troops should have to resort to eating garbage while attending any form of military training!" He looked at both of us and said, "Your funding problems are about to come to an end. What is the telephone number of your commanding officer?"

After we gave the general the telephone number, he picked up his telephone and called our commanding officer. The general started the conversation calmly and pleasantly, telling our commanding officer about how well we were performing on his base, and he wanted to know what kind of sailors that we both were. Our commanding officer said that we were both professional and dedicated sailors. The general then asked our commanding officer about his standing order of no travel or training funds for advanced training in order to save his command money on training.

When our commanding officer confirmed our story, my God, the way the general cussed out our commanding officer, you would have thought he was a member of the Hells Angels prior to joining the military. I mean, this general was calling our commanding officer everything that was slimy, low, and shameful!

When the general slammed down the phone, he looked at us and started to laugh out loud saying, "I'll bet your commander shit his pants! What do you gentlemen think? Can you imagine the look on that son-of-a-bitch's face?" (In truth, we could) "What say we go for an early lunch and laugh some more about this, and maybe I'll make another phone call to shake up his day some more? Are you gents up for that? I sure am!"

We both looked at each other and said, "You're the general."

The general busted out laughing again and said, "You're damn right I am! Come on, chow and a couple of beers are on me!"

That general was a genuine, down to earth, good man, and because of him we all got the funds for our training that we needed. Our commanding officer also paid back the $100.00 that the general gave us. Thanks again General, you are always welcome by our fire!

Chapter 19

Stealth Vehicle

Whoever said that, "Necessity is the mother of all inventions," was never a U.S. Navy SEAL. I say this because, in the SEAL teams, "Boredom is the mother of all inventions and the necessity for a well-played practical joke." When Steve and I were assigned as camp guards for one week out at the SEAL team training camp in the California desert (for you SEALs out there that know me - yeah I know, what were "they" thinking, leaving the two of us alone with our imaginations, out in the middle of the desert without adult supervision), we had to do something to keep ourselves entertained, besides guarding the camp all day, shooting bats with our shotguns at night and watching them spinning to the ground like a helicopter after it had been shot.

You have to understand that being a camp guard out in the middle of the desert is a monotonous and mind-numbing assignment. So one day, while Steve and I were sitting around drinking a few beers, we came up with the idea to affix two jeep headlights to a steel pole with wire cables that went to our jeep battery. When we would activate the on-off switch on the pole, the pole mounted jeep lights would come on. This was a true masterpiece!

Satisfied about the workings of our new invention for a joke, we sat around and waited until dark. As soon as it got dark, we locked up the entire camp and set all the alarms. We then loaded up our jeep with our "light pole" and began driving down a long flat desert highway in southern California. It was a beautiful warm starry night, but there was no traffic to be seen. We were both beginning to wonder if we were ever going to use our new invention.

As we continued driving down this long stretch of a road in our military jeep, we finally saw the lights of an oncoming vehicle way off, in the distance. My partner in crime jumped into the back seat of the jeep and waited for the right moment to turn on our pole mounted jeep lights. As the oncoming vehicle got within the proper range, Steve turned on the pole mounted lights and slowly swung the light pole out to the driver's side of our jeep. From a distance, and at night, it looked like another vehicle was trying to pass us.

As the oncoming vehicle got closer, the oncoming vehicle started to flash his headlights at our phantom vehicle to warn it that he is in danger of a head on collision. Steve waited until the vehicle was about 100 yards away, and shut off the jeep lights on the pole, and then he climbed back into the passenger seat of our jeep.

To the driver of the oncoming vehicle, it must have appeared that our "phantom vehicle" was still in the outside passing lane and coming straight at him, because the oncoming vehicle slowed to a stop, and pulled off on the side of the road. When we passed the oncoming vehicle, Steve and I looked at each other and uttered the words, "Shit, a state trooper."

I guess the state trooper was still waiting for the other vehicle that turned off its lights, because he never came after us. We put our jeep in four-wheel drive, shut off our headlights, and headed off road out into the desert, and to a place where we felt secure that the state trooper could not see us.

As we watched from a distance, we saw that there were now two state troopers, and they were both using their searchlights to scan the entire area of the road where we had turned off our pole lights. They were scanning with their searchlights for the vehicle that had shut off its lights.

I guess they were looking for any signs of that stealth vehicle. It was funny, but we never did that again.

Chapter 20

Toad Sniping in Honduras

Sometimes, a few of the overseas assignments on which U.S. Navy SEALs deploy, are of the "civic action" nature. I will never understand why someone would want to send a bunch of trained killers on a mission of peace (unless it is peace through fire superiority). Don't get me wrong here, because there are, and have been, many times when SEALs will stop to help someone, or contribute their time and money to help a cause. However, and for the most part, when it comes to international affairs, U.S. Navy SEALs will have an affair with any international woman, or SEALs will travel to exotic countries, meet exotic people, and kill them. In war, it is after all, what SEALs are trained to do, and SEALs "do it" so very well.

Back at headquarters the higher ups, for whatever their reasons tasked our platoon with a "civic action" mission to a river near Puerto Lempira, Honduras. Our mission was to free up a six-mile long logjam, which was comprised of fallen mahogany trees in the Rio Limpa River. What do SEALs know about logjams? Nothing! However, there is an old saying among professionals who use explosives "There is no problem that cannot be solved with the right amount of explosives." So, on the cargo plane, we brought down about 800 hundred pounds of C4 and TNT explosives that we were going to use to unjam the logs that were in and near the river.

When we all had arrived at the landing strip, we boarded a helicopter and flew over the area of the river that was jammed with logs. We were amazed at the sight, and once we got on the ground we figured out why they sent us to do this job. It was like building the Panama Canal, the area was so heavily infested with mosquitoes. The days were long and the work was extremely hard, the logjam on this river was several miles long, and swimming in the alligator (the locals call them Caimans) infested river to attach the explosive charges was not particularly a comforting feeling. These Caimans were everywhere along the river, and we did have armed lookouts, but the water was very muddy, and when the Caimans submerged they could no longer be seen by our armed lookouts.

All of us decided that it was a waste of time and manpower to have armed lookouts, so we stopped using them. We all agreed that if someone was going to be eaten by a Caiman, there was little if anything we could do about it, so we just concentrated on doing our job, which was to secure massive amounts of explosives to the logs that had jammed up the river in order to clear them out.

The job of "rigging" the explosives to the logjam was extremely dangerous because you had to feel all around, and under the logs while holding your breath in order to tie your 200r40 pound explosive charge to the deepest floating log in the logjam. Hopefully, it was a log and not a Caiman that you were feeling. If you were lucky, the logs would not shift in the water and thus trapping you underwater with no way to swim to the surface. In order to relieve the stress of a day from evading all the Caimans, and rigging explosives underwater in a river that was so muddy you could not see what you were doing, at night, we all would go out toad sniping around the banks of the river.

There were so many of these toads (in the thousands) that it was difficult to sleep at night because of all the noise they would make. Being the loving and caring environmentalists whom we all are, and knowing what the environmentalists do to the goats that threaten the habitat of a certain fox on an island in the Pacific ocean, we thought that we would take a page from an unknown environmentalist handbook on what to do when there is an overpopulation of a species that may threaten another species. To hell with the greater numbers of that species, just thin out the herd.

We did not use any of our weapons, as that would be a waste of good ammunition. Besides, how hard could it be to shoot a big toad at night with a flashlight in his eyes? Instead, our weapon of choice would be an eight-pound sledgehammer. For this night mission, everyone was paired up as a sniper team. The teams would consist of one sniper and one spotter per team.

Each spotter had to have a flashlight (instead of a spotting scope), his Sig Saur 9mm pistol for killing the occasional Caiman that would invade our camp area, a note pad to record the winds, humidity, and temperature. The spotter would also recommend the proper elevation for each "shot/swing" and of course, each spotter was there to confirm the total number of all the kills by his "sniper."

Squashing these toads with a sledgehammer was very cool, one swing, and you could squash them down into the mud almost two feet! One of our guys sounded like he was Bill Murray from the movie "Caddyshack" as he would call out, "Here he is ladies and gentlemen.... The Cinderella kid at Augusta… the gallery goes quiet as he takes out his driver, he lines up his shot…" "Thump, "it's in the hole! It's in the hole. No one can drive a toad into the ground like this kid!"

It was a great stress reliever; we did not make a dent in the toad population, but we sure had fun trying.

Chapter 21

Broken Dick

On some SEAL deployments, for whatever the reasons, the deployment can be more physically demanding on a platoon than on other deployments. During our SEAL platoon deployment to the western Pacific, several members of our SEAL platoon, including myself, were beleaguered by numerous random accidents. These "accidents" took place on operational missions and exercises. The injuries were comprised of dislocated shoulders from conducting "drop and pickup." Drop and pickup is a maneuver where you would roll off a rubber boat that is tied to the side of a patrol boat at designated intervals into the water at a high speed. Once in the water, You would then swim into the shore to gather intelligence on the surface and subsurface about what is near or on the beach, and then swim back out to sea to get picked up by the same patrol boat.

When the patrol boat approached you on the surface of the water, you would be snatched out of the water by a guy inside a small rubber boat that is attached to the side of the patrol boat, and he would be holding a garden hose with a nylon rope through it. This garden hose was called a sling because it was in the shape of a sling/loop, and the guy with the sling would snag your arm, that you were holding above your head, with the sling, and pull you out of the water and back into the small rubber boat. This tactical maneuver for inserting combat swimmers works very well. However, if the boat is traveling at high speed, it will dislocate your shoulder when your arm is snagged by the sling.

There were many broken ribs from rock climbing, broken arms and legs from parachuting into the trees (not by choice), and head injuries sustained from falling off the sides of a ship at night that we had to climb up (hitting a steal deck with your head is never a good idea). All the various missions and training exercises that we had conducted throughout our entire deployment had left scars on many of us, not to mention the invisible emotional scars.

Near the end of our tour of duty, and as was customary at the time, we all had a platoon photograph taken. One photo was taken for ourselves, where we were fully suited up for combat (so cool), and one that was to be displayed on the quarterdeck of the command where we had served our tour of duty. The photograph that we were going to present to our unit commander was to reflect all of our injuries that we had acquired during our deployment while assigned to his command.

In preparation for this particular platoon photo, we all went over to the base medical clinic and had plaster casts put on all the various parts of our bodies, as well as bloody bandages to resemble all of our other sustained injuries. When we were all done getting bandaged up, we looked like we had just escaped from a field medical hospital in a combat zone.

The best reflection of an injury was made for Tommy. Tommy came out of the base clinic with a cast on his dick (When Tommy was rapelling down the side of a cliff, he accidentally came down on one of the many tree branches that were protruding out of the cliff, and it stabbed his penis). The cast was in the shape of a horizontal "L" about 18 inches long (his dream not ours) with the short end of the "L" facing down. Tommy had a supporting wrap attached to it that went around his broken dick, and around the back of his neck to help support the cast in its horizontal broken dick position.

When Tommy walked out of the medical clinic to join us for the platoon photo, a female lieutenant walked by and said, "Oh my God, you broke your penis?"

Tommy, seeing the female lieutenant, snapped to attention and rendered the female lieutenant a hand salute, which she returned (ahh military protocol). Looking at the female lieutenant, Tommy said, "Yes Ma'am, but it only hurts when it gets hard and starts throbbing Ma'am." The female lieutenant turned beet red. Shaking her head, she turned away from Tommy and entered the medical clinic.

Tommy looked at all of us and said, "That was a stupid thing for me to say! I should have asked her for some physical therapy!" We all laughed, and then we headed off to get our platoon photograph taken. When we presented the photo of us all in plaster casts and bandaged up, the commander loved it, and said that he was going to keep this one on display in his office and when it came time for him to transfer, he was going to take it with him.

It was a great photo, and in retrospect we all wished that we had kept a copy!

Chapter 22

TNT Robbers

When it comes to calling in air support to blow the crap out of an enemy position or anything else, for that matter, no one does it better (in my opinion) than an air wing from the US Marines. In the days before all these high-tech smart bombs, these guys were so good that they could drop a 200-pound bomb in your glass of beer from 30 thousand feet, vaporizing your ass, and the only thing left would be your boots inside a huge bomb crater where you use to be.

When we were overseas in another country, our platoon had a great opportunity to go through some close air support training provided by the US Marine A6 (intruder) air wing, and in my opinion, the A6 attack bomber may not have been pretty or fast, but it was probably the best attack bomber ever built.

Our platoon was situated on top of a mountain that overlooked this huge military bombing range where we were going to utilize the A6 attack bombers by calling in air strikes on several old World War II trucks and tanks that were in the valley below us. These tanks and trucks had been bombed so many times, by other aircraft that they all just looked like metal junk heaps.

While scanning the bombing range for a particular target that I wanted the A6 intruders to drop their bombs on, I spotted something interesting, as I was looking through my binoculars. There were four indigenous personnel (people who are native to the country) that had tied ropes to a 200-pound bomb, which had not exploded on its intended target, and they were dragging this 200 pound bomb behind them, and away from the bombing range.

I reported to the Marine Captain, who was assigned to be with us as a forward observer, about my sighting of the indigenous personnel out on the bombing range, and that they were dragging a 200-pound bomb behind them. The Marine captain explained that the reason they were doing that was so that they could drag the unexploded bomb to a place where they could cut the bomb open and pilfer the TNT (a High Explosive) out of the unexploded bombs that they found. They would then sell the stolen high explosives that they got from the bombs on the black market or use it themselves.

"Hmmm…. Ok." I said.

Our entire platoon was sitting around scanning the bombing range below us for targets until we got word that the A6 attack bombers were in our operational area. The Marine captain told all of us to pick a target that we wanted the A6 attack bombers to hit, and to make sure that it was away from the TNT thieves.

So, I picked a grid area on the map (a grid is something like a house address) that was away from the TNT robbers and in an area where I thought thieves might have a base camp, as I could see drag marks that were made by other bombs that they had dragged behind them leading around a small hill, and into a narrow valley.

I called in my target grid location on the radio to the A6 pilot...

Pilot — "Roger inbound..."

I requested two snakes (these are 200-pound bombs that are released at a low level, and they have fins attached to them that act like speed breaks to slow the bombs down, giving the pilot time to escape the blast area)...

Pilot — "Roger two snakes, wings level..." (wings level tells me that he is inbound and in line to the target that I had given him, and that he is ready to release the bombs on my command).

Just then, the Marine captain yelled at me, "Hey, where is your target?"

"Down there!" I yelled.

Pilot — "Inbound on final approach to target..."

"Clear and hot," I said (Clear and Hot tells the pilot that he is clear to release the bombs on the acquired target).

The Marine captain was quickly glancing at his map and looking at the narrow valley where the insidious indigenous asses were dragging the 200-pound bomb. The Marine captain grabbed the microphone to the radio and yells, "Wave off, wave off!" (Wave off tells the pilot to abort his attack, and not to drop any bombs). No bombs were dropped, and I was as pissed off at that Marine captain as he was at me.

The Marine captain yelled at me, "What the hell do you think you were doing, those are civilians down there!"

"Not in my book sir! People who steal TNT to sell or use against us as bombs or improvised explosive devices (IEDs) are not civilians, they're guerrillas!" (Nowadays we call them terrorists).

The Marine Captain canceled the entire aircraft bombing exercise with us, as he felt that we could no longer be trusted to order bombs to be dropped on the old targets that were on the bombing range. He was right, and those damn guerrillas sure got off lucky that day. Nevertheless, one can only wonder, at what cost.

Chapter 23

Wax On Wax Off

As you might well imagine with all the "A" personalities in a SEAL platoon, or for that matter, all the SEAL teams in general, there are bound to be a few ruffled feathers about any number of things between SEALs.

We had a platoon officer who thought that our platoon jeep (left over from WWII), which he drove as his own personal vehicle, needed to be waxed and shined (it was painted a non-reflective flat olive drab color). He called a platoon meeting and said, "Guys, since you are not doing much right now, I want you to go outside to wash and wax my platoon jeep."

Now mind you, we were in the Philippines, it was 95 degrees in the shade, the humidity is 80 percent, and he was asking us to wax a World War II jeep that was painted a flat olive drab color.

"Sir" I said, "Are you feeling ok?"

"Yes, I am, now get your lazy asses out there, and do what I told you to do!"

"Yes sir," we all said.

So, off we went to wash and wax our/his platoon jeep. I told two of our platoon members to get a hose, soap, and water and start washing the jeep; I was going to go buy some wax, and Jim and I would wax the jeep when we got back.

As we were driving to the store, Jim and I were talking about the lunacy of what our officer was requesting us to do, and all of a sudden, we had an epiphany about what we needed to do. When we got to the store, we purchased four cans of simonized floor wax for wood. Those of you who work with wood know how great this stuff is, and that it is never intended to be used on metal, as it is a real pain in the butt to get off any metal or even to try to polish a vehicle's paint job in order to make it shine. We were both laughing about our plan and when we got back to our/his platoon jeep, we saw that the guys had done a fair job of getting most of the mud off the jeep that was most likely left over from WWII.

It was high noon, under a blazing hot sun, when we started applying the floor wax onto the flat olive drab paint of the jeep. Jim and I were both amazed to see how the wax melted right into the paint finish, filling every scratch and all the small dents as the wax flowed onto the hot metal of the jeep. After we finished applying all four cans of floor wax on the jeep, we told our officer that the job was completed. Our officer came out to look at his jeep and said, "Wow, nice job! But, is this wax still wet? Is it some sort of new liquid wax?"

Jim and I looked at our officer and said, "Well sir, the heat from the sun will make it melt into the metal. It will look great tomorrow!"

The next day, we all had another platoon meeting with our platoon officer, and for some reason, he was really pissed off. I do not know why, but he came right to me. Our entire platoon knew that our officer had little patience for practical jokes, especially by me.

Our platoon officer asked me if I thought my joke was funny.

"Joke sir? What joke are you referring to, sir?"

"The f--king jeep, you asshole!"

"Jeep? What about it sir?"

"Go look at it, you smart-ass!"

As I stood there shrugging my shoulders, and looking at my platoon officer, as if he was speaking a foreign language, I said, "Ok sir, let's go check it out."

We all walked around back to where our/his platoon jeep was parked, and there it was, parked in the shade from the tropical sun, a completely white WWII jeep! Looking at that completely white jeep (we even waxed the tires), I said, "Wow sir, I didn't know wax could do that! Cool!"

Our officer barked at me, "Cool? You think that a white military jeep is cool?"

"Well, yes I do, sir, if this was Alaska. Remember sir, you were the one that told us to get our lazy asses out there to wash and wax your jeep.

"Therefore, the way I see it sir, because we were following your orders, it is not our fault that the jeep turned white from being waxed. Besides sir, we purchased all the wax with our own money just so we could fulfill your orders. We put the wax on in the heat of the mid-day sun just as you ordered our lazy asses to do sir. So, as I see it, some of this blame for the white jeep belongs to you sir."

Our platoon officer was clearly pissed, and he turned and walked away. However, the platoon jeep remained white. What was really cool about that jeep being so white was that you always knew where our officer was!

Chapter 24

I Parked My Jet Outside the Bar

My dad always told me that common sense is not so common, and those who have it, wish that others did too. Many years ago, when I was an instructor at SEAL Team One, I was assisting in the training of a platoon out in the California desert.

During a two-day break in the training cycle, I stopped in one of our town hangouts (the Road Kill Café) for a beer or two, or three. It was hot outside in the summer heat, and the cold beer tasted very good. As I was sitting there and enjoying my beer, a woman who was the local drunk and the biggest malcontent of the town, came in and sat at the bar.

This woman started complaining to anyone who would listen to her about all the bombing going on out on the bombing range (go figure) from the jets that were flying around for no apparent reason, other than to disturb her by dropping their bombs on the military bombing range.

This woman was clearly pissed off, and she was complaining specifically about the explosions from the bombs that were shaking her trailer home, and sometimes her dishes would fall off her countertops and break. (Really? What do you expect when you park your mobile home next to a bombing range?)

This woman was one of the locals that we call "lizard people" (because they have lived out in the desert for so long that their skin looks and feels like lizard skin). The woman began looking around the bar, and she spotted me in my jungle green uniform and slurred, "Hey you, you owe me money!"

"Oh yeah, for what?" I said.

"You owe me money for all the dishes that you broke in my house from your damn bombing!"

I said, "What? Are you serious lady?"

She snapped back, "I want my money! You broke my dishes so give me my money!"

Her verbal attacks on me pissed me off. I got up and walked over to her and I said, "You are right, lady, I was out there dropping bombs from my jet in the hopes of breaking your stupid dishes, and while I was flying around I thought a cold beer would really taste good right about now. I saw this bar down here, so I landed my jet outside in the back parking lot so that I could come in here and drink a few beers before I fly back out on the bombing range again. By the way, where do you live so I can drop my bombs on your house?"

The woman got up and went outside looking for my jet in the parking lot! When she came back in, I said, "Well? Did you see my jet out there?"

She was still in her pissed off drunken mode and slurred, "Maybe it wasn't you, but I am sure that you were with them."

I could not believe this woman — she lives right next to a bombing range that is clearly marked "Government Bombing Range." What are you supposed to expect to fall from military jets? She has skin like a lizard, and the desert heat had fried all but the two brain cells that she had left, which she was trying to cool off with beers.

I gave her five bucks and said, "Buy a liquid plate on me!" I left the bar and drove to a restaurant across from the bar and I waited for this bimbo to leave the bar so that I could follow her. (Because payback was on my mind.)

An hour or so had passed, and I watched as she struggled to get into her pickup truck. As she started to drive away, I jumped into my jeep and followed her from a distance. She drove straight to her motor home, and I drove back to my base camp to prepare myself for a nighttime payback mission on this lizard woman.

When I got to camp, I took some thin, black, nylon line (about 200 feet), six large rubber bands, two thumbtacks, and a steel nut. I tied one end of the black nylon line to the steel nut, and I tied all the rubber bands together. I then ran one end of the rubber band through the center of the steel nut, and I slid the steel nut until it was in the center of the rubber band. My "window knocker" was now staged and ready.

When it was dark, I got into my jeep and drove into town. I parked my jeep about six blocks away from the bimbo's motor home, and I went the rest of the way on foot. When I got near the lizard women's motor home, I sneaked up to her window, and I quietly pressed one thumbtack through the end of the rubber band and into the left side of her window frame. I then stretched the rubber band over to the right side of her window frame and pressed in the other thumbtack. I made sure that the steel nut was in the center and being held against the glass window by the tight rubber bands, which was held in place by the thumbtacks.

Once I had the rubber band and steel nut in place on the lizard woman's window, I started to feed out the black nylon line to a concealed position about 150 feet away from her window. Once I was in place, I tugged on the nylon line several times making a tapping sound on her window. "Tap, Tap, Tap."

It was funny to see her come to the window looking out to see who was there every time I "knocked" on her window. I did this several times until she got so pissed off that she threw her window open and yelled, "I know you damn kids are out there! I called the cops!"

She slammed her window shut, and I did it again. "Tap, Tap, Tap."

This time she opened the window and yelled, "I got a gun, and if you bang on my window again, I will shoot you!"

Well, that sounded like an invitation to me, so I just had to do it again. "Tap, Tap, Tap." True to her word, she came out of her motor home with a gun. She ran around her entire motor home, and she even looked under it, but found no one. As soon as she got back inside her motor home, I pulled on the line to tap on her window, "Tap, Tap, Tap." I guess that was the last straw, because she came running out of her door yelling, "I'm gonna kill you sons-of-bitches! Do you hear me? I'm gonna a kill you!"

I was satisfied that I had paid her back, and after she went back inside, I sneaked away back to my jeep. As I was driving back to camp, I was feeling good about my payback on the lizard woman. At least she won't be complaining about military jets dropping bombs for a while. Now it will be "those damn kids banging on her window."

Chapter 25

Mandatory Officers Party

Thank God Commanding Officers (COs) come and go, although certain COs needed to go sooner. Like the one that made us pay out of pocket for any advanced training, or the one that sent over 30 enlisted (not officers) SEALs to the fleet (the infamous dirty 30), because we were over-manned at the end of the Vietnam War. Though not all COs are bad, there were/are some COs that are so great, you wished that they could stay forever, and those commanding officers are the ones for whom there is nothing you would not do.

Many years ago, a certain CO on the West Coast would throw monthly "officers only" parties. These parties were for only the officers under his command (thank God), and they were always held at the commanding officer's home. The attendance was mandatory (so you know that kind of party is going to be very boring), and ALL of the officers under his command, including their wives and girlfriends, had to attend, unless they had an emergency or some important prior obligation that was cleared through the CO, which excused you from attending.

My assistant platoon commander (Oliver) displayed a lot of grit when he attended one of the CO's "mandatory parties" with a pretty girl that had booming career in downtown San Diego. Oliver told me about his pretty date (her unique career was unknown to the rest of the partygoers) that he took to the CO's party. Oliver said that the funniest part about the whole evening was how well his date was getting along with all the other officers' wives, and that she seemed to be so well accepted by everyone.

Oliver said that the CO told him his girlfriend seems to be really hitting it off well with all the ladies, and she appears to be of military wife material. Oliver said, "Oh yes sir, she has an uncanny ability to make any man happy, sir."

"Really Oliver? You are such a lucky man to find that kind of a woman!"

"No sir, I don't think that luck had anything to do with it; I think that it is more about location, sir."

"You are right, Oliver, she is a high-class woman!"

Oliver replied, "Sir, you have no idea."

It was when all the women were congregated in the kitchen, that Oliver's date was asked by the COs wife, "Where do you work?"

Oliver's "date" replied, "In the city."

"Oh? What do you do in the city?"

Oliver's date replied, "Well, I'm a prostitute!"

At first, all the officers' wives started to laugh, but when Oliver's date did not respond to the laughter, the COs wife realized that she was serious about being a prostitute.

The CO's wife looked at Oliver's date and said, "You're really a prostitute?"

"Yes, I am. Do you have a problem with that?"

The CO's wife completely lost her composure and yelled at Oliver's date, "YES, I do have a problem with someone like you who earns her money by sleeping with men! It is immoral and it's disgusting!"

The prostitute replied, "Really? How am I any different from you? You sleep with your husband, and he gives you money, a car, this house, clothes, and whatever else that you want. It seems to me that you charge more for sex than I do!"

The whole corner of the house exploded with screams and accusations by all the women. The CO was so pissed off at Oliver that he told Oliver to leave, and to take his tramp with him. As Oliver was leaving the CO's house, the CO's wife yelled at Oliver, saying, "I cannot believe that you brought a prostitute into my home!" The CO told Oliver to see him in the morning.

The next morning when Oliver met with the CO, Oliver was given 30 days of extra duty (guard duty) for bringing a prostitute into the CO's home. Whenever someone would ask Oliver about why he got so much duty, Oliver would explain what happened, and then he would smile and say, "It was worth it! Because I am banned, now and forevermore, from all of his future mandatory parties!"

Chapter 26

Where Is The Groom?

Should a Navy SEAL ever want to keep from getting hazed by his SEAL brothers, then there are two bits of personal information that every U.S. Navy SEAL will always try to keep from his fellow teammates, and they are: his birthday, and the day that he is going to get married.

Our platoon discovered that Sam was getting married to his beautiful fiancé, and that her entire family was flying in from Texas for the big event at a Catholic church in San Diego. Before Sam was to get married to his lovely fiancé, on the Eve of their wedding day, and against the wishes of his fiancé, our platoon had to have a bachelor's party for Sam. Because Sam's bride-to-be protested so strongly to all of us about giving Sam a bachelor's party, this was certainly going to be a great party.

Our entire platoon chipped in and rented an entire bar in downtown San Diego. We did this so that no one else could enter our little party, except for any of our other brother SEALs. It all started innocently enough, as most bachelor parties do, with plenty of drinks, girls, and so on. I think that it was about eleven PM (With all the booze we drank, who can be sure?); we were all so inebriated that we (certainly not the groom to be) had a great idea for one heck of a joke! We all took Sam to Lindbergh Field (San Diego International Airport. Of course, this was all long before 9-11 and the TSA Nazis).

We all walked up to the airline counter, supporting Sam in his drunken stupor, and purchased a one-way ticket for Sam to Boulder, Colorado. By now, Sam had passed out from all the alcohol that he had ingested. So we took his wallet, including any change that he had, and we told the stewardess that Sam was getting married tomorrow in Boulder, Colorado, and because we had his bachelors' party here, could she please make sure that he got off the plane in Boulder. She smiled, and said that Sam was lucky to have such good friends like us, and she reassured us that she would make sure that Sam got off the plane in Boulder, Colorado. We thanked her, and we all left Sam to his fate.

It was around noontime, and on the day that Sam and his bride to be were to be married. We were all sitting together in the church in San Diego, waiting to see Sam get married. As we (the innocent) sat there, we were all looking around for Sam. However, Sam was nowhere to be found. Sam's father walked up to us and asked us if we had seen him, and we all replied, "Not since last night, sir."

Sam's father said, "I wonder where he could be."

Yes indeed, where could Sam be, as we (now, the guilty) all started looking at each other as if we were innocent of any wrong doing what-so-ever whispering, "Where the hell is Sam?"

As time went on, it became very clear to us that Sam was not going to make it to his wedding. So, we (the not so innocent) got up to go inside the side waiting room of the church, where the bride and all the bridesmaids were waiting to come out, to see Sam's beautiful bride, and explain to her what we thought would be taken as a funny joke.

Nothing could have been further from the truth. After explaining what we all had done to Sam, we watched as what was once a beautiful woman, turned into an ugly, venomous monster, snorting fire from her nostrils right before our eyes!

When the look of shock had left her face, and the enormity of what we had done had set in, she started cursing at us loudly (mind you, this was inside a Catholic church, and everyone could hear a pin drop), and she began slapping each of us on our faces. While we (the very guilty) were standing there taking in all of her venomous anger, in walks the Priest, and all of the in-laws, to see what all the yelling and cursing was about, and why the lovely bride was so upset/pissed off.

I am here to tell you that whoever said, "Confession is good for the soul" was never a Navy SEAL at a wedding and inside a church with an angry bride ready to do battle against him.

Of course, all the in-laws were astonished when they learned what we had done to Sam. The mother of the bride was furious and said that we were the ugliest people that she had ever met in her life, and then she began to curse us (like mother, like daughter we thought). As all the women were trying to console the bride, Sam's father, who was a retired Marine Colonel, walked up to us with that "you guys are so screwed smile," and in a low voice he said, "Boys, that was a good joke, but knowing how angry these ladies can get, I am sure glad that I am not any of you gentlemen." Sam's wife-to-be and her mother clearly hated all of us for ruining what they claimed to be "their wedding day." Why is it that a woman always say it is "Their" or "My" wedding day? What happened to "our" (as in Bride and Groom) wedding day? Even so, none of us were not going to throw gasoline on that fire.

Meanwhile, back in Boulder, Colorado, Sam finally found someone that gave him enough money to make a long distance phone call to the church in San Diego, to let us all know that he was all right. We paid for Sam's flight back to San Diego, and when we all got together (and away from Sam's future wife), Sam told us that he thought our joke was funny. However, his wife-to-be told him that we were not to be invited back to the wedding the next day, nor would we be welcome in their house for any dinners for the rest of our lives. (Did she actually believe that we would trust her to cook food for us?)

We all wished Sam well, and we could not resist one last joke. While Sam and his bride were inside the church getting married, we (the forever banned) rubbed limburger cheese all over Sam's car engine, and taped inflated condoms all over his car. We were all sure that after everything we had done, Sam's wife would never forget "her" wedding day!

Chapter 27

Honey and Feathers

As I stated before, there are a few things that SEALs try to keep from their teammates — weddings, birthdays, and the like. These are secrets, and as a SEAL you must guard them well, because your brother SEALs love to pull pranks on each other and all that is needed is an excuse. So, if your special day is found out, it will cost you dearly, as it did for one young U.S. Navy SEAL that thought he was capable of fending off his brother SEALs that were planning to attack him on his birthday.

Whatever it was that we were originally going to do to Frank might not have been too bad had Frank not made a statement to the effect, "There are not enough SEALs here to take me down on my birthday." (Remember a few pages back, what I said about a challenge?) Frank, who made that foolish boast, was no small man, but it is a numbers game when it comes to defending yourself. No matter how big and strong you are, you might get a few good slams in, but you cannot beat everyone, and eventually you will go down.

We all waited until the end of the day, and as Frank was walking out of the SEAL locker room, we all jumped him! The fight was on, but as I said, it is a numbers game. There were a lot more of us then he could handle, and after a lot of struggling and fighting, we finally wore him down.

We tied Frank up and dragged him out to the beach behind the SEAL Team One compound. Frank was a big boy and a great fighter; it was no easy task for us to duct tape his arms and legs in a spread eagle fashion to the Yellow One beach marker (Two poles sunk deep in the sand with a large yellow marker for landing vessels to guide on as they approached the beach).

When we had finished taping his arms and legs to the steel poles, we cut all his clothes off his body, stripping him naked. Frank was cursing up a storm and threatened all of us with death as we poured honey all over his head and body. When he was totally covered with honey, we tore open a feather pillow and threw the feathers all over him.

We left him taped to the beach marker cussing and pledging death threats against us. As we approached the quarterdeck area (the main entrance in and out of the SEAL compound), our Commanding Officer came out to see what the screaming and cursing was all about.

Our Commanding Officer looked at us, and then he looked at Frank honeyed, feathered, and taped to the beach marker. Our CO started to laugh, and then he said, "Cut that man down!"

Zack spoke up first and said, "Are you serious, sir? I would wait a bit, Frank is really pissed-off, sir."

The CO replied, "I agree, he is a big boy. Well, at least cut the binds on one of his hands, and then get the hell out of there."

"Yes sir," we all replied. We all drew straws to see who would go back out there; Pete lost (poor Pete). As Pete approached Frank, Frank said that after he got free, he was going to bury all of us that night. We were all a bit concerned as Frank usually did what he said he would do. So we all split for the safety of our homes and those who had wives told them to shut off all the lights, lock the doors and windows, and not to open the door for anyone!

Frank never came around, but we didn't get any sleep that night either, as we were all waiting for Frank to come around! Nice one, Frank.

Chapter 28

Payback for Flying First Class

Now, do not get me wrong here, I have had my fair share of flying first class like most people have, and yes, it is nice on long trips. However, for those self-appointed "elite snobs" out there that fly ONLY first class, do not look at the rest of us boarding the plane, as if we are the underlings while sipping on your mixed drink with its cute little umbrella in it, or burying your face in a newspaper pretending to be engrossed in some story or the results of some stock, as if we are disturbing you when we walk by.

The truth of the matter is, if 600 dollars pays for a round trip ticket in coach, the price of a round trip first or business class ticket would be about 1,400 dollars. So, that "free" mixed drink that you are sipping on with the cute little umbrella just cost you 800 dollars! Enjoy it.

The other truth about flying in first class or business class is, if and when we crash, those of us flying in coach have a better chance of survival than you do in first class. Because, if you think about it, you never see the front of the airplane intact after an airplane crash, do you?

So, if we all do crash, please be sure to kiss the pilot on his butt cheek before you fly through his ass on your way through the front end of the airplane on an impact, and know that you will be providing a nice cushion for the rest of us who are ALL sitting behind you!

As U.S. Navy SEALs do a lot of traveling around the world for missions, special schools or training, the smart SEALs will join one of the many frequent flier programs so that he can get upgraded to business/ first class. Because the government is not going to put an enlisted man who serves his country, even if he is returning from combat, in business or first class. Those seats are reserved for senior level officers, business executives, contractors, and the affluent. Get your butt to the back of the plane, solider!

On one such training trip, a SEAL was ribbing another SEAL because he had accumulated enough frequent flier points to fly first class, and the other SEAL had to fly in coach. His brother SEAL was going on and on about all the free drinks he was going to have, and the hot meal he was going to eat while sitting in his nice soft seat with all that legroom.

Well, I guess that his conscience had gotten the better of him because while they were airborne, the SEAL in first class had the flight attendant send back a mixed drink to the SEAL that was flying in coach.

When the flight attendant went back to where the SEAL was sitting in coach, and offered the mixed drink to him, the SEAL in coach asked, "Who is this from?" The flight attendant replied that it was from the gentleman in first class. The SEAL replied, "That guy will just not leave me alone! I'm very sorry miss, but could you please return that drink to him, and please tell him that I am straight, I like women not men, and tell him that I am not interested in having any sort of an affair with him."

The flight attendant replied, "I will certainly tell him, I am very sorry to disturb you, sir!"

The SEAL replied, "It is not your fault that he uses people like you to try to get what he wants."

When the stewardess returned the mixed drink and told the SEAL in first class what the SEAL in coach had said, the looks that the SEAL in first class got from the stewardess, and the others flying in first class was priceless, especially when the gentlemen sitting next to him in first class, got up and moved to another seat. Ahhh, paybacks can be so much fun.

Chapter 29

When Seals Cock Block Other SEALs

When you are a single guy, and doing the bar scene, it is a tough enough game to play without someone undermining your efforts. Because not only do you have to contend with all the other competition inside the bar or nightclub, but also you never know who has your back, especially if you are in the SEAL teams and "out-on-the-town" in a SEAL platoon.

Our platoon was drinking in a local bar and having a great time together. Sitting at a table with some women were a few of the SEALs in our platoon, and they were making great time with the women who were seated with them. Myself and two other members of our platoon were sitting at the bar enjoying a few brews, as we admired the young studs making their moves on these women whom they were sitting with.

However, all of that was about to change when our platoon corpsman (Chuck) walked up to us and said, "Would you gents care to make a wager?"

"About what?" I asked.

Doc replied, "That I can make those women leave our SEAL teammates at that table over there."

Looking at Doc, and then at our SEAL brothers sitting at the table, I asked, "You're not going to make them puke are you?"

Doc laughed, "Nooo nothing like that."

We all laughed as we recalled the episode with the Marines. Doc added, "No drugs, and nothing physical."

"Ok, what is the bet?" I asked.

Doc replied, "If I win, you guys pay for my drinks, if I lose, I pay for yours."

I replied, "Nothing physical and no chemicals. Ok Doc, you're on. Go do your stuff." Doc smiled that "I got this bet" smile, and turned towards the poor souls sitting at the table.

Doc walked over to the table where the young SEALs were sitting and started chewing out the SEALs because they were sitting with the women, "Hey, I told you guys no drinking! You all got shots for syphilis, except you Greg, you got gonorrhea. You guys should not even be next to these women; you might infect them. Hey, they didn't kiss you did they? If they did I will have to give you all ladies shots as well!"

Greg stood and barked at Doc saying, "What the hell are you talking about Doc? You know that is all bullshit!"

Doc fired back saying, "Look, I am looking out for these women here, I am the medical corpsman and you guys are all infected from the hookers that you were with last week, so don't try to bullshit these women here that you are not infected! You women should take my advice, as I am their medical doctor, and leave these infected guys alone!" Doc spun around and left the table.

The women got that astonished look on their faces, and you could hear that they were shocked and clearly pissed off. The women got up from the table yelling obscenities at the SEALs. However, the funniest part was watching the SEALs trying to profess their innocence and purity to these women. SEALs... Pure? That is enough to make anyone laugh!

Doc knew that there is no rational woman on earth that would be willing to risk the chance of catching something from these guys! Doc also knew that being our platoon corpsman made him practically immune from any paybacks. Had the whole scene not been so funny, I would have been pissed off too, because the night was young, and Doc drinks top shelf Scotch.

Chapter 30

When Navy SEALs Go Fishing in the Desert

Our platoon was slotted to conduct SEAL advanced training out in a remote area of the desert for 45 days. The advanced SEAL platoon training was going to be great; however, eating MREs (Meals Ready to Eat) for 45 days was going to get very old. I don't know how dogs eat the same canned dog food, day in and day out, not to mention the fact that they wag their tails every time you open a can of that smelly stuff, like you were serving them a New York strip steak. Based on the reaction of dogs, perhaps, instead of eating MREs, we should all eat dog food.

One day, as we were all sitting around at the SEAL camp, a few of us were reading a military map, and looking for some new training areas. I was stunned when I saw a location on the military map that said, "Trout Farm." In a million years, you would never think that the desert is the best place to find trout, well not me anyway.

To see if in fact what we had read on the military map was indeed true, my team-mate Waldo and I, got into our military jeep and headed out to the grid coordinates of the trout farm to see if in fact there really was a Trout farm at that grid location on the military map.

When we arrived at the grid coordinates on the map, what we found at this area was a huge eight-foot fence that enclosed three shallow concrete pools. On the eight-foot fence were signs that said, "Trout farm, no trespassing allowed," and other words to the effect that "these trout are protected by law."

Who would have ever thought that there would be an actual Trout farm here? However, there we both were, in the California desert standing next to an 8-foot high fence with a bunch of trout that were, according to the signs on the fence, protected by law. Waldo started laughing and said, "This is like the Beverly Hill Billies with their cement pond full of fish!" I remember the TV show, but I am not sure if they fished in their pool or not. Either way, we both laughed as we got back into our military jeep and headed towards the town to buy some fishing poles, hooks, and bait.

When we arrived at the general store, we purchased a couple of fishing poles, hooks, and whatever else we thought that we might need. After we purchased all the fishing supplies that we thought that we would use, we headed back to our base camp to swap our jeep for a 5-ton truck. While we were at our base camp, we also loaded up two 55-gallon drums filled with ice and water; we were going to use these 55-gallon drums to store all the fish that we were going to catch.

What was the reason that we swapped our military jeep for the 5-ton truck? Well, remember that there is an eight-foot high fence around the concrete ponds protecting all those fish inside the concrete ponds. Climbing over the fence would be trespassing, so we thought that we would use the 5-ton truck as our "platform" to fish from because it was just as high as the fence. We loaded up all the fishing gear, including a can of corn for bait, and headed back out to the trout farm.

Once arrived there, we pulled up as close as possible to the 8-foot high fence, and parked our truck. We both got out of the truck, and grabbed our fishing poles. We climbed on top of the cab of our 5-ton truck, which was above the fence. We then baited our hooks with the corn, and we cast out our fishing lines into the trout pond. We were catching fish faster than we could bait our hooks.

We were both laughing aloud, and my teammate said, "Fishing should always be like this, you would never get bored, and you would always have plenty to eat!" We were filling our two 55 gallon drums up fast, and we were getting tired hauling in all the trout that we were catching. When we're done with "our" limit, which was well over 100 trout, we put away our fishing poles and headed back to our base camp. We had enough fish for everyone, for the next six days of training. Everyone at our camp got their fill, and it sure beat the MREs (Meals Ready to Eat) that we were supposed to eat three times a day. Thanks Trout Farm!

Chapter 31

Hey, is that Bottled Water?

When U.S. Navy SEALs deploy overseas to under developed countries, you have to expect to get the Hershey squirts from drinking the
local water, and yes, it does depend on what country that you go too if
you are going to be effected or not. As our SEAL platoon was going to
be "in country" anywhere from six months to a year, and as you cannot
bring bottled water with you. The best thing that you can do is just
drink the local water and get over whatever is going to happen to your
internal system.

When we were on a deployment to a country in Central America, our
squad was stationed near the front lines of a guerrilla movement. We had
a nice building that was reinforced to give all of us a lot of protection
from small arms fire, which we would need should the guerrillas ever
decide to attack our position. Our mission was to train the commando
forces in counter guerrilla warfare, and to deal with the guerrilla warfare
threat that was oppressing thousands of people in their country.

The training was intense, and we were all putting in many long hours
to ensure that the commandos were going to be as well trained as possible for the missions that they were going to be tasked with. The one
thing that would always set us behind schedule in our daily training,
were the VIP visitors who consisted of congressional representatives,
senators, State Department people, Department of Defense People, and
so on, and these VIPs would arrive about every week from the USA.
After awhile, we all got a little tired of all these VIP visitors, because
they would take up valuable time away from our scheduled training
with the people that needed our training the most, the commandos. We
could care less about the VIPs, because we wanted the commandos to
be ready to deal with any and all combat threats that they were going to
face on a daily bases, in order to stay alive.

Whenever the VIPs would arrive at our location, it is no small affair,
as it was usually a group of up to 20 persons, depending on who the
VIP was, and the reason for their visit. They would sit in on a situation briefing, given by our lieutenant, which was about the situation of
the war and the effect that our training was having on the commandos'
ability to combat the enemy. While the VIPs all sat around drinking
their bottled water, and eating all of our food that we paid for (and they

usually wanted shrimp), they would make promises to deliver whatever support that we needed, which in truth, they rarely if ever delivered on any of their promises of support. We all came to realize that politicians are professional liars, and they would not deliver on a promise, unless it benefited "them," or it created a "photo opportunity for them," using us as window dressing for their photos.

So, in preparation for these "VIP" visits, we decided to have a little fun with "them" at their expense. As we were all accustomed to drinking the local water, and we never used or had any need for any bottled water. We purchased a five-gallon office type water cooler; we filled up our 5-gallon water bottle to our water cooler with the water from our team house's garden hose. This water was crystal clear, hillside runoff water, which went into a huge green moss lined concrete tank filled with all kinds of microorganisms, insects, and a few occasional floating dead rats. This water was then pumped through the underground city pipes that were installed back in the early 1900s.

When the VIP visitors would ask us if the water cooler was bottled water, we could honestly reply, "Yes, it is." Hey, it was water, and it was in a bottle. They would drink our bottled water to their hearts' content, and then they would fill up their empty water bottles with the water from our 5-gallon water jug until it was empty.

The reason that they would fill up all of their empty water bottles was to prepare themselves for their next stop, and their long flight back on a military cargo plane that had only one toilet. Never once would ANY of these VIPs offer any form of payment for the food that they all ate, nor did we get any of their support that they had promised.

So, for their lack of support, we wished them all "Happy Trails," and we all hoped that the line to that single toilet in the rear of the C-130 cargo plane that they were all flying back to the USA on, was long, and that they had all ran out of toilet paper!

Chapter 32

It's All in Your Perception

During one of our many training missions in the swamps of Florida, and as usual, we were playing the role of the enemy (for SEALs this is a common theme). We were evading several of the US Army units that were sent out into the swamps to try and capture or kill us. We patrolled all night, in waist deep swamp muck water, while being bitten by just about every insect that Darwin could name, and evading all the Army units that were sent out to find us. We came to a nice grassy area that had low shrubs and trees, which afforded us concealment from any land or air units that were out looking for us.

As dawn was breaking, we heard a lot of yelling and screaming that peaked our attention. I told the guys to stay alert, while Paul and I go out and investigate what the source of the activity was that we were all hearing. We crawled a good way through the tall grass until we could see that we were in an affluent area of Florida.

There was a young woman who was cursing up a storm at this guy, and when she finished, she got into her red Ferrari and sped off. The guy whom she was cursing at leaned against his black Mercedes Benz and started crying. Paul looked at me and said, "Can you believe this shit?" Paul got up from our concealed position and started walking over to the man, with me following behind. We gave the man quite a scare, as we had our guns with us, faces painted, and we were reeking from the smell of swamp muck.

Paul looked at this guy and said, "We are out here playing war games, and we couldn't help over hearing your little domestic problem, are you ok Bucky?" The guy replied in slobbering voice, "My wife just left me for good, and now I don't know what to do!"

Paul paused for a moment, looking around, shaking his head slowly up and down and slowly repeating the mans words, "You don't know what to do." Paul took in a slow deep breath, and let him have it. "You stupid asshole, look around you! You got a beautiful car, a beautiful house, a garage with an F--king airplane in it, and she left you? F--K her! You can have ANY woman that you want! You think you got problems. My wife took a sledgehammer my motorcycle, and after she smashed it all to shit, she poured gasoline on it, and then she set it on fire! If that wasn't enough to show how pissed off she was at me, she went into our house and threw all my clothes out on the front lawn, and told me never to come back, or she would set me on fire! I am out here in the F--king swamps hiding from the bad guys who want to capture or kill me, I am getting my ass bitten by everything out here, I am cold, wet, tired, and hungry. Your wife leaves you with ALL of this shit, and you think YOU got problems? Wake the F--k up stupid, she did you a favor!"

Paul must have struck a nerve with this guy, because he stopped crying, and I watched as a small smile came to his face, and he said, "You're right, I guess things aren't so bad for me after all. Hey, you guys want to come in for a bite to eat or something?" Paul and I both declined his offer. He thanked Paul, shook both of our hands, and then he watched as we both disappear back into the swamp from where we came.

I can't imagine the stories that this guy tells, about the day that two guys came out of the swamp, to his friends.

It was true what Paul said about his wife, I was there helping him pick up his clothes off his lawn, and I saw the bike lying in his driveway on its' side smoldering, and looking like it was hit by a train.

Chapter 33

Payback for Being an Asshole Platoon Chief

From time to time, every SEAL platoon will get a chief assigned to their platoon that is, quite frankly, just an asshole. Not that a platoon chief should always be a nice guy, but he should know that there is a time and a place to be an asshole to his men, and only when his men have asked for it (like any parent who has children). I received great advice from an officer who once told me, "Always praise your men in the open, and always chew their asses in private."

I remember one particular SEAL platoon chief named "Walter," and he did not quite master the fine art of knowing when and where to discipline his men, and he would rule them with an iron fist. The consequences for this type of "leadership," was not sitting well with the men in his platoon members, and "they" were forming plans to make Walter's life a bit interesting. So, his men, when faced with their platoon chiefs open verbal abuses and usurpations, and feeling that they have been reduced to a form of despotism, his men decided to give their platoon chief, paybacks.

The first payback to this chief came when one of his SEAL platoon members took a crap inside a plastic resealable bag, he then stabbed it numerous times with a pin, and then he sewed the "turd bag" inside his platoon chief's" pillow. Three of his SEAL platoon members then, waited until lunch time, and with one acting as a lookout, the others snuck inside the chiefs' quarters onboard the ship, which was taking the SEAL platoon to their next area of operation that was about 30 days sailing time away. Once they found the rack (bed) that their chief was using to sleep on at night, they switched their chief good pillow for the turd pillow.

Every night, Walter would go to sleep with his head on that smelly pillow. After a few days, the other chiefs that shared the chief's sleeping compartment started moving away from the area where Walter's rack was, and they commented to Walter about the foul odor emanating from his rack. Thinking that he had an old and somehow rotting mattress, Walter swapped out his old mattress for a new one. Walter thought that this would cure his smelly problem. However, for some illogical reason, he kept his "special" pillow.

One night, while Walter was sleeping in his bed, the plastic bag inside his pillow burst open and oozed out its smelly contents inside his pillow. The overpowering stench from the foul ooze woke Walter up, and he began to gag, and curse. Realizing that this had to be the actions of his own men, he punished every enlisted man in his SEAL platoon by putting all of them to work washing dishes in the ships' galley (better known as KP duty "KP" meaning Kitchen Patrol).

When Walter's SEAL platoon arrived at their debarkation destination, I was there with my SEAL platoon to do a turnover of duties, after which, my SEAL platoon was to be transported to another operational area. Both of our SEAL platoons were to spend about two weeks together, so there would be plenty of time to complete the turnover of duties and to have a few good times together as well.

One night, as I was returning from my night out in a local town, I was walking past the sauna room in our barracks, what caught my attention was a faint voice calling for help followed by a "thud" sound, "help... thud... help... thud... help..." When I walked into the room where the sauna was located, I saw that someone had tied the handles of the sauna door, which effectively prevented anyone on the inside of the sauna from getting out, and the temperature gauge to the sauna had been jammed on high. When I cut the rope away from the door handle and opened the door, there laying on the floor was Walter. Walter was very weak, and I had to take him to the base clinic for an IV, as he was dangerously dehydrated from being locked inside the sauna for so long.

As we were sitting there in the recovery room, I asked Walter how things were between him and his platoon. "Why, you think I got problems?" Smiling, I replied, "No, not at all Walter, I think that you being an asshole to your men all the time is working out great for you don't you?"

Walter stared at the ceiling for some time while slowly nodding his head, he then said, "So, this is payback for me being an asshole to all of my men?" Yup, I replied, "It's up to you Walter, you can sit down and work things out with your men, or you can continue being an asshole to them. Just remember this Walter, the next time you might not be so lucky, because Lord knows, and from what I have heard from your men, they are willing to go to any length with their great imaginations to pay you back for being an asshole!

I was glad to hear that Walter had eased up on being such a hard ass to his men in his platoon, and as a platoon, they were all doing a lot better.

Chapter 34

Foreign Exchange Program

I often wondered why the SEAL teams did this, exchange one officer and one enlisted man, for a foreign officer, and a foreign enlisted man as observers to each other's training. On the West coast, the foreign officers would be put "in-charge" of our training department, and the US officers would only be "observers" in their foreign training department! Now, I grant you that there is some merit to the foreign exchange program, but overall, the guys in the SEAL teams were never placed in command of any foreign personnel, unlike their counterpart's who came to the SEAL team on the West Coast in United States.

For example, there was an Australian Army SAS captain (Special Air Service), who was assigned to the training department at SEAL team one. Now, almost all the Australian guys whom I have met and worked with are spot on professionals in every sense of the word. Nevertheless, even the SAS will tell you that (just like in the SEAL teams) a few loose screws always fall off the table (in both enlisted and officer ranks).

However, let's get back to this SAS captain. This SAS captain was an unusual fellow, he openly thought of himself as being far superior to any of us in the SEAL teams. As far as "our women" in the USA were concerned, he would never miss a chance to tell us that when it comes to your "American women," he would say, "American women are the ones who wear the pants in what should be the man's house, and in your marriages." He would also say that it is the American women who have the last say in any argument (might be true, but don't say that crap to a bunch of SEALs when their women are not around).

This captain justified his remarks by saying that the reason American women rule in a household is because, all the American men are afraid to stand up to their women. The captain would say, "Our Australian women always know their place in a marriage, because we Australians have not been "de-balled" by our women like you American men have!"

Well, of course a payback was in order for those comments. So, while out we were out at our remote training camp in the desert, and training a SEAL platoon, the SEAL platoon training session was coming to an end. In preparation for going back home the next day, this SAS captain was jamming all of his dirty laundry into his kit bag to bring home to his missus so that she could wash his dirty clothes.

While the SAS captain was busy packing, a few of us got together and formulated a plan to payback this cocky SAS captain. In preparation for the Australian captain's departure for home, we thought that we would drive into the small town and purchase the SAS captain a little "welcome home" warming gift. When we got into town, we went to the department store, and we purchased a fancy, frilly bra, and some cheap ass perfume, which we spilled on the bra that we had purchased.

We took our "gift" back with us to our barracks, and while the cocky SAS captain was on his way into town to drink a few brews with the rest of the boys, we went into his room, and we stuck that fancy bra deep inside his kit bag, in the center of all his dirty laundry. Once we had accomplished our payback deed, and high fived each other, we headed back to town to join everyone else for a few brews. The next day, we all woke up and departed for our return trip back to Coronado, Calif.

While I was sitting around my apartment that night, I got a telephone call from the SAS captain, and he was distressed about an apparent joke that had been played on him. He said that he knew that I was the one responsible for this stupid little joke, which now has his wife deeply upset with him. He said that he was going to put his wife on the phone, and that I had better clear this matter up and tell her that it was indeed a joke. I said, "Sure captain, put her on."

When his wife spoke on the phone, I could hear the stress, and coldness in her voice. "Hello…" Hello, this is Billy; I was out in the desert conducting platoon training with your husband. Look, I don't know what your husband has told you, but the truth is that we all warned him to get rid of that stupid trophy bra that he took from some woman before he went home to see you, but he said piss on it, the wife knows her place, and…." She slammed down the telephone!

After a moment or two, my telephone started ringing like crazy, but I did not answer it, and as I did not want any "surprise guests" to show up at my apartment, I left my apartment to go out for a few beers.

After a few hours, and a few beers, I called the SAS captain's house, and I spoke to his wife later that night to reassure her that it was indeed a joke. However, I did not get the feeling that she totally believed me.

Perhaps if she is reading this now, she will. However, you should remember this lady, had your husband not insulted all the men and women in the USA, we would not have played that joke on him.

Chapter 35

A Bad Sound to Hear During a Night

Combat Equipment Jump...

Whoosh Thump... Whoosh Thump!

Whenever SEALs conduct their night combat equipment parachute training, being on the drop zone during the night of a combat equipment parachute jump can be more nerve racking than actually jumping out of an airplane at night. Mostly, because it is dark and when you look up into the night sky you cannot see the parachute jumpers that are sky diving from 20,000 or 30,000 feet, unless they are all wearing strobe lights on their parachute equipment bags.

One night, while a few of us were on the drop zone (DZ) waiting for a SEAL platoon to fly over and jump out of the C-130 cargo plane, we began setting up all the lights in the shape of a "T." The reason for the "T" is so that the SEALs, who were going to jump out of the airplane, can spot the location of the DZ and steer their parachutes to our location on the ground, after which they would then load up our vehicles, and we would take them back to the base.

To communicate with the aircraft that the SEALs were going to jump out of, we had our radio on a speaker so that anyone on the DZ could hear the aircraft when they contacted us on the drop zone. It was not long before we all heard the Aircraft jump master (he is the man in command of telling the jumpers when to jump out of the aircraft at the right moment) on our radio letting us know that they were inbound, and five minutes away from releasing all the parachute jumpers.

The SEALs were jumping from an altitude of about 25,000 feet with combat equipment bags (these are bags full of ammunition, food, water and other electronic equipment needed for their mission). We heard the jump master say on our radio that all jumpers are out.

On the drop zone, we were all looking up into the night sky trying to spot the strobe lights (these are bright flashing lights that are attached to each man. This makes it easier for us on the ground to spot them for safety reasons) attached to each jumper as they fell through the night sky. (Of course, on a real mission they would not be wearing any strobe lights because if they did the enemy would see them, and start shooting at them).

As we were able to see all the SEAL jumpers from the ground because of the flashes from the strobe lights, we informed the jump master that we counted all members of the SEAL platoon falling to earth. When the SEAL jumpers got close enough (about 5,000 feet), you could hear the opening of their parachutes. What caught our attention next, was the flashing strobes that were not falling slower, as they should be when a jumper is under a parachute that had opened. We watched, as the two SEAL jumpers were getting closer and closer to the ground, and they were falling at about150 MPH.

All of us on the drop zone could see that something was horribly wrong, as the flashes from the strobe lights were falling extremely fast, and we all knew that their parachutes had failed to open. We all started yelling, "Pull... Pull... Pull!" (Each parachute jumper had to pull his own ripcord, which would then open his parachute), and then came the rushing sounds from the jumpers falling at high speed through the air and towards the ground, which was followed by the horrible sounds of the speeding impacts made by two parachute jumpers, Whoosh THUMP. . . . . . Whoosh THUMP.

I once saw a brother SEAL, who I had gone through training with; hit the ground at 150 miles per hour. I can tell you that what the impact does to a person's body is not a pretty sight. We all ran over to where we heard the sounds of the jumpers that had impacted on the ground. Their strobe lights were still flashing so it made it easy for us to find their bodies quickly. When we arrived at the location of the "thuds" made from the sounds of the impact by the jumpers, we saw the flattened remains of two combat equipment bags.

Apparently, two members of the SEAL platoon thought that it would be funny to send two combat equipment bags loaded up with weights, out of the aircraft at the same time as the jumpers. When all the SEAL jumpers had finally landed, they all got a good laugh about us running to give aid to dead equipment bags. It was funny, but it was also a feeling of great relief!

Chapter 36

Jumpmasters Should Never Say "No,"

When Everyone is Ready to Jump!

As I said earlier, having to jump out of a perfectly good airplane or a helicopter was never any form of enjoyment for me, especially when I knew it was capable of landing.

When our platoon traveled too Florida to a remote base to conduct nighttime HALO parachute training (HALO = High Altitude Low Opening). After our safety briefing about the parachute jump, our platoon suited up with all of our parachute equipment for our nighttime HALO jump, we then all boarded the C-130 aircraft. Our platoon was sitting inside a C-130 (Large cargo aircraft) flying at 25,000 feet on our way to our drop zone, and we were all breathing pure oxygen (as there is little or no breathable air above 15,000 feet).

As we were all sitting around breathing pure oxygen and waiting for our aircraft to approach our drop zone, We started to double check all of our combat gear, to include all of our water, food, bullets, explosives and operational equipment that we would need for our training mission. We had our parachutes on, and as I said, we were just sitting around waiting as almost all jumpers do, for the jumpmaster to tell us to get off of our butts. We were all waiting for the jumpmaster to give the two-minute warning that would be followed by a one-minute warning given by the jumpmaster, and then everyone would stand up, make their way to the back ramp of the aircraft, wait for the 10 second warning, followed by the jumpmaster yelling "GO!" Then all of us would jump off of the back ramp of the aircraft and out into the night sky.

It was nighttime, and inside the C-130, it is warm and noisy from the four turboprop engines. Some guys were telling stories, while others pretended to be sleeping. Then all of us were tuned in when we heard the jumpmaster yell out "Two Minutes!" Everyone sticks two fingers in the air in acknowledgment that we heard his two-minute warning.

We all know that we are approaching the drop zone (a place on the ground where we would all steer our parachutes too, and land). In preparation for jumping out of the aircraft, we all stand up, and we check each other's parachute equipment, as if any of us would really jump without a parachute properly rigged to your bodies.

Actually, when you are this advanced in your jumping career, it is just to make sure that no one has any bent pins on their parachute containers/rigs that would prevent their parachute from opening. Ok, there is a bit more to it, but this is a book on the amusing side of Navy SEALs, and it is not a training manual, so all of you sky gods out there will just have to get over yourselves, and those of you who know me, know that I could not care less about jumping out of a damn airplane!

After checking each other's parachutes and the combat gear rigged to your parachute harnesses, the jumpmaster yells out "One Minute!" We all stand up and move to the back of the aircraft. The jumpmaster opens the back ramp of the aircraft, and all of our goggles immediately freeze over from the cold (yes it is extremely cold up there. At 25,000 feet, depending on where you are in the world, it could be as low as 22 degrees below zero, even in summer).

We all crowded up on the back ramp of the C-130 in preparation to jump off of the back ramp and out into the night sky while waiting for the jumpmaster to yell, "Go." The jumpmaster yells out "10 seconds!" You feel your heart pumping faster in anticipation of jumping out into the night sky from the noisy aircraft.

As we were all standing there staring out into the black night sky, listening to the roar of the C-130s turboprop engines, and feeling the rush of cold air hitting our bodies while our hearts pumped adrenaline through our veins. We were all preparing to jump out into the night sky. As we were all standing on the edge of the ramp ready to jump out, the jumpmaster yells out "NO!" and our entire platoon jumped out into the night sky!

Now I ask you, inside a noisy aircraft with your butt puckering up, your heart pounding out of your chest, and the adrenaline pumping through your veins, doesn't "NO" sound like "GO?" Hell, even the simplest of poets can rhyme "NO" with "GO!"

Well, there we all were, falling to the earth at 150 MPH and looking for the drop zone. Unlike the Army where the whole world is a drop zone; we were all looking for lights on the drop zone in the shape of a "T." There was nothing but a few scattered lights, and darkness below. When we fell down to about 5,000 feet, we deployed our parachutes and drifted down to earth. When we all landed, we got a headcount of everyone, and we took out are maps and compasses to find out where we were (there were no GPS units at that time). When we figured out where we all were on our maps, we saw that we were about eighteen miles away from where we were supposed to be.

On the ground and about twenty miles away from where we were all supposed to be meant that there was no way we were going to be able to hit our target within our allotted time frame. After cussing the jumpmaster, we collected up all of our parachutes, got another head-count of everyone, and we all walked through the pine forest to a main road where we waved down a friendly 18-wheeler truck driver that was hauling smelly pigs to be slaughtered. We told him of our predicament, and the truck driver said that if we could find a spot among the pigs, he would give all of us a lift to where we need to go. We all started climbing onto his rig as he chuckled out loud saying, "Wait until I tell this story, I hauled 40 smelly pigs and 14 smelly SEALs!"

It was indeed funny from his and our point of view. However, it sure beat walking the twenty miles that we all needed to go, and we hit our target on time!

Chapter 37

Want to Go on a Parachute Jump? No Thanks!

Jumping out of an airplane might sound like a lot of fun to some of you guys/gals out there, but after 500 free-falls and God only knows how many static line parachute jumps, I never got the adrenalin bug. To me, jumping out of an airplane into an operational area on a mission was just another method of insertion to start our mission, and nothing more. Besides, I never liked the idea of flying into a bad guy's territory, and then jumping out of a perfectly good aircraft.

I figured that the bad guys could shoot down our airplane with a missile or at the very least, if I was coming down under a parachute, there would be some bad guys on the ground, and they would love nothing better than to fire a few bullets up my ass. Besides, if I ever had a need for an adrenaline rush, I would much rather run across a busy highway, and dodge on-coming cars, as I feel that would be a lot safer than jumping out of an airplane at night over an enemy controlled area with a bunch of bad guys firing their guns up at you while you slowly float down to earth under a parachute.

Another reason why I do not like jumping out of an aircraft (go figure the career I chose), was because I always knew that the aircraft was going to land. Why jump? Besides, they make helicopters, fast attack vehicles, and fast patrol boats don't they?

As I never really cared about jumping out of an aircraft, there was a time when I was in the SEAL teams that almost two years had passed since I had made a practice parachute jump (sweet).

Nevertheless, all of that was about to change when I transferred to Red Cell. Red Cell (Please read the book "Red Cell" by Richard Marcinko) was a make-believe terrorist unit within the US military. This mock terrorist unit was comprised mainly of U.S. Navy SEALs, who played the role of terrorists. During one of our daily meetings, I was informed that we were all going to go to Puerto Rico via a C-130 aircraft, and we were all going to make three parachute jumps a day, off the back ramp of this C-130 every day for one week.

Flying to Puerto Rico is great, a beautiful country with great food and people. However, to me, jumping out of a perfectly good airplane that is going to land there, was senseless. I was told that we were going to be jumping square parachutes (the last time that I did a freefall parachute or skydived, the parachutes were round).

It is so presumptuous how everyone in the SEALs assumes that you love jumping out of airplanes or helicopters as much as they do. Although, if anyone had looked into my eyes when they were talking about skydiving, they would have known that for me, nothing was further from the truth.

Not wanting to let on that I had never jumped a square parachute before, because you had to go through the proper training first, and anytime that you did something for the first time in the SEAL teams, it would cost you a case of beer. So, I would watch how the guys packed their square parachutes instead of asking for instructions on how to do it. I have also listened to enough BS stories about flying a square parachute, to know that once you were 100 feet off the ground, you could not pull down on the steering lines of your parachute to do any turns because if you did, you would be swung out like you were a sitting on a swing and then you would be slammed into the ground. In addition, you had to "flair" (a term meaning to pull down on both of your steering lines to stop your forward movement) your parachute just before landing; this would slow you down so that you did not fly into the ground at 30 miles an hour, breaking your legs.

On the day that we were loading up all of our jump gear to fly to Puerto Rico on the C-130, I was being asked by a few of my team-mates about doing some "relative work" (this is where the cool "sky gods" fly into each other, and hold each other's hands or each other's feet while falling to the earth at 150 mph, Awww so sweet).

I never understood the big deal about "hooking up" while falling at 150 mph to the earth. As I said, for me, jumping out of an airplane is just another method of insertion so that you can begin your mission to go after the enemy.

Well, as I am not a sky god, I said, "If any of you guys feel the need to hold my hands while we are falling to earth, you need to check your manhood." A few of the guys thought that I was joking and tried to press me about hooking up, so I made it crystal clear by saying, "Should any of you decide to "hook-up" with me while I am falling to earth, I will take out my knife and cut your parachute off of your body!" My remark seemed to instill the proper "the chief is crazy, so we had better stay away from him" looks on their faces.

When we got near our drop zone in Puerto Rico, we all put on our parachutes, and the back ramp of the C-130 was lowered in preparation for all of us to jump out. All the sky gods were whooping it up and high five-ing each other like this was the biggest event of their lives. As I stood there on the back ramp of the C-130 flying at 12,000 feet above the earth, I was anxious as hell!

The one-minute signal was given, and everyone crowded on the end of the back ramp, and prepared to jump off the ramp of the C-130 aircraft from 12,000 feet all at the same time. The green light came on, and we all jumped out into the sky, falling to the earth at about 150 mph.

Thankfully, no one tried to hook up with me. As I was falling to the earth, I looked at my altimeter (a do-hicky that tells you how high above the ground you are before impact), and I decided to open my parachute at about 4,000 feet above the ground, normally everyone opens their parachutes at about 2,500 feet. At 4,000 feet above the ground, I thought I would be a safe enough to mess around with the square parachute before getting too close to the ground where I could get hurt.

The square parachute was a nice parachute, and it was easy to fly. As I got close to the ground, I flared my parachute and landed softly. Cool, I thought, this was going to be easy. Now all I had to do was repack my square parachute, and get back on the C-130 to do it again.

Having never actually repacked a square parachute before (remember I only watched the guys doing this), I was slowly and methodically taking my time to repack my parachute. I was never into the phrase, "All that matters is that you have a "canopy" (opened parachute) before impact."

As I was slowly repacking my parachute, our officer, and senior "sky god," was yelling "Hurry up! We can get three jumps in today if we all hurry up on repacking our parachutes!" I was in no rush to jump again, and I was taking my own sweet time to repack my parachute, because my life depended on it, and I wanted to do it right.

My slowness in repacking my parachute must have really pissed off the senior sky god, because he walked up to me and he said, "You are too F--king slow Billy! You are going to miss the plane!" It always amazed be how one persons ego/passion can be another person's pain in the ass.

I looked up at our officer and said, "Sir, I would much rather take my time repacking my parachute, and miss that plane, then to hit the ground at 150 mph!" I was told to stay back, and that I had better be ready for the third flight (I thought to myself, oh please, don't throw me in that briar patch). So, I stayed back, sweet!

When I had finally finished repacking my parachute, I diverted my attention skyward to observe all the jumpers that were coming down under their square canopies (opened parachutes) flying towards the drop zone. The senior sky god was flying with the wind, and he was way too low to the ground to change his course and make his approach into the wind, which would give him a soft landing. Because he was flying too close to the ground, and he could not change his course of direction (Because of the swing out effect like a pendulum), he flew right into the side of our bus, WHAP!

The scene was so funny that it reminded me of Wiley coyote chasing the roadrunner, and hitting the side of a cliff, and then slowly sliding down. The sky god was bruised badly, both externally and to his ego. He also left a nice dent in the side of our bus. I walked over to where he was laying on the ground, moaning in pain, and I said, "You sure know how to stop a bus sir, are you hurt bad sir? That looked like it hurt really bad." As he laid there still moaning and groaning in pain, I said, "Hurry up and repack your parachute sir! We can get one more jump in today if you hurry up!"

It felt good to give him a hard time, and I hoped he finally realized that rushing to get more jumps in a short time frame would equal great pain! Our officer was ok, but his ego took longer to heal than his bruises did.

Chapter 38

Some Marriages were Just Not Meant to Be

In the military, any marriage can be difficult because of the separation issues. Even so, marriages to guys in the U.S. Navy SEAL teams are extremely difficult. Most of the SEALs (the good ones anyway) do a lot of training and deploying, and it is a well-known fact that marriages in the U.S. Navy SEAL teams have the highest divorce rate in the Navy. You can ask any SEAL about marriages that they were a part of, which have gone bad, and usually there is a funny story behind it. (Well, it is funny after some time has passed).

Like the story about Paul, when his ex-wife took a sledgehammer to his motorcycle, then set his motorcycle on fire, and then threw all of his clothes out on the front lawn. Or, the officer who came home to his house after finishing a long deployment, only to find his house filled with new furniture, and a new couple living in what was once his house. As most SEALs give their wives a "Power of Attorney" (in the event a SEAL is killed or deployed for many months), this officers' ex wife had sold the house, and his dog while he was away on his deployment. He later learned that she left him for another man who would be at home more than an officer in the SEAL teams.

Such was the case with Mike, and his soon to be ex-wife. Mike's wife kept demanding that he stay home and stop deploying, or she would make his life in the SEAL teams extremely miserable for him, and she did. His wife would call the SEAL team compound everyday while Mike was deployed, and ask to speak to the Commanding Officer. She would say that it is an emergency, and she would tell the SEAL commanding officer whom she was having anxiety attacks, and chest pains, and if the CO did not bring Mike home, that she was going to die!

As you can imagine, this did create a few high profile problems for Mike. So, when Mike returned home early from his deployment at the request of the Commanding Officer. The Commanding Officer told Mike to straighten out his home life or choose another career. Mike, not wanting to leave the SEAL teams, tried to reason with his wife, explaining that his SEAL career would be filled with deployments to other countries, and combat zones.

If she could not accept his career in the SEAL teams, then perhaps the best thing for the both of them is to divorce each other. To Mike's (and to the rest of us) amazement, she refused to accept his life in the SEAL teams, and any thought of a divorce. She told Mike that she was going to get her way, and not that F--king SEAL team.

Well, this started the infamous poop war. Everyday, Mike would take a crap in their pet's cat box, and leave it for his wife to clean out, or he would take a crap from his upstairs condominium porch onto the porch of the people living below him before he went off to work every morning. When Mike was questioned about the poop on the porch, Mike would blame it on his wife.

I had asked Mike, "Don't you think your neighbors will know that it is you, and not your wife who is taking a crap on their porch?" Mike replied, "Hey, she makes my life at the teams' a living hell, so I am making her life at home a living hell. Besides, what are they going to do? Take the turd-a-ballistics to see if it came from my ass?"

This war went on for about a month, and the final straw came when Mike fell asleep after returning home from a night out with his teammates. The next day, when Mike did not show up for work at the SEAL team area, two SEALs from Mike's platoon were sent to Mike's house to check on him. When the two SEALs got there, they banged on Mike's door, and they heard Mike screaming from inside his house. The two SEALs kicked in Mike's front door, and they ran down the hall to where they heard Mike screaming.

When they got to Mike's bedroom, there was Mike tied spread eagle to the four corners of his bed, and Mike was raving mad. He said that he had fallen asleep after some heavy drinking, and after he had an argument with his wife. When Mike woke up to go pee, he found that he could not move his entire body. Not only were Mike's arms and legs tied to the four corners of his bed, but his wife had also wrapped his body in plastic, and poured six bags of ready-mix concrete over his stomach, crotch area, and his legs.

Mike's SEAL platoon members had to use a sledgehammer to free Mike from the hardened concrete. When Mike was finally cut free from his bonds, he took a much needed shower as he did more than just piss on himself. When Mike came out of the shower, he called his wife at work to say that he had packed up all of his stuff, and that he was never coming back home. (After what she had done, what sensible man would?)

In the end, she lost! (However, in reality, she won, because in court, she got everything, the car, the house, well everything except Mike).

Chapter 39

Hey, Go Get My Bags

Based on the fact that all officers and enlisted men go through the same type training together, it is amazing to me how some (not all) "staff" officers (Staff officers are in the SEAL teams, they are NOT in a operational platoon, but they work on the special warfare staff to help in the planning of a SEAL platoons mission and other special operations), would milk their rank among the enlisted. Don't get me wrong here; as there are a few officers in the SEAL teams, whose bags I would gladly carry anywhere, and anytime! When our platoon was in a foreign country, we were sitting around waiting to depart on a new assignment. Everyone had gotten up early in the morning, and loaded all of their personal bags onto the trucks so that we could head out to the airport to load up the aircraft that we were all going to depart on to our next operational area.

As we were sitting there, taking a break from loading up all of our operational equipment, one of our staff officers came up to us and said, "Hey, you three guys, go up to my room at the officer's barracks with this truck and load up my bags." I said, "Sir, you were supposed to have your personal bags down here and loaded on the trucks three hours ago." I got the expected response, "Just do as I say, ok?" "Yes sir, three bags full sir." I responded, and off we went.

We drove our truck up to the officer's barracks, got his room key from the front desk, and we went up to the fourth floor where his room was. When we went inside his room, there in the center of his room where the three kit bags that he wanted us to load up onto the truck. I looked at his three bags, and I looked at the window and said, "Open it." We all smiled as we tossed his bags from his fourth-floor room, out through the window of his room. We missed our truck entirely (not that we were aiming for it, because the truck was parked on the other side of the officer's barracks).

When we got down to where we had thrown his kit bags, we then picked up all three of his bags and threw them onto the truck. With his bags now secured inside our truck, we drove back to the departure area where we all left for the airport. Once we were all onboard the C-130 aircraft, I was watching the staff officer, who told us to fetch his bags, as he was speaking with our platoon officers about what he had purchased out in town.

Raising his finger, the staff officer went over to where everyone's bags were secured with cargo netting inside the loading platform of the aircraft. He undid a few of the straps and pulled out one of his kitbags, he slowly unzipped his kitbag in preparation to show our platoon officers what he had purchased. I watched as the face of the staff officer turned white at what he was seeing inside his kitbag.

Reaching into his bag, he slowly pulled out several broken pieces of fine porcelain that was once a part of two vases that he had purchased. Oooh shit, I murmured, and I closed my eyes pretending to be asleep. When we landed, the staff officer pulled the three of us aside and he asked the three of us if we knew how his two porcelain vases got broken inside his kit bag. I said, "I'm not sure sir, your kitbags looked ok to us when we loaded them, you might want to talk to the air force loadmaster sir, as they unload our trucks and put everything onto the loading pallets to go inside the aircraft." He stood there nodding his head, and said, "Ok, thanks!"

The three of us watched as the staff officer walked away, and as we all looked at each other, Steve said, "I bet that is the last time he will ask us to be his bag boys." I said, "You might be right Steve, but now we have to figure out a way to slip him the money that it cost him to pay for those two vases that we destroyed."

When we arrived at our new operational area, we waited for a couple of weeks to pass before our planned mission to pay back the money for the broken vases. One night when the SEAL staff officer went into town with our platoon officers, we broke into his room by picking the lock on his door and the lock to his wall locker. We left an envelope with $800.00 in it, to pay for our crime, and a note written in crayon that simply said, "Payment for what was broken."

Thank God, he never questioned us, or mentioned anything about the money. However, it was not surprising that whenever a very crappy job needed to be done, we were always the three that ended up with that job.

Chapter 40

Oysters in a Can

While attending advanced training at a school on Eglin air force base in Florida, I had the opportunity to indulge in some wonderfully tasting Apalachicola oysters. These oysters were so good that I purchased six cans of them to take back with me to Coronado, Calif. At about 50 oysters to a can, I didn't want to run out of them anytime soon. This was back in the late 1970s when they were about 25 cents an oyster, and during "happy hour," at the Seagull restaurant, you could get them for 10 cents each! God, I miss those days!

On the day that I was to fly back to San Diego, I placed all six cans of these wonderful tasting oysters inside the bottom of my duffle bag, and I stuffed all of my clothes around the cans to protect my precious cargo of Apalachicola oysters. At the designated time, I went to the airport and got on the plane for my flight back to San Diego, California.

When I arrived at the San Diego airport, I was pleased when I saw my duffle bag on the carousel of the baggage claim area. However, to my horror, I saw that the whole bottom of my duffel bag was soaked and oozing the fishy smelling oyster juice out of my duffle bag. Many of the people who were waiting for their bags were rightfully pissed off, as my duffel bag had soaked their bags with my fishy smelling oyster juice that was leaking out of my duffle bag and onto the carousel itself.

When I approached my duffle bag to pick it up from the carousel, one passenger came up to me and said, "Are you an idiot? What the hell do you have in your bag? Look at what you did!" I said, "I know, I think all these oysters are ruined now, what a waste right?" He looked at me and said, "Oysters? You put oysters in your bag?" I said, "Yeah, But I am hoping that a few of the cans did not open, and that they are still good!" He just looked at me, as if I was an idiot.

I am sure that his was not the response that he was looking for because he walked away from me" shaking his head. But, I bet he never had such great tasting oysters either. I slung my wet, smelly, and leaky duffle bag over my shoulder and walked out of the airport to grab a taxi cab before the passengers revolted against me, and with a hope that I could make it home with at least a couple of good cans of oysters.

On the ride home, the cab driver commented on the fishy smell, as my duffle bag was now leaking on the floor inside his cab. I gave him a twenty-dollar tip for a fifteen-dollar fare and I said; "Now you know why they call us Squids."

I saw from the expression on his face that he was not amused, and he left me with the feeling that my tip was not enough money. He got back inside his fishy smelling cab, shaking his head while he drove away with all of his windows rolled down. Oh well, at least I had two good cans of Oysters left to enjoy!

Chapter 41

Surf's Up, Let's Go Die!

Many years ago, the eggheads who invented the IBS (IBS: Inflatable Boat Small, this rubber boat has been used since World War II), they intended this rubber boat to be used as a means of water transportation for "special units" or transporting personnel from a submarine to shore for a late-night mission or to another vessel while out at sea.

For the most part, they would pull the rolled-up rubber boat out of the storage holding area onboard the submarine, inflate the boat and paddle to shore to do their mission, after completing their mission, they would paddle back out to the submarine, re-stow or sink the rubber boat and submerge the submarine. I am sure that these same eggheads NEVER intended for this small inflatable rubber boat to be used to take seven guys through waves who are FIFTEEN-FOOT high in the surf zone! Nevertheless, that is exactly what one of our officers wanted us to do.

So, there we all were with our UDT life vests on (The Underwater Demolition Team life vest is an inflatable life jacket), knowing that one of us was surely going to die. Standing on the edge of the beach, while facing these monstrous waves with our paddles, and our rubber boat, we waited for a low set (about 14 feet high). As we stood knee deep in the water watching this monstrous wave crash, and begin to surge in towards the beach, our officer said, "Ok men, let's go!" We jumped into our rubber boats and all started to paddle out to meet our doom.

The first wave plunged down in front of us, and we dug into the water with our paddles, stroking as hard as we could to try to make it past the next oncoming wave before it plunged down on top of us.

I guess that it was not meant to be, and thank God, that God protects fools and SEALs, because the force of a 15-foot wave crashing down on you is an experience you will never forget. It makes your heart pump fast with adrenaline, while your lungs scream for air as you are being tumbled and held underwater by the force of the wave.

When the giant wave hit us, my paddle was ripped out of my hands, and all of us were tossed backwards and out of our small rubber boat. It is difficult to know if you are swimming up or down under all that turbulence inside the wave. Once you make it to the surface, you try to swim for shore so that you can escape the next oncoming wave.

However, the force from the water of the first wave, which is return-ing back out to sea (called a rip current), pulls you back into the next oncoming wave. You see the next wave coming towards you, and it looks like it is 10 or 20 feet higher than it really is.

Looking at this huge wave, you know that when it crashes down upon you, you are going to be eaten by tons of seawater. In order to live, you try to suck in all the air on the planet. Because, you know that the wave is going to take you back down, and smash you on the bottom coral before spitting you out again. You also realize that if you do not make it to the beach, this process will repeat itself until you make it to the beach, or you die.

Once we all made it back to the beach, bruised, scrapped, but other-wise alive. We all got busy collecting up all the paddles and our rubber boats. Our officer walked up to us and said, "Ok men, not bad, let's try it again!" We all looked at him, as if he had lost his mind. Thank God our platoon chief spoke up and said, "Sir, I see no reason to prolong the agony here, don't let those huge waves deprive you of what you want to do to all of us, take my knife and kill each one of us yourself!"

Our officer ignored what our platoon chief had said, and replied, "Chief, we are going back out there until we make it through those waves!" Our platoon chief looked at our officer, and then looked at his knife that he was holding, and we all watched as our chief walked over to the IBS, and he stabbed it! To make sure that we could not repair it, he cut a hole in both sides of the IBS, and each cut ran the entire length of our rubber boats.

We all watched in astonishment at what our chief was doing, under the loud protests of our platoon officer. When our platoon chief was done cutting up our rubber boats, he turned to our officer and said, "Sir, I will pay for those boats, as I am the one responsible for destroying them. Tell me sir, how will you pay for the lives of these men as you are responsible for ALL of them?"

Our platoon officer looked at our chief, and at the shredded boats on the beach behind the chief, and then our platoon officer looked at us and said" "Point well taken chief, let's pack up and go men, the drinks are on me!" "Hooya!" said our chief, and we were off to do the most sensible thing we would do that day!

Chapter 42

This Page Intentionally Left Blank

While attending one of our many formal military schools, I started to notice a theme in our issued military manuals. On the supposedly blank pages inside the manuals, the blank pages were marked with the statement, "This Page Intentionally Left Blank." Now, to me, this is just about the dumbest statement to be placed on a page. You will find this statement on nearly all military documents or military manuals. In my opinion, it speaks to the arrogance or lack of intelligence of some people in administrative positions! I had to include this asinine statement here for no particular reason other than to show my disdain for stupid things that the military requires a person to do.

I mean, come on you administrative types! The mere fact that the word "This Page Intentionally Left Blank" is on the page, shows that the page is NOT blank! Who really cares if the page is blank or not, I mean, is someone NOT going to turn the page? Does anyone, with half a brain, really care that you intentionally left the page blank, and if the page IS blank... Why leave it in the book or manual?

Unlike the military protocol for numerous documents and manuals, I did not waste an entire page of a document just to put "This Page Intentionally Left Blank" on it!

Well, I guess I did on the chapter page, geezus, now I'm an idiot! Let us continue!

Chapter 43

What Do You Do with a Drunken SEAL/Frogman?

Now, who among us has not done something stupid whenever alcohol was involved? Well, besides having your fingernails painted with nail polish, or having a couple of eyes tattooed on the head of your penis, or had your penis pierced and then attached a tiny dinner bell to it (you know who you are). Because, when you get drunk, who wouldn't do those things?

When our platoon was deploying to a certain country in the Western Pacific, and we had a stopover in Hawaii, a few of us thought that it would be a great idea to "go-out-on-the-town and have a great time trying to visit as many bars as we could before the light of day warmed our smiley faces." After all, who knows what perils awaited us at our final destination.

I must say that although Hawaii is a nice place, it is also extremely expensive to have a great time as a sailor out on the town. We found the cheapest bars that we could, where the beer cost us 1.00 a bottle (In the 1970s, the same beer in a similar bar in San Diego would have been around .35 Cents). Prices be damned, we were all having a great time, and Lord knows where the time goes when you are having so much fun. To this day, I am not sure what possessed us to go swimming in a small fountain in front of this huge house. However, at the time I guess that it seemed like a good idea.

There we all were, sitting in this fountain, singing songs, and sharing a bottle of scotch, when we were so rudely interrupted by two huge figures. The largest figure spoke up first and said, "We got a tank, but it isn't full of water!" We all looked up at him through the water spraying down on us from the fountain, and you could make out a badge, a gun, and a car with pretty flashing lights on it. "Hooya police officers!" we replied.

Tim spoke up and said, "We don't mean no harm officers, tomorrow we are shipping out of here, and this was just a little celebration is all." The officers looked down at us and said, "That's fine boys, but this fountain is part of our Governor's mansion, how about, we take you gentlemen back to your base, or would you like us to take you to our tank to finish your swim?" We all replied, "Oh the base would be great officers, thank you very much, yes the base, we must go back to the base!"

As the police officers were driving us back to the military base, a car pulled up alongside of us at a traffic light, and the people inside that car started to look at us in the back of the police patrol car. Tim yelled at the people, "Hey, What the F--k are you looking at? I got your license plate number you assholes, and when I get out, I am going to come to your house!"

The people in the car made a left turn and sped away from us. Tim was laughing, he apologized to the officers saying, "Sorry officers, I just couldn't resist." The officers were laughing too and said, "No problem, we decided that we are going to take all of you to jail so you can sleep it off.

Thanks a lot Tim!

Chapter 44

Whale Shark Bait

When it comes to training foreign troops, a school of thought that we like to share with the people that we are training is, "All work and no play makes for a boring day." Sometimes, as instructors, you have to make your own fun at the students' expense. We were training a group of Pilipino Underwater Demolition Team members in the fine old art of drop and pick up. What "drop and pickup" means is, swimmers are dropped off into the water at designated intervals by a patrol boat moving at about 20 knots, parallel to a beach. After all the swimmers are dropped off, they are then picked up by the patrol boat traveling at about 15 knots with the help of another guy inside a rubber boat that is holding a looped rubber hose to snare the arms of each swimmer, and haul them out of the water and into the IBS, which is tied to the side of the recovery/patrol boat.

With an IBS tied to the side of the patrol boat, you can jump into the small rubber boat by twos and roll off into the water on a command from the cast-master at designated intervals, making it easy for the swimmers to be recovered again by the same patrol boat.

While all the Pilipino UDT guys were going through this drop and pick up training exercise, a 30-foot whale shark happened to visit us. We (the SEALs) thought that it would be great fun to do the drop and pickups near the whale shark. So, we told the Pilipino UDT members about our plan to drop them off into the water next to the whale shark. You would have thought that the way they were looking at us that we had totally lost our minds.

As we were approaching the location of the whale shark, we told them to "Get ready!" As soon as we said, "Get ready," all the Pilipino UDT guys went to the front of the patrol boat and started shaking their heads and saying, "No, No way GI!" We tried to insist, but they held firm to their belief that they would be eaten alive by this whale shark if they went into the water.

So, we told the boat coxswain (the guy who steers the patrol boat) to position his boat just ahead of the whale shark, so that when the wale shark got close to us, we would jump into the water and pretend that the whale shark is eating us, just to see how all the Pilipino UDT members would react. So, we cruised alongside the shark until we got ahead of it, and when we were in the right position, my teammate and I dove into the water next to the whale shark. We had a great time next to this whale shark, splashing, screaming, and yelling as if we were being eaten alive, and then we stopped our thrashing about in the water, we lay calm pretending to be dead from the whale shark attack.

We could see at a distance, all the Pilipino UDT guys on the back of the boat looking at us, waving their arms, and trying to direct the boat coxswain back to our position in the water (we were told later by the boat coxswain what was said). The boat coxswain said, "Let em die, they knew it was going to eat them!" The Pilipino UDT guys insisted that the boat coxswain go back to recover our bodies. The boat coxswain said, "Ok, I will go back over there. Someone grab that pole to pick up the body parts!"

Two of the Pilipino UDT guys were in the IBS with a hook to fish us out of the water. When the boat came alongside Steve, one of the Pilipino UDT guys tried to put the hook around Steve. Steve suddenly grabbed the pole and screamed. Steve's actions scared the hell out of the Pilipino UDT member so much that he fell back screaming inside the boat. When they finally realized that we were alive, they all started to laugh; it was then that they all realized that they had more to fear from Steve and I, then from a whale shark. Nevertheless, they still would not get into the water next to the whale shark that was swimming nearby.

Oh well, at least Steve and I had fun!

Chapter 45

To All You College Kids on Spring Break… Fear the Father!

Spring break is a time for most college students to let off a little steam and break away from the daily routine of studying and taking exams, as they all try not to fail out of the their college of choice, and not to piss away their parents hard earned money.

It's not that these kids do not enjoy life on the campus. However, ALL that studying and testing must really take a toll on their brains. So much so that all their common sense (which for them is not so common), seems to just fade away when any amount of alcohol is ingested (Amateurs).

As it would happen, a few of us were sent to Mexico to assist the Mexican Navy in the recovery of a maritime asset, and it just happened to be during spring break. The town was filled with all kinds of young female talent and male bozos, hell bent on trying to impress all the young females by showing them how much alcohol they could consume in the least amount of time (I guess this younger generation of females has a different set of standards for men than when I was young).

As we were still in our reconnaissance phase of the maritime asset that we were sent to recover, we all decided to take a break for one night, and go out to the local club where we could observe America's future leaders in action.

When we entered the club, we all went to the upstairs level where we could look down on the entire dance floor. It was quite the sight, and I am sure that the way some of these kids were dancing and sexually carrying on, their parents would have snatched them up by their ears and brought them right back home. No mom/dad, we're just sitting by the pool everyday and relaxing in the sun… Yeah right!

While we were drinking our beers and observing all the kids hell bound on destroying all their brain cells in one night, Fred saw something that really caught his attention, and like any good SEAL teammate, he pointed out what he had spotted to the rest of us.

There in the corner of the club was a young girl straddling a young stud, and they were clearly engaging in sex. As we stood there watching this "floor show," it was not long before they were finished. When she got off of the young stud, we all gave her a standing ovation. Looking at all of us applauding her, she turned a deep red from embarrassment, and spun around to run off to the women's restroom.

As the young stud was zipping up his paints, we all watched as Fred slowly approached him. The kid looked at Fred and said, "Is there a problem?" Fred gave the kid a mean look and said, "That was my daughter you little son-of-a-bitch!" The kid was not sure if Fred was serious or not, until Fred slammed him against the wall. The kid was so fear struck by Fred saying that he was the father of the girl whom he had just had sex with that he started to pee his pants.

Fred looked at the kid and said, "Get the hell out of here before I kill you, you little son-of-a-bitch!" The kid took off running so fast that his own heals were kicking his ass as he ran out the door of the club. We were all laughing at what Fred did to this young college kid, as we were sure that this kid would tell all of his friends about "his encounter with some chicks' dad at a nightclub."

Hey kid, if you're reading this, it was a joke, you can stop running now!

Chapter 46

Dog and Pony Shows

Everybody who has ever had to prepare for or has been an active participant in hates the Dog and Pony shows, or the so-called petting zoo. What is a Dog and Pony show? Well, it is a formal show where we would exhibit all of our capabilities as U.S. Navy SEALs to foreign dignitaries, heads of state, senior officers, or officers from the war college. Now there is a scary thought... War College. What if you don't graduate or what if you finished last in your class? Does that mean you will suck at war? A petting zoo is where we would set up/display all of our communications equipment, weapons, and so on for all the VIPs to pick up and handle.

As you may well imagine, there are a lot of preparations that go into these things, and there is a lot of pressure on all the participating SEALs to look and do their best, and to get every part of the SEAL demonstration correct.

However, if you know anything about "Murphy's Law," you know that nothing goes exactly according to your most well laid plans, and Mr. Murphy was in total and complete charge on the day of this "demonstration of our capabilities."

It all started on a beautiful sunny day on the beach, with only a slight breeze and small waves in the surf zone. As the foreign officers filled the bleachers that were set up on the beach, the SEAL operations' officer walked up to the microphone and introduced himself to the audience, and then he read off all the day's events that were scheduled to take place.

First, the operations' officer displayed the "lead line" (a 30-foot line with knots tied at every foot, which was secured by a lead weight). The UDT/SEAL swimmers use the lead line to measure the depth of the water starting at 30 feet as they swim towards the beach taking measurements every so often until they reach the hide tidemark on the beach – hence the name "lead line." When the operations' officer tossed the lead weight out to show the attached line with all the knots spaced every foot, it snagged up like a fishing reel and swung back and forth like a pendulum in his hand to the amusement of all the foreign officers.

Next, on the list of demonstrating our special warfare capabilities, was the 7-man boat crew in the famous IBS, paddling to shore through the surf zone. The seven-man crew caught a two-foot wave, and began to surf the wave into the beach, but the coxswain (the guy who steers the boat) was not paying attention, and to the astonishment of our operations' officer, the entire boat crew was flipped over in the surf zone by the two-foot wave.

The coup de grâce came when the final event began, a platoon of SEALs were repelling from a CH-46 helicopter in front of all these foreign officers. As the first SEAL out was in such a hurry, he only ran the line through his carabineer once (a steel ring that is attached to a harness on the man who will be sliding down the rope), instead of wrapping the line through the carabineer three times.

When the SEAL jumped off the back ramp of the helicopter, he fell 100 feet to the ground at high speed, breaking both his ankles, more impressive than that was that the SEAL got up and walked away. As the SEAL was walking away grimacing in pain, one of the foreign officers said, "These guys are all crazy!"

Yes indeed, I am sure that all the foreign officers were extremely unimpressed by all the U.S. Navy SEALs demonstrating their "special capabilities" on that day! Our operations' officer topped it all off at the end of the demonstration by saying in the voice of Porky pig, "A B, A B. That's all folks!"

Chapter 47

Kicked Out of France

Now, one might find it difficult to be working in a foreign country where some of the people are arrogant, speak a different language, and do not care for Americans. However, you should realize, like in most countries, there are always some bad people mixed in with the good, and not everyone hates Americans. However, in human nature, the ones that do hate Americans leave a bad impression on you about the rest of them.

Our platoon was sent to a base in France, where we were all going to conduct joint training with the French Navy Commandos. The French Navy Commandos are the Special Forces of the French Navy. When we were stationed on their military base, many of us had to adjust to their military protocol. The French Navy commandos were all about military rank. For example, inside their dining hall facility, everyone eats and sits according to military rank, i.e.; all enlisted eat according to their military rank. The first to eat among the enlisted ranks are the E-8 and 7s, then the E-6s, then the E-5s and E-4s and so on down the military rank scale. There is no difference in the amount or the quality of the food, which everyone eats. Nevertheless, I did not like the idea that the lowest ranks ate their food last, as it is our belief in the SEAL teams that you take care of your men, and you lead by example.

As I was the chief of our platoon with the Enlisted rank of E-7 (E-7 is on a scale from E-1 up to E-9, with E-9 being the highest of the enlisted rank), I entered the French dining hall in my dress white uniform as per their military protocol. On this particular French military naval base, eating was a formal affair. I sat at the designated seating area for E-7s, and the meal started pleasantly enough with French bread and bottles of red wine being placed on our dining tables.

As I did not speak French, I asked the Chief Sergeant, who was sitting across from me, to "pass me the butter."

The Chief Sergeant responded to me in English by saying, "You stupid American, it is called beurre! Say it! Beurre! You are in my country, you stupid American, so speak my language! Say beurre!"

Of course, his attitude really pissed me off. As I began to feel the rage of my anger swelling up inside me from his insulting demeanor, and being the wonderful diplomat that I am, I looked at this asshole and said,

"Ok, Burr, like a Burr in my ass!" I came across the table; I knocked him out of his chair and threw him on the ground. I began punching his face and yelling, "Here's a burr for ya, Frenchy!"

I guess a logical man would have surveyed his surroundings and seen that he was greatly outnumbered, and a logical man would have ignored his insults and walked out. However, at this point in my anger, I was way beyond being logical. Before I knew it, the French navy commandos, who were all inside the dining hall, came to the rescue of their comrade and began kicking and punching me from all sides. I felt pain in my rids, and the occasional slight blackout from being kicked or punched in the back of my head. I knew that I was going to be in a lot of trouble if I did not make my way to an exit door and escape.

I was trying to fight my way out to the exit door as best as I could, but I was getting beat really bad. When I finally made it to the exit door, I was on my hands and knees, I pushed the dining hall door open, and I crawled outside. I heard one of my guys yell, "Chief! Those bastards are beating our chief, come on, let's get em!" It took all I had to yell at my guys to stop, and when it was all over, I was in handcuffs being led away to their brig (jail).

When my officers came to see me in the brig on the French navy base, they wanted to know how it all had happened, and I told them the truth. They said that they were going to see the base Contre-Amiral (an officer in charge of the entire French navy base with a US military rank equivalent to a Commodore or rear admiral), and try to straighten this whole matter out. My officers sent our platoon corpsmen into my cell to check me out and treat my wounds. The corpsman said that I probably had a couple of busted ribs, and he gave me some pills for pain. In a low voice so that our officers could not hear, he asked me about payback for what happened to me. I looked at him and said, "I like the thought, but do not do anything yet."

When my officers returned that night to give me an update on my dilemma, they informed me that at 0800 hours in the morning, I was to go before the base rear admiral for a formal hearing on my serious misconduct in the dining hall. I was also informed that due to the serious nature of this "international incident," there was going to be a representative from the US embassy military group that would also be in attendance.

The morning came as it always does, and at 0800 sharp there I was standing at attention in the rear admiral's office wearing my torn, bloodstained, dress white uniform with both of my officers, and the gentleman from the US embassy military group, who was one of our senior US military representatives in France.

The rear admiral was slowly shaking his head while looking over the report about the incident that took place in the dining hall. When he had completed reading the report he took in a deep breath and exhaled with a slow frustrated sound. The French rear admiral looked at me, and asked me to explain my actions. As I began my explanation, the rear admiral leaned back in his office chair and stared up at his ceiling fan while listening to my entire explanation about my actions in the dining hall. While I was explaining my side of the story about what had happened, he began to frown and shake his head. The more details that I brought to light about the incident in the dining hall, the more aggravated the rear admiral became about what I was saying.

When I had finished explaining about how the entire event had unfolded, the rear admiral leaned forward in his chair, looked at me in total disgust, and said, "If you are to remain here on my base, you will write a formal letter of apology to me about this incident. You will also apologize to my entire commando unit for your insubordinate, disgraceful, and disrespectful actions as a representative of your US military. Should you choose not to carry out what I am demanding from you, I will request that this gentleman, from your US embassy, to escort you off of my base, and out of my country."

While I was standing there at attention, and looking at this rear admiral, I started to feel that what this rear admiral was requesting me to do was a lot of bullshit. I truly felt that I was not the guilty one here, as I was not the one who set the entire event in motion inside the dining hall. Well, as I am a warrior and not a diplomat, I looked at both of my officers who were standing next to me, and they both appeared to have that "It's up to you chief" look on their faces. Saying nothing, I smiled at them both.

I then looked at the rear admiral and said, "Sir, nothing would please me more than to go to another country, where the BULLSHIT doesn't stink like it does right here in your office!"

Upon hearing this, the rear admiral shot out of his chair yelling, "OUT! GET HIM OUT OF MY SIGHT! GET HIM OUT OF MY COUNTRY!" The rear admiral yelled a few other words at me in French that I am sure were not complementary, but in French, somehow it sounded that way.

As I was being escorted away by the gentleman from the US embassy, my officers looked at me and said, "Jesus, Chief, we didn't expect you to say that!"

I looked at both of my officers and said, "Sirs, take care of the men, and tell them that I do NOT want any of them to do any paybacks for this!"

For my sins, I was sent to Spain for three weeks, where I waited for my platoon to join me after they had completed their joint training exercises with the French commandos.

Ahhh, Sangria, Pialla, and the sweet sounds of Spanish guitars.

Chapter 48

Death or Crap

On the other side of the world, far away from the good old USA, there is a wonderful country called South Korea. In South Korea in the late fall it is windy, cold, wet, and an icy place to be. Now, you will never see that description of South Korea in any travel brochures from any travel agency, but ask anyone who has spent time there, and they will tell you that just about sums it up.

Working with the South Korean UDTs is always interesting duty to say the least. I can truly say that they are a hard-core bunch of guys, who are dedicated to the total success of any mission that they are assigned to carry out. Their motto should be, "Screw safety, and to hell with all protocols, just accomplish the mission, and should you survive the mission, it is a bonus!"

We were going to conduct joint training exercise on one of the many South Korean islands. Our mission was to parachute in with our boats and motors, get into a well defended radio relay station and attach some fake explosive charges to the power generators, which supplies electric power to the communications station, and then make our way back out to sea and rendezvous with a submarine. Once onboard, the submarine would then take us back to our operational base.

After parachuting into the water at night with our rubber boats, we climbed into our rubber boats, engaged our motors, and navigated our way into this island in three four-man teams. Each team was comprised of two Americans and two South Koreans. The small island that we were to attack had several military foot and vehicle patrols that were out looking for us, and the communications relay station that we were to attack was heavily defended. After we had all made it to the island, we buried our boats, split up into our four-man teams and we all headed to our target. We all made it undetected to our target and we all attached our fake explosive charges to the power generators.

Once we had accomplished that part of our mission, we again split up and headed to where we had buried our boats. However, to our bad luck, someone guarding the communications relay station found one of our explosive charges on the power generators, and activated the general alarm. This was not a good thing as the island was small, and our escape with our rubber boats was not going to happen. We all knew that the first place that they would send their civil defense and military forces was to the water's edge to look for any boats or people trying to escape the island. We contacted the submarine by radio, and we informed the submarine that our pick up time would be rolled back 24 hours, and if we were lucky, we would be at the designated rendezvous point for extraction. We also informed the submarine that if they did not see or hear from us at the designated time, to consider us dead or captured and to move out of the area.

All of our four-man teams tried to find hiding spots on the island, because daylight was coming in a couple of hours, and on this small island, there were no trees and very few hedges or bushes to conceal ourselves. One of our teams hid inside a large haystack, and the other team hid inside one of the many outhouses (in the pit area). My team found a nice cave-like mound. We removed a few large stones and crawled inside; after crawling inside the cave, we then replaced all the large stones. It was a great spot because we all barely fit inside and our closeness kept us warm, and we were out of the wind and rain.

While we were hiding from all the search parties that were looking for us, one of the teams alerted us by squad radio that they were about to be captured. It was the team that was hiding inside one of the haystacks that were scattered about the island. They came out of the haystacks because the villagers, who were all members of the South Korean Civil Defense Force, were stabbing all the haystacks that they came to with very large pitchforks.

While I was telling everyone to shift frequency to the alternate net after one of our teams was captured, I started to notice a smell that was similar to a rotting dead animal smell. When I turned on my flashlight to look around inside the small cave area where we were all sitting, thinking I would find a dead animal, what I discovered was that our hiding spot was actually the inside of a grave, and the smell was coming from its permanent resident.

I can tell you that 24 hours inside a tomb with a rotting corpse is a long time to wait, and when we finally got back to the submarine, no one knew who among our little group smelled the worse. Was it death from the grave that we had hidden inside, or was it crap from the outhouse ditch where the other team had hidden inside?

I can tell you that both smells got us the same result, banishment to the forward torpedo room of the submarine until the smells in our clothes, and on our bodies, could be eliminated from us, and the rest of the submarine.

Chapter 49

When Hypnotism Goes Bad

Sometimes, the guys in the SEAL teams come up with some truly great ideas for a joke that the normal person would never dare carry out. Probably because most SEALs have seen and done such terrible things in the performance of their duties that most would do anything for a good laugh to help them forget all the tragedies of war.

Our platoon was on a training mission at a remote area out in the Imperial Valley of California, where several groups of Marines were trying to locate and destroy or capture our platoon before we reached our intended target. Our mission was a success, as we had just completed the 16-day reconnaissance patrol evading all the Marines, and we were all ready to just relax over a few beers at our base camp. As we were sitting there telling funny stories about a few of our SEAL brothers, one of our platoon members started telling us about a bar in El Centro, California that he had been to before. According to Ben's story, it would seem that this particular bar had a hypnotist for their main act. It seems that this particular hypnotist could hypnotize men into thinking that they were pregnant. We all thought that it would be funny to take his act to the next level, without the knowledge of the hypnotist.

So, we loaded up the Moulage Kit. This a medical training kit made up of fake wounds that you would attach to your body. These fake wounds had the ability to pump out blood from wherever the wound was attached by the person wearing the wound. After loading up all the fake wounds that we would need for our practical joke, we jumped into our pickup truck, and we all headed to the bar in El Centro that had the hypnotist as their main attraction.

Little did this poor hypnotist know that this was going to be one hell of a night for everyone who was going to be there to see his act, to include our act as well. We were all laughing in the parking lot outside of the club as Ben and Paul opened the Moulage Kit and took out what each of them wanted for wounds, and put them into their pockets. Ben and Paul walked inside the club ahead of us and headed to the restroom to fill up their blood mix bags, and to put on their simulated wounds, which they concealed under their shirts.

It was also agreed that Doug and Steve would conceal their K-Bar knives (these knives had a six-inch blade), and when Dr. Moore asked for volunteers, Doug and Steve would go up on stage to be hypnotized by the "Great Dr. Moore." There all we were, sitting at the front row table, drinking and going over our plan, laughing at what was about to unfold.

The announcer came out on the stage and introduced the "Great Dr. Moore." After Dr. Moore went into some BS details about how only a person with a sophisticated mind can be hypnotized. Ben and Paul went to the bathroom to glue on their wounds for our performance.

When the great Dr. Moore asked for a few volunteers to come up on his stage to be hypnotized, of course Doug and Steve jumped up, and went onto the stage. The prearranged signal that we had for Doug and Steve to show us that they were indeed NOT hypnotized was to keep lifting their right finger every ten seconds.

Once Dr Moore had everyone hypnotized (or so he thought), the audience was having a great time laughing at whatever Dr. Moore requested his hypnotized subjects to do. Even so, things were about to go very wrong for this poor doctor, because when the great Dr. Moore said, "Now, all the men are pregnant and are about to give birth," Steve and Doug pulled out their K-Bar knives and started screaming that they were going to kill the guys who got them pregnant!

Doug and Steve yelled obscenities to the back of the room where Paul and Ben were standing by the restroom. Doug and Steve pulled out their knives, and jumped off the stage and charged towards Paul and Ben in the back of the room and started attacking Both of the with their knives.

Some of the people thought that it was all part of the act, until there was a lot of screaming by Ben and Paul. The spectators who saw the blood squirting out from Ben's wounds made everyone's screaming worse. When several people saw Paul's fake knife wound squirting out blood, one woman screamed, "They're really killing them!"

The great Dr. Moore was in shock standing on stage with his mouth open as he watched the entire bloody scene unfold in front of him. Dr. Moore kept yelling, "When I clap my hands you will awaken!" CLAP CLAP. "When I clap my hands, you will awaken!" CLAP CLAP.

Steve and Doug chased Paul and Ben out of the club, as people were screaming and running everywhere, especially away from Steve and Doug with their knives, and they were still screaming that they were going to kill the guys who got them pregnant. We all ran out of the club and got into our truck. We waited in the parking lot for a few moments as we heard and saw everyone in the place screaming, and running out of the exit doors.

None of us knew what had happened later, as we had all sped away in our truck, and returned to our remote desert camp. We enjoyed laughing and recanting the evening's events about our little joke while we drove down the road to our base camp. We were glad that no one got hurt in the stampede of people making it for the exits, and we were all certain that the great Dr. Moore's career got a boost from our acting.

Well, it is either that, or he will not be telling men that they are pregnant anymore.

Chapter 50

Drunk Again Chief? Well Now It's Payback Time

Training out in our desert base camp was always great. Why? Because for any of our SEAL training, we had a 360 degree free-fire zone for shooting live ammunition, we never had to pick up any brass (the expended bullet casings), and we had no limit on the amount of explosives we could use or where we wanted to place them. It was also great because everyone trained hard and everyone played hard.

Going through the final phase of your SEAL pre-deployment training is long, about four to six weeks (depending on the type and location of training). As instructors, we all had a great time out there training platoons in the desert, and every Saturday night we all went into the small desert town and enjoyed the local culture at the bar.

Whenever you drink, most of the guys know when enough is enough. Carl was a good SEAL, and he was also a good training chief, but he had a small problem finding the toilet whenever he got really drunk. One time, when Carl came back from the town, thinking that he was in the restroom, he peed on my wall locker and on my bed, waking me up to a golden shower. I yelled at Carl, "You asshole, what the f--k is wrong with you?"

Carl slurred, "Oh crap, Billy, sorry man, I thought I was in the toilet!"

One night, I decided to stay back at camp, because I felt that it was time for a little payback on Carl for having peed on me, my wall locker, and my bed. After all, fair is fair. So I got a small roll of thin wire and a 50 cap blasting machine (a 50 cap blasting machine is capable of producing up to 100 volts of electricity, enough power to fire 50 blasting caps at once). I stripped down Carl's bed, ran the wires to the center of his mattress, and stripped the ends of the wires bare. Once the wires were in place on the center of his mattress, I poured water on his mattress and put his sheets back on the bed. I hid the rest of the wire under his bed and rigged a quick disconnect (so that I could pull on the wires, and they would come lose, and Carl would not be able to trace the location of the operator... me). I then ran the wire leads behind several lockers and beds to my location, and taped the wires to my bed for easy access. When I was finished, I joined the rest of the guys in town.

After a good time in town, we all returned to our base camp. I climbed into my rack (bed) and pretended to drift off to sleep. It was about two hours later when Carl came stumbling in. He took off his clothes and fell into his bed. As Carl laid on his stomach in his bed, I quietly removed the electric blasting machine from under my pillow. I slowly connected the wires taped to my bed to the electric blasting machine and pushed down on the green button. When I pushed down on the green button, I could hear the internal capacitors charging up.

When the amber light came on, this alerted me there was enough electricity to fire 50 blasting caps (or 100 volts of electricity). I pushed the red button down to release the 100-volt electric charge...

"UGH," came the verbal sound of success!

I watched as Carl rolled over and sat half up in his bed, and he was feeling his stomach area. He lay back down on his bed, only this time he was on his back. I waited for a few moments for Carl to get comfortable, and again, I pushed down on the green button. I could hear the capacitors charging up. The amber light came on alerting me there was enough electricity to fire, so I pushed the red button again...

Carl screamed out "AHHH, What the f--k is shocking me!" I could hardly contain my urge to laugh aloud.

Carl got out of his bed and pulled his mattress off the frame of his bed. While Carl was doing that, I pulled on the quick disconnect and reeled in all the wires as quickly as I could. He found two thin wires in his mattress and started cursing at everyone around his bed. I pretended to wake up and asked, "What the hell is going on?" Carl was blabbering something about wires, and getting shocked by someone. I turned on the lights and said, "Do you see any wires going to someone's bed, Carl?" Of course, there were none to be found. I told him to go back to bed, and we would all talk about it in the morning.

When everyone drifted off to sleep, I took my blasting machine and wires back out to the bunker area, as there was surely going to be a search in the morning. When morning came, there was no evidence, and no proof. Carl was only left with suspicions. (Well, until now. Sorry Carl, but now we are even!)

Chapter 51

When a SEAL Brother Steals Milk or Ice Cream

Whenever SEALs deploy to a remote area to conduct training, where certain items will be hard to get, a few of us would stock up on those items so that we could enjoy them after a day of hard training out in the field or after coming in from the heat of the desert sun.

Drinking someone else's milk or eating their ice cream might sound a bit inconsequential to some of you out there. However, I can tell you that among certain members in the SEAL teams, it really IS a big deal. You have to understand that when you are going through advanced training in a SEAL platoon or as instructors out in the hot desert for a month or more on a limited budget, you may have little funds for luxury items like milk or ice cream, and you cannot run into town every night, because you will most likely be out in the field training at all hours.

Sometimes, during your training, it can get up to 120 degrees under the hot summer sun, and for lunch or dinner, you eat MREs (you remember those... MRE = Meal Ready to Eat — you just add hot water to the freeze-dried food in the plastic bag, shake it up — yum!). However, instead of eating a hot MRE, you might want to come in from the heat of the day and sit down to a little ice cream, or chug a few huge gulps of your cold milk before eating. Because these items are rare in a training environment out in the middle of the hot desert, let alone in combat.

With that in mind, when SEALs deploy to a remote training area as instructors, they would all put their foodstuffs into common refrigerators that are inside the instructors' lounge. This creates an environment where there will be one or two guys who will steal food and drinks from the other guys. This is all because they did not bring enough money to support themselves. In the old days of the SEAL teams (late 60s and early 70s), if a SEAL put a lock on his locker, a brother SEAL would ask him, "Why are you putting a lock on your locker? Are you calling me a thief? It is sad to see that times and events have changed people.

Eric was that typical petty thief, and everyone knew it was him when it came to helping himself to our foodstuffs. Eric was a good SEAL, but he was a weasel when it came to our milk and ice cream.

I give total credit to my SEAL brother Frank for coming up with the best deterrent for a food and drink thief. One day, during our lunch break, Frank came into the instructors' lounge where we were all sitting around and talking about the day's training events. Frank went to the common refrigerator, and took out his one-gallon jug of milk and his container of ice cream. Frank then placed the milk and ice cream on the table in front of everyone.

What happened next was pure genius. Frank unzipped his pants and took out his penis. Frank proceeded to rub his penis all around the opening of his milk jug; he then stuck his penis inside his ice cream container and into his ice cream. Frank then put his milk container and his ice cream back into the refrigerator.

Frank looked over at Eric and said, "If you want to taste my dick Eric, help yourself!" We all laughed out loud. Then, as we were all sitting there, it hit us. We all got up and went to the refrigerators to do exactly what Frank had done in front of Eric.

It must have worked, because none of us were missing anything after that.

Chapter 52

Your Actions are On the Wheel

Many moons ago, I had deployed to Africa with members of the Special Warfare Mobile Communications Team. The men of the Special Warfare Mobile Communications Team are true communications professionals, and they are deeply dedicated to ensuring that the men in the SEAL teams are able to communicate with the higher-ups through them, anytime, and anywhere.

When the Mobile Communications Team had arrived at our designated forward operating base, all the electricians quickly got to work setting up all the electronic communications equipment. Their work was essential to ensure that everything was hardwired correctly and that the radio equipment had the right power. When the electricians had completed their tasks, it was left up to the radiomen to rig all the various antennas, and to load all the crypto codes into the radio equipment for secure voice and video communications.

During this lengthy and tedious process, a SEAL lieutenant came up to me and said that he had an important message that he needed to go out ASAP (As Soon As Possible). I told the lieutenant that his message could not go out right now, as we were all still in the process of setting up the communications equipment.

The lieutenant looked at one of the electricians who happened to be flying one of his model airplanes. Upon seeing this activity, the lieutenant said, "Why isn't that guy helping? Can't you see that he is screwing off?" I told the lieutenant (LT) that he was doing exactly what he was supposed to be doing. I told that electrician that he could fly his plane because his phase of the job was finished.

The LT. looked at me and said, "I am giving you a direct order, you will send this message out right now, got it?"

I looked at the LT, and I responded, "Yes sir!" I then took his message and made a paper airplane out of the message, and I tossed it into the air.

The lieutenant looked at me with crazed eyes and said, "Your career is over, Chief!"

The LT. went back inside the operations building, and in a few moments, I was standing face to face with the operations commander. The operations commander looked at me and said, "Ok chief, I heard the

LT's side of the story and before I take any harsh action here, I would like to hear your side of this."

"Yes sir," I said, and I repeated the entire story as it had happened, and when I was finished, the commander asked me where the message was that I had made into an airplane and tossed into the air. I removed the LT's message from my shirt pocket, and I handed over the paper message that I had made into a paper airplane to the operations commander.

After the commander read the entire contents of the message, the commander commented that it was just a simple status report. The commander turned to the LT. and said, "LT, there was no need for this message to go out with such urgency. Apologize to the chief, and do not interfere with the chief or his men again. Chief, when you and your people are ready, please let me and the LT know."

I said, "Yes sir, thank you sir, and LT, your apology is accepted sir."

Two years later, that same lieutenant and I would cross paths again. The LT. (who was now a Lieutenant Commander - LCDR) was seated on the Warrant Officers Review Board. I had been selected for the warrant officer program. So when I walked into the warrant officers review board, there before my eyes I saw the LT from my Africa deployment days (now a LCDR) sitting there as the head of the review board, with the final say on who will or will not be promoted to Warrant Officer.

I looked at the Lieutenant Commander and said, "Sir, I guess there is no need for me to be here, is there?"

The LCDR looked at me and smiled, saying, "None whatsoever, Chief." I turned around and walked out of the review board.

You see... it's all on the wheel, what goes around comes around!

Chapter 53

Submersible Delivery Vehicles (SDV)... S U C K!

In the profession of being a U.S. Navy SEAL, sooner or later (if you are unlucky) you will end up riding inside an SDV. Just what is an SDV? Well, without going into a lot of details, I can tell you that an SDV is a mini-submarine. NOT like what you see in the movies; this stupid thing is way worse! First off you climb inside this underwater coffin and close the lid. You are not dry because it totally floods out. The SDV driver turns on its electric motor and away you all go on your way to do your mission, and hopefully you will all survive the trip riding along inside this underwater deathtrap.

Whoever it was that thought up these underwater coffins, they were NO friend to ANY U.S. Navy SEAL. There are no creature comforts inside these things like heated water; if the water in the ocean is cold, so are you. If you need to go to the restroom, you go in your wetsuit; if you are hungry, too bad, you should have eaten before you got into the SDV. There is no getting around, peeing or crapping in your wetsuit. Because when you are on a mission, you will be underwater for hours if need be, and as I said, there are no toilets.

When our platoon was overseas, we were tasked with conducting a training mission to sink a cruiser (a very large warship) that was docked inside a harbor. We all got our mission briefing to include a briefing on the systems of the SDV, which all the operators told us not to touch. The SDV does have an underwater intercom system for listening and talking, which is cool, but there are no tunes or movies.

We were all briefed by the SDV navigator that the underwater transit for our mission was going to take a few hours, and once we had reached a certain position under our target ship, we would be told by the driver as to when we could exit the SDV so that we could attach our explosive charges to the target vessel.

When our "mothership" got to a pre-designated position out at sea, and out of the electronic visual range of our target vessel, we all got inside the SDV, submerged, and began heading toward our target vessel. There we all were sitting inside this dark underwater coffin freezing our asses off, and wishing that we were warm and dry (SEALs are rarely warm or dry). We could all hear the navigator on the internal communications system as he called out the range to our target. When we got close to our target ship, the navigator said that he had lost the image of our target on his scope. I am sure that my entire platoon was thinking what I was thinking… How the hell can you lose an image of a cruiser on your scope?

We were still proceeding at full speed ahead on our compass bearing to our target vessel; a few moments had passed, when all of a sudden we crashed into the hull of the cruiser at full speed like a torpedo. We hit the side of our target vessel with a loud bang! We then descended at full speed straight down into the muddy bottom of the bay causing everyone's ears to rupture from the rapid increase of water pressure, as we were all descending too fast to stay ahead of the water pressure building up on our ear drums. The driver of the SDV hit the emergency blow on the SDV to make us all come to the surface.

We shot back up to the surface, and we had to exhale to keep from blowing out our lungs. We surfaced right under the hull of the cruiser with a banging and scraping sound as our SDV made its way to the ocean surface. Once we were on the surface, I slid the overhead door open and swam out; the driver of the SDV laughed and said, "Well, I guess we found the ship!" Like most of us, I was in pain from my ruptured eardrums and pissed off. I felt that this was no laughing matter. I started to swim over to the driver of the SDV; I was cussing at him for his poor performance. Realizing that I was probably going to drown him, he started to swim away from me yelling, "It was the navigator! It was the navigator!"

All this commotion did not go unnoticed by the crew of the cruiser that we were supposed to sink; they were all out on deck and shining search lights down on us, and yelling out that we were all dead, as they were throwing simulated grenades into the water near us. Thankfully, this was a training exercise, and no one was killed (not even the driver of the SDV).

Our platoon commander told the SDV unit that we were done using them (or them using us as Guinea pigs) for training, and should a real mission ever develop that would require using SDVs, we would parachute in and then swim the rest of the way to our target using rebreathers, as none of us wanted to experience riding in an SDV again.

As a few of us were not done with this SDV unit, and we worried that we might have to use them again, we planned a mission on the SDV building. The plan was simple, just disable the SDVs. When we got inside the building where the SDVs were stored, we looked around and saw huge containers of fiberglass. We took the 55-gallon drums of fiberglass and mixed them. We then poured the active fiberglass inside where the driver and navigator would sit. When the fiberglass hardened, it would render the floor controls (that make the mini-sub go up and down) useless. We all left feeling good about our mission; after all, we were protecting our own lives.

The next day you could cut the tension in the air with a knife. Our platoon officer informed us that apparently someone had broken into the SDV building last night and poured a lot of fiberglass inside the SDVs.

Dave yelled out, "Say it isn't so sir!"

Our platoon commander said, "The commander of the SDV unit said that no action will be taken against those who were involved if, whoever it was, will confess and returns to the SDV building to undo what they have done."

It took until about 3am, but we finally undid our mission of disabling the SDVs with the fiberglass. From time to time, when we get together over a few beers, we all laugh about that day, and the days of itching afterwards from removing all of that fiberglass.

Chapter 54

Foggy Ice Cubes

During one of our many Joint Unconventional Warfare exercises that are held overseas, our platoon was tasked with conducting a few joint training exercises with several different Special Forces units who are our allies from various countries. All of the missions are extremely challenging, and after each mission, there was a good time to be had by all who were involved. After one of our joint missions, at one of our "letting off steam" beach parties, one group from a certain country thought that it would be funny (without us knowing about it) to piss in a few of the pitchers of beer that the Aussies (Australian - Special Air Service or SAS) and ourselves (the SEALs) were drinking.

The next day, this particular Special Forces unit all had a good laugh at us when they told us what they had done (Big Mistake). Now, I enjoy a good prank as much as the next person does. However, the thought of this particular prank still makes me gag. What was going to be the vengeance for pissing in our beer? Well, the Aussies and a few of my SEAL platoon members got together and made some foggy ice cubes (just wait). Four days had passed since the piss in the beer joke on both the Australian SAS and our SEAL platoon. On the evening of the fifth day the Aussies, and my platoon members decided to throw a party on the beach with bottled beer, hard mixed drinks, and of course, the foggy ice cubes to go with all the mixed drinks.

When I arrived at the beach party, an Aussie friend came up to me and told me to drink only the bottled beer, and under NO circumstances whatsoever was I to ingest any of the ice cubes!

As the night went on, the guys who pissed in our beers were having a great time drinking the mixed drinks and chewing on the foggy ice – cubes; all through the night, they kept mixing more drinks and adding more foggy ice cubes to their drinks. The Aussies and my platoon members would laugh whenever they saw one of the guys that pissed in our beer chewing on the ice cubes. It all seemed pleasant, and everyone was having a great time. So, I pressed my Aussie friend for information about why I could not drink anything with the ice cubes.

What he whispered to me was something that was so gross that maggots would gag if they had heard. He leaned close to me and whispered, "Well mate, it would seem that a couple of days ago, a few of our boys got together and had a "wanking" party in the ice-cube trays, and unlike those blokes that pissed in our beers, we aren't admitting to nothing. So, sit back mate, and enjoy our little payback for the piss in the beer."

I could hardly contain myself about the whole matter. It was no wonder that the Aussies and my guys would laugh whenever they saw a guy chewing on the ice cubes, or take a sip from his mixed drink. There is no doubt that drinking piss in beer was much better than this.

Note to self: never use ice cubes if you do not know who made them!

The following day was an exercise in low-level terrain flying inside a C-130 aircraft. This aircraft, in my opinion, is just about the best thing to fly in if you are going on a tactical mission, and the relationships that any special unit has with the C-130 crews are always professional ones. The C-130 crews are well known professionals that will do anything to get you in or out of a target area.

Flying inside the C-130 is a wild ride, as the C-130 would fly just a few feet off the ground or what the Air Force calls, "nape of the earth terrain flying." All the hair would stand up on the back of your neck when you saw how close to the ground you were flying. The reason for flying this low is so that the aircraft can fly under the enemies' radar, and get you in or out of your target area, undetected.

Each group of special operations personnel boarded the C-130 to be flown around in a racetrack pattern that went over the ocean, through a huge valley, and then back to the landing strip. These low level flights took a lot of time, and it was getting late. By the time that it was our platoon's turn to go on the next flight, the loadmaster on the C-130 came out and said that we were going to be the last ones to go on this flight because it was getting late. This meant that the Australian SAS team would not get the experience of the low-level flight.

As our platoon had done this many times in the past, we asked the Aussies if they would like to take our place on the last run. They were very grateful to us for offering, and they said that when they got back from the flight that the beers would be on them.

We watched as our Aussie friends took off in the C-130 and flew low level across the ocean towards the designated valley. The C-130 was almost out of our sight when we all witnessed a huge fireball. Our entire platoon was stunned at what we were seeing and we all knew that it meant only one thing; the C-130 had crashed. We all ran to our truck to go over to the boat unit and take a couple of our swift boats over to what we knew was going to be a crash site.

When everyone finally got the word out about the crash, we had several boats and helicopters covering the entire crash area. At the crash site, we found chunks of debris from the aircraft that were scattered and floating about, and it was indeed a miracle that we found an air crewman who was still alive. The sad part was that he was the only one that we had found; there was nothing but a few chunks of debris floating in the water and any other bodies, or body parts, were nowhere to be seen or found.

Our platoon felt bad that we had offered up our turn on the C-130 to our Aussie friends who were now all dead. Even so, we also knew that they would have done the same for us. It is always difficult to lose friends. However, we will never forget them, nor will we forget the jokes and good times that we had all shared together as brothers in arms, for when we close our eyes we can see their young faces, and if we listen hard, we can still hear their laughter as we watched those guys chewing on the foggy ice cubes.

Chapter 55

Missing "C" Rations

I know that I am giving away my age here when I write about "C-rations" (C-rations are canned rations of food). In my opinion, C-rations were the best (unless you are operating in subzero temperatures). You could make all kinds of stuff out of the empty cans, like stoves that you could use for cooking, and you would use the canned peanut butter as a fuel/fire source, and so on). You also had favorites like pound cake, and a few dislikes such as the can of eggs and ham that was pressed together; most of the time it came out green in color.

While our platoon was deployed to South Korea, and conducting a few training missions with the South Korean Underwater Demolition Teams, two of us were assigned to a South Korean coastal patrol boat for 30 days (I am sure we both did something that pissed someone off, to deserve that). As we were going to be out at sea for a month, the two of us were provided 30 days each of C-rations that were to last us while we were stationed onboard the coastal patrol boat. Our C-rations were stored in a lockable compartment onboard the coastal patrol boat, to which we had attached our own combination lock.

As we sailed out of the port, we made our way up the South Korean coast to our operational area. Our mission was to watch for any air, surface, or subsurface traffic, and report any sighted activity. We were also there to relay any radio communications traffic for our SEAL squads that were on reconnaissance missions in the operational area.

On or about our fifth day at sea, we went down to our food locker to retrieve a few C-rations. When we opened up the locker where our C-rations were stored, we saw that all of our C-rations were gone. From what we could see inside the storage locker, it would seem that our hosts had used a cutting torch to cut through the steel bulkhead (wall), removed all of our C-rations, and welded the hole back up again.

We were both pissed, but we also knew that we could not go to the captain of the coastal patrol boat accusing his South Korean sailors of thievery, as we were both sure that hanging or walking the plank is still in their sea laws. More importantly, we were the only two Americans onboard the South Korean coastal patrol boat. If we went to the ship's captain accusing his men of stealing, payback would have been extreme (on both sides).

As we were the guests, we decided to say nothing and just eat the ship's daily rations of fish head soup (with the fish head in your soup bowl) and rice. We chalked up the loss of our C-rations to a good operation on behalf of the South Korean sailors. Hey, it was only food and besides, seeing and smelling the kind of food that the South Korean sailors on board were eating everyday, which we now had to eat, we could hardly blame them for stealing our C-rations.

It was during our second week at sea that the menu had changed; we were now seeing food (from our C rations) added to the rice that we were now all eating. When we asked the cook about the added food to the rice, he just smiled and shrugged his shoulders. We thought best to let the matter go, as it is never a good idea to piss off the cook.

When our mission was over, we were invited to dinner by the captain of the coastal patrol boat. Finally, we thought, a good meal. We were taken to a restaurant in town where they served us rice, fish, and some sort of veggies; this was all heaped on one plate that was prepared in front of us. Our plate of "food" was then topped off with a live octopus, which was killed just before they laid it on top of our food dish. It was somewhat amusing to watch this octopus, as the tentacles were still flopping and moving around on our plates like a bunch of waving fingers. We looked at each other and said, "When in Rome." It was difficult to chew as it was like a mushy rubber, and when I swallowed it, I was sure that I felt the suckers on the tentacles sticking to the inside of my throat.

As we were both honored guests of the captain at his table, we acted like it was the best food we had ever tasted in our lives. Nevertheless, deep down, we both truly missed our C-rations. Well, at least it wasn't camel testicles that we were being served.

Chapter 56

Five Day Land Navigation Compass Course

Navigation, with a map and compass during the daytime or at night, is an essential part of any SEALs training. Our SEAL platoon was sent on a five-day compass course to test and evaluate our navigational skills. This compass course was set up by our SEAL training command in the Cuyamaca Mountains of California. This was long before handheld GPS units. In my day, all we had was a military map and a compass. For safety, we were paired up and given a radio; we also had enough food and water for five days in the field, to include a poncho and liner, a map, and a compass.

The course was set up with seven individual tracks that would zigzag each of the seven two-man pairs all over the entire Cuyamaca Mountain range. The course was also designed so that it would take you about a day to cover/reach all three of your assigned and designated grid points on the map (a grid point is like a street number/house address). At each "grid point" there was a small metal 6"x6"x6" box container that you had to find. Inside this small metal box was your next grid point destination, and a slip of paper that you had to sign as proof that you were there. Everyone had to sign their names at all fifteen points in order to pass the five-day compass course.

This compass course might sound like fun to some of you out there, but trekking through the mountains, and blazing your own trail through Manzanita bushes under the hot summer sun (as there were no trails) is not fun. Besides, this was California and not some foreign country where we had to look for or evade the bad guys. John and I set out to find our first grid point, and I must say that it was a stroke of good fortune to find that our first compass point was near a horse ranch. I mean come on, what were those SEAL instructors expecting us to do once we saw the horse ranch? Did they expect us to keep on walking? Remember, if you aren't cheating, you aren't trying!

We went into the main building of the horse ranch, and asked if they rented horses, "Yup, we sure do sonny, fifty dollars a day."

John smiled and said, "We will take two!" We straddled our gear over the backs of our horses, took a compass bearing to our next point and off we went at a gallop. We were hitting all of our designated compass points in record time, and before we knew it, we had completed the entire five-day compass course in just one day.

It was nighttime when we brought the horses back to the ranch, and we both agreed it was the best $50.00 we had ever spent. We took a compass bearing to our last point and camped out on a ridge that over-looked our last compass point. Every day and night, we would hide from the other teams and the instructors, so that they would never find us.

On the 5th day, we walked out to our extraction point no worse for the wear. The instructors looked at us and said, "You guys don't look like you have been through the bush at all."

We just smiled, shrugged our shoulders, and said, "This compass course was easy; next time let us know when you got something a bit harder!"

Chapter 57

Navy SEALs Blow Up a UFO

One of the many times that I was a camp guard out at our remote training area in the California desert, I got to thinking about how to mess with the minds of the local lizard people that lived near our training area. Remember kids, every good joke is achieved with a good plan and good preparation.

One day while Roger and I were just sitting around, bored and having a few beers together, we came up with the idea to create a UFO out on the bombing range near the base of Lion Head Mountain, in an attempt to scare the people who were living in nearby "Slab City." Slab City got its name from all the concrete slabs left over from a WWII camp, "Camp Dunlop" that had supported the now long gone wooden structures of the deserted camp.

We had plenty of target material to blow up, which was left over from the last SEAL platoons' training cycle, and we also had a small portable field generator, which we used to power our targets for training. After identifying everything that we needed for our UFO, we then loaded up everything around our camp to build our UFO, including all the explosives to blow it up. Once our truck was completely loaded, we headed out onto the bombing range near Lion Head Mountain (about 4 miles from the location of our intended spectators).

The access road that led out to Lion Head Mountain is near Slab City, the place where all the lizard people or snowbirds live (people who park their motor homes and live near the bombing range to escape the snow up North). It was about 4 pm when we arrived at our chosen site at the base of Lion Head Mountain, and we got right to work constructing our UFO.

We strung up white and blue lights that would slowly pulse on and off, and we set timers to shoot starburst flares that would launch sideways. We also set up a system to drop white smoke grenades that once they started smoking we thought the lights would reflect off of the white smoke, creating an eerie glow. We also hooked up an old siren that we adjusted to make a low "wobbling" sound. When we were all finished constructing our UFO, it was just about dark.

We started our portable generator, and set the final timer for 30 minutes, which would activate all the lights, timers, and the siren. When we were satisfied that everything was set up and would function properly, we got into our truck and headed to Slab City where most of the lizard people lived in their motor homes.

When we arrived at Slab City, we walked up to the top of a large sand berm, which was left there from the construction of the Coachella canal. We looked at our watches, and we noticed that we had about five minutes left before the timers would activate everything on our UFO, so we started jumping up and down and yelling in excitement, "UFO! UFO!" People started to leave their motor homes, and they ran up to where we were standing and pointing.

"Where do you see it? Where's the UFO?"

Roger yelled out, "It just landed over there!" All the lizard people and snowbirds were scanning the desert area trying to sight the UFO.

When the timers activated, and the lights came on, the low wobbling sound of the siren could be heard. You would have thought that Jesus Christ himself had just appeared. One of the lizard people yelled out, "Oh my God! There it is! There it is!"

" Listen, you can hear it! Hey everyone, it's an honest to God, UFO!"

More snowbirds and lizard people came running up to the top of the sand berm where we all were all standing and pointing at the UFO, listening to the wobbling sound, and watching the lights pulse on and off through the haze of the white smoke from our smoke grenades.

"What do you think they are doing out there?"

My partner in crime said, "I don't know, but we are going to go out there and find out. This is a government bombing range, and we are the only ones who are allowed out there. Everyone remain calm, and stay here until we get back!"

As we walked down the berm towards our truck, someone yelled out, "You boys be careful now!"

We got into our truck and drove out to our UFO site. As we got near it, Roger started to turn his headlights on and off, and when we got close to our UFO, he left the lights off as if the UFO had caused some sort of power loss to our truck.

We got out of our truck just as the starburst flares went off. It was so funny, because we could only imagine what the lizard people were all thinking, and saying. We planted our explosive charges and cut the time fuse for two minutes. We got back into our truck and drove off in a different route, across the desert towards our base camp with our lights off so that the lizard people could not see us leave the UFO area.

When the explosive charges went off, we started laughing. Roger said, "Many people will tell you stories about UFOs, but few will tell you they actually saw one land, and then be attacked by the government," or so we thought.

In town the next day, the news in the bars and the restaurant were buzzing about the UFO that had landed out in the desert, and how the Navy SEALs went out there and blew it up. We heard comments like, "This is just another damn government cover up, just like that flying saucer that crashed out in Roswell!" and "I guess those Navy SEALs do not know a damn thing about diplomacy!" "Those SEALs always just shoot first, and ask questions later!"

OK, you snowbirds and lizard people, if you are reading this, I know you won't believe it, but it really was a joke!

Chapter 58

Combat is Easier than Politics

Being in the SEAL teams or for that matter, any special unit, will bring you in contact with all kinds of people, though mostly it will be the bad guys. However, there will be a few occasions in a Navy SEAL's career, when it is not just the enemy that will look at a Navy SEAL or a "special warfare operator," as a bad guy. Sometimes, it will be the very people that you (as a member of the US military), have been sworn to protect and defend that will look at you as if you are the bad guy, or an expensive item that needs to be cut out of the Department of Defense's budget.

A few years back, when I was in Central America, and during the course of my many intelligence briefings and debriefings, I became friends with our US Ambassador. One day, he invited me to one of his formal "Ambassador balls." To my credit (and defense), I tried to refuse the ambassador's invitation, not once, but several times. I told him that I did not think I would be comfortable in a political setting, as the Ambassador's guests were to include the host countries' President, members of his staff, and members of his family, high-ranking officers and their families, and other high officials of that government.

The US Ambassador said, "Nonsense, these people would love to meet someone like you, and to talk with you about what you have accomplished here for them."

Again, I stressed, "Sir, you should really reconsider, as I am very rough around the edges."

The Ambassador simply responded, "You will be there in your dress uniform with all of your medals, and that is that."

I replied, "Yes, Mr. Ambassador."

On the night of the ambassador's ball, I boarded a military helicopter, and I was off to the capital to attend the ambassador's ball. Arriving at night in my dress white uniform, I felt like such a target. I thought to myself, If I came under an enemy attack, I would have to jump into a mud puddle and roll around in it to darken my uniform so that I would be able to hide from the enemy. I arrived at the designated location for the ambassador's ball; I had gotten there early, and luckily so did the bartender.

I do not know why people go to these types of functions, unless they are ALL obligated to go. I thought they must be. When the Ambassador arrived he walked up to me, and we briefly greeted each other. Again I stressed my concern about being here, and again, he said, "Relax, just be yourself, and enjoy the night!"

Ok, a word of advice to all you political types out there, those words should never be spoken to any U.S. Navy SEAL at a formal function, unless he is ONLY there with other SEALs or Spec Ops (Special Operations) types. As I was leaning on the end of the bar, and looking around, I realized that the evening was nice but it was terribly formal. Everyone was nodding at each other, adhering to proper political protocols (of which I knew very little), letting out the occasional phony laughs, and pretending to be interested in whatever conversations that were going on with each select group of people.

As I was finishing my drink, and planning my clandestine escape out of this place (but not soon enough), I watched as a young woman approached me. She was quite lovely, all dressed up in her beautiful gown and jewels. Smiling at me, she said, "I am Miss Constanza." She then asked who I might be. I told her that I was one of the US trainers in her country, and that I was working with the navy commandos in the southern part of her country. I was shocked by her response. With a slight frown on her face she said, "Really? I find the enlisted men, in our military, to be poor and uneducated fools, don't you?"

Well, a smarter man (who would know when to keep his big mouth shut) would have excused himself to the restroom. But hey, I never walked around saying that I am a smart man, and those of you who know me, know that given this woman's statement, I could not just walk away or stand there and say nothing about her remark.

I looked at this young woman of wealth and stature, all dressed up in her jewels and flowing gown, and I said, "Poor and uneducated fools? Lady, I would much rather be with those poor and uneducated enlisted members of your military than to be standing here next to a woman like you, who thinks so little about the people fighting for your country and your freedom. They may be poor and uneducated fools to you, but to me, they are the salt of the earth, and you señorita, you're nothing more than a spoiled little snob, so do me a big favor and piss off."

A look of utter contempt for me came over her face, and she threw the contents of her glass (red wine) on my dress white uniform (staining my white uniform and my white shoes). I watched her as she spun around, and walked directly over to the President of her country.

"Oh shit," I whispered to myself, as I watched her speaking with the President and pointing at me. The President looked at me (with one of those "You're so screwed looks"), and then the President motioned with his finger at the US Ambassador (like a parent to a kid who did something wrong).

As I watched the US Ambassador, with a look of concern on his face, he walked over to the President. I was beginning to feel ill as this large group of high-ranking officials, and the President of the country were all looking at me, and listening to the young woman whom I had just insulted, and who was now crying and pointing at me. It was then for the first time in my professional life among so many political people that I saw it happen; the proverbial shit hit the fan. Remember how you felt when you knew you were in trouble? Well, this feeling was much worse.

This entire group of high-ranking officials all walked over to me, and as I stood there in my wine stained dress white uniform, the US Ambassador spoke first. "Chief, please tell me that this was just a simple misunderstanding, and please tell me that you did not insult the president's niece."

I thought to myself — The president's niece? I am so screwed!

As I began to speak, the president interrupted me saying, "Stop." He then looked at me as if I was next to be executed and in a very cold voice he said, "Chief, please repeat to me exactly, word for word, what you said to my niece."

As I was repeating the entire encounter that I had with the President's niece, I subconsciously realized that I could turn up missing, or I could have some plausible fatal accident ordered by anyone in this group of officials.

When I was finished explaining what I had said (and not why I said it) to the President's niece, I looked at the president and said, "Mr. President, had I known that this beautiful young lady was your niece, I would have chosen my words much more carefully. I apologize to your niece, to you, Mr. President, and to all of you here for my harsh and disrespectful words to Miss Constanza."

The US Ambassador looked at me with a look of disappointment, (which as his friend, hurt. Because I was the one that was the source of his embarrassment) and then he turned to the President and said, "Mr.

President, allow me to escort the Chief out of here, as his presence is no longer welcome."

As the ambassador and I walked towards the exit, I said to the ambassador, "I tried to warn you sir, but you insisted that I come here."

The ambassador looked at me and said, "You're no diplomat, Billy, but I admire your heart. Have a safe trip back to your base."

Safe trip back, I thought. Yeah right. I did not sleep that night as I moved from hotel to hotel with all my weapons, waiting to be attacked by anyone. When I got back to my base, I slept armed, and inside my barricaded room.

The next day I received a radio call from the office of military intelligence. I was ordered to go up to the military command post and to wait there. I was further informed that there was a major from intelligence coming in on a helicopter, and this major wanted to speak with me about a personal matter. A feeling of doom washed over me as I got into my jeep and drove up to the helicopter-landing pad next to the military command post where I was to wait for my "visitor."

I parked my jeep at the end of the helicopter landing pad, and I waited there with my submachine gun and my 9mm pistol. If I was to die, I was going to go down fighting. It was not long before I heard the unmistakable sound of the UH-1 helicopter flying in. The helicopter circled around the command post once, and I watched as the helicopter slowly landed facing me. Four military guards from the command post ran up to the helicopter to provide security for its occupants.

A female from intelligence, wearing the rank of a major, stepped out of the helicopter, and all the military guards snapped to attention. I watched as this female major slowly looked around the helicopter landing pad area, as if she was evaluating the security around her.

When she spotted me standing next to my jeep, she started walking towards me with her armed guards. When she got near, I saluted her, and I identified myself. She did not return my salute as per proper military protocol. She took off her flight helmet, looked at me smiling, and said, "I am Major Constanza, and I am the mother of the young woman you insulted at your Ambassador's ball the other night."

As I was looking at her, I thought to myself, shit, this is it, they are going to toss me out of a helicopter flying at 5,000 feet.

"My daughter has told me about the comment she made to you, and what you said to her at your ambassador's ball. I flew down here to personally thank you for your passionate words, about how you feel about our men with whom you are training in our military. My daughter has a lot to learn, and I am sorry for her actions the other night."

Looking at the major, I said, "Ma'am, there is no apology necessary."

Smiling, she added, "I am also ordered to pass on to you from my brother, the President, he wants you to stay away from my daughter. I do not think that this will be a problem. Do you?"

Taking in a slow deep breath, I said, "No, Ma'am. None whatsoever."

Again, she smiled at me, and after putting her flight helmet back on, she saluted me and said, "Goodbye Chief, and take care of yourself."

As she started to become airborne in her helicopter, I saluted her again, and I was thinking to myself - Combat is so much easier than politics.

Chapter 59

Stick Lizard

When I was in the SEAL teams, I always enjoyed traveling to different countries and places, meeting all kinds of people and enjoying their culture. There is always something different to be enjoyed. Many SEALs will tell you that even in combat, there is appreciation for the food, view of scenery, sunrises or sunsets.

Many times, after our platoon would finish checking into a military base or a hotel, we would go and search out a local bar to unwind, and the more rustic the bar, the better. I do not know very many SEALs that go to high-class "foo-foo" bars or clubs. Those places are for all the "pretty boys" (A pretty boy is a term that we give to guys who are full of themselves. They talk forever about themselves, and they talk about all kinds of bullshit, but deep down inside them, there is nothing of any substance about them) and girls looking for guys to buy them drinks.

I remember one bar that we went to in a small town in Arizona. It was really cool, because this particular bar was more like a saloon than a regular bar. Anyway, we walked into this bar and sat down at one of the tables, and we ordered up a few cold beers.

Looking around, I saw two old geezers that were sitting at a table and having a friendly argument about a "stick lizard." To hear this old guy tell the story, it would seem that this particular breed of lizard could carry a small stick, curled up in his tail, and while running across the hot desert sand, if his feet got too hot he would drop the stick from his tail and jump on the stick until his feet cooled off. Once his feet were cool enough, the lizard would pick the stick up again with his tail, and scurry off across the desert sand.

While listening to these two elderly gentlemen telling that story, I became intrigued, and I decided to ask them about this unique lizard. I introduced myself, and asked them where they had seen this stick lizard. They both looked up at me and started to laugh, and one of them spoke up and said, "You are not from around here are you boy?"

"No, I'm not." I said, "Why?"

"Because, if you were, you would realize that we were just pulling your leg son!"

They sat there laughing at me while I was thinking about ipecac, but I smiled and said, "Good one."

I returned to our table and while the rest of us had a good laugh about me being made fun of by a couple of old timers, I had a couple of beers sent over to their table. As we were drinking, telling stories about our brother SEALs who were killed or were still alive, and laughing aloud about them, these two old timers came over to our table and asked us if we were in the military. We said that we were in the Navy, and again, they both started to laugh. One of them said, "What happened to your ship, boys? Did it get stuck out there in the desert? You boys must be really off course!"

Being in the SEAL teams, we were all used to being made fun of by people who know nothing of SEALs (We get comments like – "You're a seal? How long can you balance a ball on your nose?"). We all sat there and let these old gents have their fun. The other gentleman spoke up and said that they used to be in the Army. Jim asked them what unit they served with, and they both replied, "The 501st Parachute Infantry Regiment, we were Airborne during World War II." We invited them to join us, and to our greatest pleasure, they did.

As we were all brothers-in-arms, we asked them about the rocks, bows, arrows, and spears that were issued to combat soldiers in WWII. They laughed, and then they told us about operation "Market Garden." (This was an operation that called for a combined armor and airborne assault to capture and hold key enemy bridges deep behind German lines in Holland. The operation consisted of capturing five bridges ahead of the Allied armored forces that were to land at Normandy). The movie that came out many years ago that was titled, "A Bridge Too Far," never even came close to what these guys were telling us about what had really happened. We all thought, why is it so difficult for Hollywood to tell a true story which would have been better than the one they produced?

We all had a great time together comparing what they had for combat equipment in WWII, and what we were using today. What was funny (and sad) to us was their expressions, and deepest concerns about what they all had done for our country during the war would, in fact, one day all be forgotten.

How odd, I thought, America forgetting what soldiers do/did for their country, and all the sacrifices that they made/make, some being their lives, all the sacrifices that generation had made for us, would indeed one day all be forgotten? These gentlemen genuinely felt that with each younger generation coming up, that generation as would the next, would care less and less about all the sacrifices that were made for them, let alone understand why those sacrifices were even made. This was hard for us to understand because we deeply appreciated their sacrifices and we all totally understood why their sacrifices had to be made during those times.

Jim was sitting there like the rest of us, silently smiling in admiration at the WWII veterans. Jim broke the silence by saying, "Would you two fellows care to go for a ride with us?"

They looked at all of us and said, "Where you boys want to go?"

Jim said, "To our training camp. It is not far from here, and I think we got a few things out there that you guys would get a kick out of." They both agreed to accompany us out at our training camp, so we all got into our vehicles, and we sped out to our training camp with our two honored guests as fast as we could.

When we had all arrived at our training camp, we went into our weapons storage locker and took out a few of our various weapons, and some ammunition so that they could fire the weapons. Of course, they liked the M14 rifle and the M60 machine gun, but what they really liked was our LAAW rockets (Light Anti Armor Weapon). They both agreed that if they had these weapons in WWII, they would have ended the war a lot sooner. They asked if they could fire the LAAW rocket again. We all laughed, and Jim said, "Sure you can." Jim handed them both another LAAW rocket and said, "Pick any target out there!"

Saying pick "ANY" target was Jim's biggest mistake. The target that they both chose was one of our flatbed trucks parked out on the firing range, and it had our target material on it, which we were going to use for our training. They both fired at it and blew the entire truck right to hell; the explosion was followed by a huge fireball and smoke.

We all stood there with our mouths open, and the two World War II veterans were now laughing like little kids. We all watched as our lieutenant came running up to the berm and yelled, "What the f--k is going on here?"

Jim spoke up and said, "Sir, I would like to introduce to you two members of the famed 501st Parachute Infantry Regiment that were present during Operation Market Garden in World War II." The two former members of the 501st Parachute Infantry Regiment snapped to attention, and saluted our officer.

Our officer looked at the two men saluting him, and then he looked past them at our smoldering truck. Our officer saluted them back and said, "Gentlemen, it is an honor to meet the both of you. Would you care to fire another round?" We all laughed, and the two men from the 501st Parachute Infantry Regiment fired a couple more LAAW rockets into our smoldering flatbed truck.

We all had a great time together on that day firing all of the weapons. The next day, we expected to get our asses chewed out by our officer. Instead, our officer brought us all together and simply said, "About the two WWII veterans that were here yesterday, I will only say this. My grandfather was a ball turret gunner in WWII. It is good that warriors meet and share their stories so that they will live on within us; we shall never forget them or their deeds of honor for our great nation."

Not to mention our truck that they blew up!

Chapter 60

Pirates Wear Black

On one of our many training exercises along the coast of California, we were tasked to play the role of the bad guys, and take out a communications site guarded by a unit from the US Marines. Our training mission required us to launch from a troop carrier out at sea, motor in by rubber boat, and simulate blowing up a radar site using timers attached to grenade simulators. As this was all to happen in one night, we all wore black military shirts, blue jeans, dark-green head bandannas, and we used military face paint, so we could all blend into the shadows of the night.

After our tactical mission briefing, we were all standing on the deck of the ship, waiting for our ship to cruse within range of the coast before we launched our small rubber boats that we would use to take us into the shore to start our mission. As we were waiting on the deck of our ship, a Marine major approached us. The Marine major looked at all of us suited up for our one night tactical operation and said, "Who the hell are you men? You all look like a bunch of God Damn Pirates! Your uniforms are a disgrace to the military!"

Our officer spoke up and said, "Sir, we are Navy SEALs, and as to our uniforms, my men are wearing what I ordered my men to wear for this operation. Now if you don't mind sir, my men and I are on a tight time schedule, as we have a date with some bad guys, and we don't want to be rude by showing up late for them."

The major was clearly pissed off and replied, "You men have no respect for the uniform."

I never saw our officer get so upset at another service member. Our officer turned around and walked up to the major and said, "Sir, if you have a problem with any of my men, I suggest that you address it with me in private, and as we ARE on a tight time schedule here, may I suggest that you make it fast."

The major looked at our officer without saying anything for what seemed like about a minute. The major then turned around and walked away, before the major got ten steps, our officer yelled out, "Major!" The major stopped and turned to face our officer. Our officer saluted the major and said, "Arrr be garr narr, sir!" After that, we all started talking like pirates as we walked away to get into our two rubber boats, and we all started off on our mission.

It was a dark and cloudy night, as we were motoring into the shore at night from our ship in one of our two rubber boats. The night was cool and with the seas kicking up a bit, we were all getting wet from the ocean spray coming onto us from our boats as we bounced on the waves.

All of a sudden, there was a loud thud followed by a few small boulders hitting the rocky beach near us. It was Spanky, and he was in bad shape. The impact of the fall had caused him to break his femur. Spanky was in a lot of pain, and our corpsman injected Spanky with a shot of morphine; he then started to splint Spanky's leg. There was no way for us to go back out to sea as it would have taken hours for us to find the ship, which was heading out to sea after they had dropped us off. As Tim was our backup rock climber, it was now up to Tim to make the climb up the cliff. When Tim made it to the top, he threw down the climbing rope, and each began our ascent to the top of the 300-foot cliff.

Our corpsman was the last to come up as Spanky was pulled up ahead of him. Once we were all at the top, we used our radio to contact the field exercise controller to get a medical pickup for Spanky. As we all did not want to fail our mission, we left Spanky with one of our platoon members (Jeff). Jeff told us not to worry, as he would make sure that Spanky and he were indeed picked up, and that Spanky would be given medical care, while the rest of us continued on with our mission. Spanky was in LaLa Land from the morphine, and telling us that we had better accomplish the mission, or he would tell everyone that we broke his leg.

While patrolling to our target, we were informed over our radio by one of the exercise referees that Spanky and Jeff were declared prisoners of war. Spanky was taken to the local hospital to treat his fractured femur, and Jeff was taken to be interrogated by his captures. Jeff gave his captures a lot of misinformation as to where his SEAL platoon was going, and what our intended target was. Jeff finally told his captures that we were going to their command post to capture their general. Upon hearing this, the entire base went on alert and recalled several of their field patrols to strengthen the security of their base area.

I guess that was the reason why we got into the communications site without seeing a lot of bad guys patrolling around it. We were able to place all of our explosive charges, set the timers, and depart without firing a single shot from any of our weapons. Thanks Jeff!

Chapter 61

Ride a Camel? I'd Rather Walk!

To me, the northwest part of Africa is one great big sandbox dotted with small villages and wandering nomads. Working with the nomads was very interesting to say the least. Our platoon was assigned to blend in with a nomadic tribe, and to conduct a long-range reconnaissance mission in the desert (yeah, there is more out there than just sand). First we had to learn from the nomadic people as much as they would teach us about the Sahara desert. Our platoon was to learn how to survive in the Sahara desert by finding food and water. In addition, we were to learn how to use and ride a their camels.

The nomads were tolerant of us, and to start things off, they prepared a huge meal for us consisting essentially of goat meat and some fruits. We all sat around the blanket where the food was spread out. What was impressive was how all the food was covered with flies, and I do not mean just a few flies — there were literally thousands of them covering all the food.

The way you would serve yourself the food from the blanket was to wave your hand over the food and pick up a piece of goat meat (not with your left hand, as that is the hand you wipe your butt with, at least over there). You had to keep waving your hand near your morsel of food all the way into your mouth to keep the flies off your food and out of your mouth. However, this action did not keep the flies off your lips or out of your eyes. After the meal, some great conversation and strong tea, we were all instructed on how to ride the camels.

Now, you would think that riding a camel is no different from riding a horse. Well, I am here to tell you that there is a world of difference between them. Camels, at least these camels, were the dirtiest, and the smelliest, beasts I know. Our officer wanted to be the first person to try, and rank does have its privileges (and an officer should always lead by example), so he went first.

We all watched as our officer got on the camel; that part was easy, because the camel is lying on the ground (like a dog, but not on its side). Our officer looked at us and said, "This wooden saddle feels like you are straddling a 2x4." The nomad instructor said something to the camel, and the camel got up fast. As camels get up ass first, it flung our officer head-first into the desert floor. This action was followed by a few comments like, "That was impressive Sir," "You're a natural!" "Hey, I wasn't looking sir, can you do that again?" Aside from a bloody nose and a little injured pride, our officer was in good shape.

Once we all had mastered the fine art of getting on and falling off the camels it was time to load up, and head out to our reconnaissance area. It was a good four days' ride with the camels, and I must say watching a camel walking along in front of you as he unloads his smelly, gooey, diarrhea that runs down his backside will cure any hunger pangs that you might have.

The pain from riding on the wooden saddle was starting to get to me. I thought that I would move my blanket under my butt to sit on it as a cushion. So I stopped my camel, and made him get down on his knees. I started to move the blanket when my camel turned his head at me. When the camel did this, he flung all his slimy spit from his mouth onto my face. Picture having the worst head cold you have ever had, and then blowing your nose on someone's face, and you will have a clear picture of how I looked.

Now I know where that phrase "the straw that broke the camel's back" came from. After a few remarks from my teammates like, "Hey I think he loves you," and "Is that your new sunblock cream?" I wanted to break that camel's back.

Instead, I grabbed the rope lead that was secured to the camel's head, and I started walking. The less I rode that disgusting animal, the better I felt. Remember that old camel cigarette commercial, "I'd walk a mile for a camel"? Well, I would walk a mile AWAY from any damn smelly camel!

Chapter 62

Hemorrhoid Patrol

Hard training in the SEAL teams is always the key to the success of any real mission, though at times some training missions teetered on the ridiculous side.

On this particular training mission, we were to simulate blowing up a bridge with simulated explosive charges. The bridge went across the Mississippi River connecting Highway 84. We had seven days to recon the bridge, and after we had assessed how much explosives that we would need to blow it up, we were to call in our requirements by radio, and a friendly agent would meet us with the required amount of simulated explosives (made from clay), and anything else that we would need to complete our mission.

On or about our third night patrolling through the swamps that surrounded the bridge area, something started to hang out of my butt, and it was not poo poo. As I am not a doctor, and as I had never had a hemorrhoid before, this was a new experience for me. Not knowing what it was, I dropped my pants and tried to pinch it off, thinking it might be a big leech or a tick. However, when I squeezed it as hard as I could, nothing came out. So, I tried to pull on it but that just increased the pain. Frustrated about what was causing me so much pain, I went to our platoon corpsman (Doc); still thinking it might be a leech or a tick, I wanted him to have a look at it.

Now, guys in the SEAL teams are not shy about a lot of things, but asking another SEAL in your platoon to check your asshole is a difficult thing to do, even if he is your platoon corpsman; it just invites too many damn jokes. The Doc took out his flashlight and after checking out my butt area, he said, "Looks like the head of a snake is trying to come out of your ass Billy. That is the biggest damn hemorrhoid I have ever seen!"

I said, "A hemorrhoid? What the hell is that, and what can you do about it?" Our corpsman said that I needed a tube of "Preparation H," but he did not have one. So the Doc recommended that I go to the drugstore in the nearby town and buy one. If I did not, the problem would only get worse.

The next day, when it started to get dark, my teammate Paul and I patrolled out of our operational area, and we headed to the nearby town that was only about 4 miles away. This town had a population of about

200 people. There we all were, muddy, smelly, faces painted, and armed. We walked into the drug store and the old druggist behind the counter did not even look surprised. He just looked at us and said, "Can I help you boys?"

I said, "Ah, yes sir, I would like some Preparation H, sir."

He handed me the box of Preparation H and said, "Damn things sure do hurt, don't they son?"

"Yes sir, they do." I replied.

I stuck my hand in my pocket to pull out some cash but the druggist said, "Son, it's on the house. If you had to walk in here from wherever it is that you came from, you are in more need of that ointment than I am of your cash." I thanked him for his kindness, and we left the store. Paul and I patrolled to a secure area, where I could use my newly purchased ass ointment.

As I was squeezing the ointment up my butt, I kept thinking, I hope to God no one puts a spotlight on us. What a picture this would make, one guy with a gun on the lookout, and another with his pants down shoving a tube of Preparation H up his ass.

Chapter 63

I Used the Spy for Protection

There is no doubt that words do mean things, and sometimes words can be taken out of context. Waldo was a new SEAL that was on his first combat patrol in a platoon that was sent out on a mission to capture an enemy spy, and to bring the spy back for intelligence information.

The SEALs patrolled for hours, sneaking and peeking through the jungle, until they came to a tiny village where they knew the enemy spy would be. While the spy was smoking a cigarette just outside of his hut, one SEAL snuck up behind him and took him down. The enemy spy was gagged, blindfolded, and his hands were tied behind his back.

When all the SEALs were ready to move out, they passed the enemy spy back to the new guy (Waldo) who was rear security (the guy who guards the rear of the patrol/squad).

When they handed the enemy spy over to Waldo, Waldo was told to take care of him and not to let him get away. With their enemy spy safely placed into Waldo's hands, the SEAL squad patrolled to their extraction point. As bad luck would have it, the platoon came under heavy enemy fire. Waldo's duty was to guard the enemy spy and prevent him from escaping, but he also had to protect his teammates and himself while taking enemy fire.

During the enemy attack on the SEAL platoon, an enemy solider was firing his automatic weapon at the enemy spy and Waldo. Luckily for Waldo, another platoon member killed that enemy solider. The SEAL platoon finally broke contact from the enemy, and upon reaching their extraction point, the word was passed back for Waldo to "pass up the enemy spy."

A few brief moments had passed and there were many perplexed SEALs saying, "What?" The word was passed up to the platoon officer that Waldo did not have the spy.

A perplexed officer went to Waldo and said, "What the f--k happened to our enemy spy? You didn't let him get away, did you?"

Waldo looked at his platoon officer and said, "Well sir, when the enemy spy was handed over to me, I was told to take care of him, and make sure that he did not get away. However, no one said that I could not use him as a shield for protection when we were all being shot at. He was shot several times by his own men sir, so I left him there."

" You did what?" replied the officer.

Waldo said, "I left him. He was shot up bad sir, and I thought that a dead spy is of no use to us, so I left him there."

Waldo's officer said, "Next time, push the prisoner down into the mud and stand on top of him, we need spies that can talk and tell us who else is a spy in our area and what the enemy is up to! You don't use spies as your own personal bullet stopper, you moron!"

Waldo felt bad about failing his first mission with his fellow teammates. However, Waldo did not feel as bad as that dead enemy spy. Well, he is dead, so I guess he isn't feeling bad now, is he?

Chapter 64

The Four "S's": SEALs, Submarines, and Sea Snakes

Working onboard a submarine is always interesting duty, and this time our platoon was going to be onboard the Diamondback. The Diamondback was an old diesel submarine that had converted its two missile storage chambers into large swimmer lockout chambers. This enabled the submarine to carry the dreaded SEAL Swimmer Delivery Vehicles (SDVs). SDVs are those miniature submarines, remember? Like underwater coffins.

The Diamondback always made our diving operations interesting, because sometimes certain systems onboard the submarine that were related to diving operations got fouled up, such as seawater entering the Hookah breathing system. This is an air hose that divers use to breathe inside the chamber while the chamber is filled with seawater. So you can imagine your surprise when you expect to breathe in air, and you get a mouthful of seawater instead.

We were conducting some joint diving operations with the Australian SAS (Special Air Service) in the South China Sea area. What was neat about the Diamondback's two missile storage chambers was that there was a lot of room inside them. These chambers were so big that you could fit a whole SEAL squad inside one chamber with all of their operational equipment, flood the entire compartment with seawater, and while submerged, the huge steel door could be opened so that everyone could easily swim out of the chamber and up to the ocean's surface.

Our joint training with the Australian SAS was always a pleasure as they were very professional, and they had the same warped sense of humor that we did. This was a training lock in and lock out (a term meaning divers go into the chamber, the chamber is completely flooded with seawater, the submarine chamber door opens, and all the divers swim to the surface, and vice versa), A small rubber boat was tethered to the periscope of the submarine. This tether line to the periscope was a thick nylon rope. Two safety personnel with a radio were inside the boat just in case someone had a problem, and could not return inside the submarine. The personnel inside the safety boat would use the radio to contact the submarine and tell it to surface, so that whatever the problem was, it could be dealt with quickly, and on the ocean's surface.

One thing you should know is that it is hard for a submarine to "hover" underwater in one spot while submerged, and as it would happen, the submarine stopped hovering and started to sink deeper, taking the two safety personnel in the rubber boat down with it. The SEALs inside the rubber boat were yelling on the radio to the personnel inside the submarine that they were being pulled underwater. For those of us who were inside the submarine, it was the last we heard from them on the radio.

The submarine tender that was stationed nearby for this training exercise saw the rubber boat go underwater and a few moments later, it popped back up to the surface. The submarine propellers were out of the water as the submarine slowly descended beneath the waves.

When the submarine had surfaced, we began our search for the two safety personnel that were in the rubber boat, and we found them swimming towards the rubber boat that had popped to the surface. The operation was delayed until we could provide them with another radio, as the one that they originally had was now sitting 4,000 feet down, on the bottom of the ocean floor.

Once everyone was all set up again, we began our descent from the surface to go back inside the submarine dive chamber. The huge steel door was open, and it was easy to swim inside. We each grabbed an air regulator, which was mounted on the inside of the dive chamber, and we all started breathing while the large steel chamber door of the submarine began slowly closing to seal all of us in from the ocean outside.

We all heard the dive master as he said, "Standby to drain water." As the seawater started to drain out of the large chamber to a level where our heads were now out of the water, we saw that we were not alone inside the chamber. Our eyes got big when we saw that two sea snakes had entered the chamber with us, and they did not seem to be happy about their new environment/location.

As the seawater got down to our chests, one of the Australians yelled out that these snakes are venomous. Just as we were thinking what else could go wrong, the master diver who was outside the chamber and operating the console said that the main drain valve pump had stopped working. By this time, we all had our knives out to defend ourselves from being bitten by the sea snakes that were frantically swimming around us.

The dive master finally fixed the problem with the valve on the drain pump and finished draining the seawater from the chamber so that we could re-enter the submarine. If you ever wanted to know if eight guys could fit through a small steel hatched door (about the size of a car tire) all at the same time, the answer is no!

The two pissed-off sea snakes that were slithering on the steel floor of the dive chamber next to our exit established the order of who the strongest ones were in our group, as that is how each of us pushed our way through the steel hatch, and no, I was NOT the strongest.

For all of you animal lovers out there, there were no animals harmed during this training operation, only our pride.

Chapter 65

Failed Uniform Inspection

A few years ago, I was a tactical evaluator for a SEAL platoon, which was on a 15-day desert training operation in southern California. My job was to follow along with the platoon, and analyze them on their overall tactical performance. As an evaluator, you do everything that a SEAL platoon does, including putting face paint on for camouflage, and you bring your own food and water. On the tenth day of the patrol, I got a call on the radio, informing me that I was to come out of the field, and that I was to be replaced by another SEAL tactical evaluator.

When I got to the road, I turned over my platoon evaluation notes to my relief evaluator. I was further informed that I had to fly to the East Coast and replace a radioman from the West Coast platoon, as he had broken his leg on a parachute jump, and the platoon was in need of another radio communicator. The guys had already packed up my bags, so they took me to the El Centro airfield where I got onboard a C-130 aircraft that was leaving for Norfolk, VA.

When I arrived in Norfolk, it was a warm Sunday afternoon, and I felt like a cold beer, but I was informed there is a "blue law" in Virginia, which meant that you cannot buy any alcohol on Sundays. What BS is that, I thought? When the driver from SEAL Team 2 arrived to pick me up from the airport, he was in his dress white uniform, and I was still in my field uniform with my face painted, and in need of a haircut, shower, and a shave. When we got to the SEAL Team 2 quarterdeck (Quarterdeck is like a main office entrance to a building) I dropped my kit bag and asked where the base club was.

A guy in UDT swim trunks, and a Blue and Gold workout shirt was lying on the couch. He looked at me and said, "You need a f--king haircut, and a shave. That uniform needs to be pressed and starched, and your boots need to be spit shined!"

I looked at him and said, "I don't know who the hell you think you are, but I just got out of the field and..."

"I am Master Chief Zeller, and you got one hour to do what I said, and get your ass back here for inspection by me." The guy on the quarterdeck was motioning at me with both of his hands to go, so I did.

I went to the base barracks, and I took a quick shower and a shave, found some scissors and cut my hair off, borrowed an iron and pressed my dirty uniform that I had been wearing for the past 10 days, borrowed some black shoe polish, and tried to put a shine on a pair of boots that looked like the desert sand.

When I got back the SEAL team 2 quarterdeck for my inspection, the master chief was waiting for me. He took one look at me and said, "You failed! You got the duty." (Meaning I was to relieve the guy, who was standing guard duty on the quarterdeck).

I said, "Master Chief, I am from the West Coast SEAL team."

He looked at me and said, "Not today you're not." I stood duty at SEAL Team 2 until I was relieved by the on-coming duty section the next day.

I got many strange looks from the members of SEAL Team 2, as no one (at that time) stood duty in their field uniforms. When All of SEAL Team Two was standing at attention for" "Officers Call" (a term meaning all officers are to report the status of their platoons and departments, and to receive any new instructions from the commanding officer), I was escorted from the quarterdeck by the command Master Chief Zeller, where I was ordered to stand in front of the entire SEAL team.

I stood there at attention while Master Chief Zeller pointed out to everyone that the way I looked and dressed is NOT the way any of his SEAL team members will ever dress or look, unless they wanted to stand the duty on the SEAL Team Two quarterdeck. After a few West Coast Puke and Hollywood Frogman remarks, I was excused, and I joined the platoon that I was sent there to assist.

Thanks for the welcome aboard, Master Chief!

Chapter 66

Styrofoam Boat

When I was deployed to Central America, and I was assigned to... well, let us just call it Unit X, I had the opportunity to meet various oddballs, and backstabbing individuals. Unit X was suppose to be comprised of intelligent personnel, or so I thought. However, what I came to realize was that most of these morons were about as intelligent as a mud fence on a beach at low tide.

When I was young, my father would tell me that common sense is not so common, and this was certainly true for Willard. Willard was an ex-army officer who had a background in logistics. Willard came to me one day and asked me if I could be a translator for him, as he was going to teach the commandos a class on the 60mm mortar. I said, "They already know how to use the mortar, why do you want to give a class on it?"

He said, "Because I said so that's why."

Ah, I see the logic in that. Ok, let me go and get a few commandos together, so that we can start your 60mm mortar class. I rounded up about ten commandos that I knew could teach this class in their sleep, and told them just to play along with whatever I would say.

Willard arrived at the training classroom with a manual on the 60mm mortar (this manual is about the size of a telephone book). I asked him, "Are you going to teach directly out of that manual?"

He said, "That's right, and I want you to translate for me word for word from every page when I read it."

Now, not only can you not translate everything from a book word for word from one language into another, but if he was going to have his way, this class was going to take months to teach.

Willard started to read from the 60mm mortar manual. When he completed about ten sentences, he then nodded at me to translate word for word for him. I looked at the commandos and said about six words in Spanish. Willard looked at me and said, "That's it? That was word for word?"

I said, "Yes it was, please continue." He read off ten more sentences and paused for me to translate. This time I said three words in Spanish.

Willard got pissed off and said, "There is no way in hell that you are translating what I am reading word for word."

"Really?" I asked. I then turned to the commandos and asked them what was the effective range of the 6omm mortar, and of course, they gave the right answer. Willard fired me as his translator, and he got someone else from Unit X to do his translating for him.

As I felt bad for those poor commandos that were left in Willard's classroom, I went to the base commander, and I asked him if I could conduct an emergency combat readiness formation of all of his men. I also requested that he instruct his officers to conduct a thorough weapons inspection of every commando's weapon. He agreed to my request, and the formation was called, much to the pleasure of the commandos that were enduring Willard's painful class on the 6omm mortar, as they also got out of his class.

The next time I ran into Willard was when he had a boat made of Styrofoam. He said that it was extremely light in weight, and it could hold six men with all of their operational equipment. I said, "Don't you mean six beers?" It was spray-painted black, and it was about as smart as that mud fence at low tide.

I looked at Willard and said, "When someone jumps in that thing, they will go right through it, to the bottom of the ocean, and if you tow this thing out to sea with anybody in it, it will fall apart."

Willard looked at me and said, "You SEALs are really stupid. Styrofoam floats, you know!"

Looking at Willard as if he had lost his mind, I said, "So does Bull Shit!"

Willard was going to prove his point, and he picked six commandos to get into the Styrofoam boat at the end of the dock, and paddle his brainless creation to shore. I told the commandos to put on their life jackets, because they were not going to make it.

I watched as the first commando carefully got into the boat, and he was leaving deep footprints wherever he walked. As soon as the second guy got into the boat, the Styrofoam boat broke in half. Willard was right, Styrofoam does float, and luckily, I had the commandos put on their life jackets, because the commandos, who were wearing all their combat gear, would have sunk straight to the bottom.

I looked at Willard and said, "Should you develop a brain anytime in the near future, please let me know. Until that time, stay away from my commandos. Because if you don't, I will make you personally follow through with your next dim-witted idea to its dangerous conclusion, and for everyone here, THAT would be a good thing!"

Willard was pissed about my remarks, but he never messed with any of my commandos after that.

Chapter 67

14 SEALs Defeat 100 Army Rangers in a

Combat Training Exercise

When the Multiple Integrated Laser Engagement System (MILES) came on the market, it was a great training tool for the US military. This equipment is similar to laser tag. You wear a harness with black laser sensors that cover the front and back of your body, and a laser-firing device that is mounted to your weapon. Every time that you would fire the blank cartridge in your weapon, a laser beam is fired to simulate the bullet. When the laser beam hits the sensors on the person's harness, an alarm goes off on the person who was shot by you, simulating that they were killed. In addition, the laser-firing device on the weapon of the person you killed will cease to function. The only way to shut off the alarm on the person that was killed is by a referee who carries a special key to reset the wearer's alarm.

As part of a huge training exercise, our SEAL platoon was to play the role of the bad guys (we always love that role) against the U.S. Army Rangers. Our mission was to attack an airfield and simulate destroying a new fighter aircraft that was inside the airfield's hanger. The mission of the Rangers was to defend the fighter aircraft. Now, 14 SEALs against 100 Army Rangers is a bit of a challenge, but we were not the ones being evaluated for this particular exercise, the US Army Rangers were. We had a plan for our mission, but we all realized that we were most likely not going to succeed, due to the fact that we would all be killed in the attack. The Army Rangers had a heavily defended position that we were going to assault, but again, we were not the ones being evaluated on this particular mission. The Army Rangers were being evaluated on their defensive positions and on their command and control during an enemy attack of an airfield.

So, after we had completed our briefing to the US Army referees on how we were going to assault the target, we were given an Army referee who was assigned to patrol with us and observe our actions. Remember, referees are the only ones with keys to shut off the alarms on the vests in the event anyone is killed. The direction of our patrol took us through a river, and as it was late November, the water was wet and cold. Our

Army referee said that he was going to take the footbridge, and he would meet us on the other side. We felt that this was a lame move on his part, but his leaving gave us an extreme tactical advantage. We were no longer under observation (or adult supervision). Our point man produced a roll of black electricians' tape, and we all covered the laser sensors on our vest/harnesses with the black tape. The reason for doing this was to block the laser sensors from receiving any laser lights that would be shot at us. Thus, our alarms could not be activated if we were shot, which would signal that we were dead.

When we got to the other side of the river, our dry and happy referee met us, and we all proceeded to patrol into the target area. After a quick reconnaissance of our target area, we saw that the Rangers had set up a perimeter around the hanger, and that they all had fortified fighting positions. We separated into two squads of seven men each, and decided to attack from two different locations. When we started the attack, all hell broke loose as the Army Rangers fired flares into the air for illumination, and we were all taking fire from everywhere.

Our squad was moving fast between the surrounding cover, and shooting every Ranger that we saw; none of us were being killed. This was due in large part to the black tape that was covering our laser sensors, as this would not allow the laser beam to activate our alarms.

John was our point-man, and he guided us to the rear of the aircraft hanger, where he was greeted by an Army Ranger that fired a whole magazine of blanks at John without killing him, much to the astonishment of the Army Ranger. John fired twice and killed the Army Ranger. We moved around to the side of the hanger, and asked the referee if he would move to another position so that he could better observe/evaluate the entire assault.

To our pleasure, the referee agreed. Once the referee was out of our line of sight, we all took off all the black tape that was covering our laser sensors and prepared ourselves for the final assault. There was only a handful of the Army Rangers left alive, and they were inside the hanger.

When our final assault was over, everyone was calling foul, that is except us of course.

To put to rest the Army Rangers' point of contention with us, the referee ordered our entire platoon to line up, and we did. The referee took out what looked like a laser ray gun and fired it at us. When he did this, all of our alarms went off. The referee said our laser gear was in good working order, so the Navy SEALs win the assault. SEALs 100 kills — Army Rangers 0 kills. (Remember, if you aren't cheating, you aren't trying.)

For all the US Army Rangers that were on that operation, we know that you would have put a major hurt on us.

Chapter 68

Payback for Failed Uniform Inspection

In my story about "Failed Inspection," it would be a few years before I became good friends with the Master Chief that gave me duty for failing his inspection (and it is indeed an honor to be his friend). As luck would have it, we deployed together to Spain for a rather large operational training mission that would involve several SEAL platoons and special operational supporting units.

As missions go, this particular mission pace was very intense. However, there were plenty of times to go off the base and into the nearby town for some great food and wine. Our living accommodations were fair and the Master Chief, because of his rank, was put up in the officers' quarters.

One day, I had to go up to the Master Chief's room and go over some operational plans for a mission on which we were going to brief a SEAL platoon. I noticed that an Air Force Colonel had a room directly across from the Master Chief, and that this Colonel was receiving four cases of expensive wine. When I inquired about the wine, the Colonel said that they were for some officers back at the Pentagon, and that he would be leaving in a couple of days to deliver them when he got back to the USA.

After I completed going over all the mission plans with the Master Chief, I departed from the Officers Quarters, and I returned to the operations center. That night, I went back to the officer's quarters and picked the lock on the Colonel's door. As the Colonel was not in his room, I helped myself to two cases of the Colonels wine. I picked the lock on the Master Chief's door and entered his room. I opened the two cases of wine and hid the wine bottles all around the Master Chief's room. Having completed my "payback" for the "failed uniform inspection," I returned to the operations center.

It was a late night, and on or about 3am at the operations center, I got a call from some MPs (Military Police), saying that one of our senior enlisted members was going to be arrested for grand theft. I spoke with the MP in command, and I asked them not to arrest the Master Chief until I got there, to which the senior MP agreed.

When I arrived, I went up to the Air Force Colonel, and I told him what I had done, and that this was my payback for what he had done to me when I failed his Master Chief's uniform inspection. To my surprise, the Air Force Colonel saw the humor in my prank, and he told me to wait here while he explained this misunderstanding to the MPs.

As I was standing there, watching the Colonel, I saw the Master Chief walk up to them. Do you remember that feeling you got when you thought that you were in trouble? This feeling was much worse. As they all started nodding their heads and looking at me, I felt a chill run down my spine.

The Master Chief saluted the Colonel, and the Colonel departed. Now the Master Chief and the MPs started walking over to me. When they were standing next to me, the Master Chief said, "Billy, first I want you to know that we are still friends. Next, I want you to know that you are under arrest! Take him away."

I tried to plead my case, but my pleas were ignored as I was hand-cuffed and taken away to jail. I sat in jail for two days, and when the Master Chief came to see me on the morning of the third day, he said, "I spoke with the base commander; he agreed to let you out until your trial."

Trial? I said, "Are you going to charge me?"

The Master Chief replied, "Tell me, Billy. How did you like my joke?"

I breathed a sigh of relief, and said, "I won't be doing any paybacks on you ever again!"

The Master Chief just smiled and said, "We aren't even."

Chapter 69

20 Second Pains

Sometimes, when you live in a foreign country, it is not always the water that can give you diarrhea; sometimes it can be the food. When I was tasked to accompany a couple of foreign officers, to observe the enlisted troops conducting various military maneuvers at their national training center, we loaded up our pickup truck and headed out to the national training center, which was about a two-hour drive away from our fortified base camp.

After observing all the troops at the center, I was then invited to have lunch with the regular troops, while the foreign officers went up to the officers' dining hall. The enlisted lunch consisted of pork, which did not seem to smell very good. However, not wanting to be rude to my host, I ate whatever was placed in front of me. After lunch, we observed some more of their great training, followed by the typical ceremonial good-byes.

We all got into our truck, and headed down the road for our long drive back to base camp. As we were driving, I started to feel a rumble deep in my stomach that caused my intestines a lot of pain. I knew I had to stop, but as we were in an unfriendly territory, I thought we had better keep driving. And then it happened — the 20-second pain.

Everyone has some kind of warning that their bowels are about to explode, and mine is 20 seconds. At the end of the 20 seconds, my bowels are going to release whatever that is contained inside them, no matter if I am ready for it or not. I did not want to stop on the side of the road, because if I did, I was sure that some bad guy would put a bullet up my ass. I tried as best I could to hold it in, but all that crap just exploded out of my butt, and it was coming out like a fire hose. It would have been okay if it was just a little bit, but it was about as much as six soiled baby diapers (those of you who have children understand).

The two officers who were with me started staring at me, and each of them had a disgusted look on their faces. The smell inside our pickup truck was overwhelming. My pants were soaked with diarrhea, and I could feel it leaking down my legs and onto the floor of the pickup truck.

We must have been quite a sight to see driving down the road with all of our heads sticking out of our pickup truck's windows, just like dogs.

Chapter 70

Purple Head

When you are an instructor in the SEAL teams, it allows you to be creative in your choices for target materials that you want other SEAL team platoons to attack or to blow up. In preparation for the next SEAL platoon training cycle, Chris and I were sent out to pick up some target material that was to be used at one of our training sites. We had a flat-bed truck, and some tie down chains, and cargo straps that we used to secure a huge diesel generator and four large transformers that we were going to use as a power sub station, which a SEAL platoon was going to use as a target to blow up.

We were heading through the Laguna Mountains in southern California with our heavy load secured in the back of our truck. Chris was driving, and I was half sleeping on the passenger side. Chris took a sharp turn, and we both heard a loud "crack" that came from behind us. Chris yelled out that we were going to roll over. I looked out my passenger window, and I saw the road pavement coming closer to my passenger window as our truck, with its heavy load, began to roll over.

What seemed to take forever actually happened in just a few seconds. My legs were sticking outside the shattered windshield when we were upside down, and Chris yelled out for me to pull my legs in. Just as I pulled my legs in the top of the cab crushed in on us completely. Had my legs remained outside they would have been cut off (thanks Chris). I heard Chris scream out in pain as the steering wheel crushed down on his lap.

We continued to roll over until we came to a complete stop. We got out of our seat-belts, and we both kicked on the passenger-side door until it flung open. We crawled out of the cab of the truck and laid down on the side of the road, looking at our smashed truck and the diesel generator, including the four transformers that were laying all over the road. We both felt lucky to be alive as our truck had stopped rolling, in the upright position, just short of a cliff that dropped 400 feet to the canyon below.

As we were both checking ourselves, I found that I was bleeding from my head and from my right leg. Chris was lying on the side of the road complaining of severe pain to his groin area where the steering wheel had crushed down on him. I undid his pants and I saw that his penis was a deep red color, and that it was swelling up. It was at that moment that a state trooper rolled up on our accident. He asked if I was ok, and I said, "Yes, but I think that my teammate here is in bad shape."

The state trooper walked over to Chris. Chris was still moaning in severe pain. The Trooper said that he needed to pull down Chris's pants to inspect the area of pain that Chris was complaining about. When the State Trooper pulled down Chris's pants, it revealed Chris's wounded penis. Upon seeing Chris's wounded penis, the State Trooper gasped, "Oh my God!" I looked over at Chris's penis and saw that it was still swelling up. The head of his penis was as big as a major-league baseball, and it was starting to turn a deep purple color.

The state trooper called for an ambulance, and when it arrived, we were both transported to the local hospital. As the doctor was stitching up the gashes in my head and my leg, I looked over at Chris in the emergency room next to me, and I could see Chris's exposed penis. It was now looking like the top of a baseball bat that was going to explode any second.

A female doctor who specializes in male genitals (figure the odds) came into the emergency room. When she started to handle Chris's penis, Chris said, "Doc, I don't care about the color, I just want you to keep it this size, ok?"

She looked at Chris, and in a flat sarcastic voice she said, "I guess not having a normal penis like the rest of the male population, you must look at this as God's gift to you. However, I am not God, and I do not perform miracles. So, when I am done with you, you will have the same small penis you always had."

Chris and I both laughed out loud. It was good to be seen by someone with our sense of humor. However, Chris's laughter soon turned into a moan of anguish, when she took out a scalpel and said that she was going to remove a large portion of his penis. Chris began to plead with her...

Again, it was her wonderful warped sense of humor, lucky for Chris.

Chapter 71

Can I Borrow that IBS Paddle?

Punishment for screwing up in the South Korean military is WAY different from the punishment that one gets in the US military. On the lower levels of the South Korean military rank structure, there are no trials to find out who the guilty parties are, as the senior military personnel that are serving within the same unit take care of their own problems right there on the spot. In the South Korean military, there IS a deep sense of honor, and when one is asked a question as to their part in any wrongdoing, the "offender" will always respond with the truth. If they were ever to lie, not only would they lose their sense of honor among the personnel within the unit where they are serving, but their punishment would be very extreme in contrast to what they would normally get.

What is normal punishment in the South Korean navy? Well, when our SEAL platoon arrived at the South Korean UDT compound for some joint training, a few of us started to unload our truck full of operational equipment. An old friend, Master Chief Park, greeted me. Master Chief Park is well known and respected by all South Korean UDT personnel, and to all SEALs from Team One. He is a legend in the South Korean UDT navy, because during his time in the Vietnam War, he had acquired 136 confirmed kills.

It was good to see Master Chief Park, and after a few handshakes and brief greetings by everyone, he asked me if he could borrow one of our IBS paddles (like a canoe paddle). I did not think anything about it, and I said, "Sure, here you go." I then gave him the IBS paddle. Curious, I watched as Master Chief Park walked over to where three Korean UDT first class petty officers were standing at attention. Master Chief Park began yelling at all three of them.

The first of the three Korean UDT petty officers stepped forward and nodded several times as Master Chief Park was yelling at him, and as this petty officer bowed, Master Chief Park hit the first class petty officer in the back of his calf muscles with the IBS paddle.

Master Chief Park repeated this beating to the other two UDT first class petty officers on their legs. (As I was watching this, I was thinking that it must really suck to stand there waiting for your turn to be beat.)

When the three First Class Petty officers recovered from their beatings, they got back into formation, and again, they all stood at attention. Master Chief Park walked up to each first class petty officer, and he ripped off the first class rank badges that were sewn onto their sleeves. As all three "EX" first class petty officers were standing at attention, Master Chief Park began yelling at them again, and then hit each of them in the back of their heads with the IBS paddle, knocking each of them down to the ground.

While they were lying on the ground, Master Chief Park started to kick each of them, as he continued yelling at them. I really felt bad for those three South Koreans, and had I known that Master Chief Park was going to use one of our IBS paddles as a beating tool, I would not have given it to him (well, maybe I would have). However, it could have been a lot worse; he might have asked to borrow our truck to drive over those three South Koreans, because when Master Chief Park got pissed off, no one knew what he would do.

When Master Chief Park returned my IBS paddle to me, I asked what those three guys did to deserve that kind of punishment, and the loss of their first class rank badges. Master Chief Park explained to me that they had all gone into a restaurant for dinner, and after eating the food that they ordered, they told the owner that they were not going to pay for their food, and they left. This was their punishment for their actions because they brought disgrace to their unit. Master Chief Park said that they must never forget that they serve and protect the South Korean people, and they always need the support of their people.

Master Chief Park also told me that when you join the South Korean navy, your ass does not belong to you; your ass belongs to the South Korean navy. We all started laughing about what Master Chief Park had said. Well, that is except for the three ex-first class petty officers, who were still on the ground moaning in pain.

A testament to the "can do" spirit of the South Korean UDT members, when we were all flying onboard a C-130 aircraft to do a water jump with our Zodiac rubber boat (the boat is pushed off the back ramp of the C-130 with its own parachute, and then all the rest of us parachute jumped out of the C-130 after it):

When we approached the water drop zone area at an elevation of 1,200 feet, the jumpmaster yelled out, "Two minutes!" We (the SEALs) could not believe our eyes. All the South Korean UDT members were getting inside the rubber boat without their parachutes, and they were tying ropes around themselves and securing the other end of the rope to the rubber hand straps on the Zodiac rubber boat!

We all started laughing and yelling, "Get off the boat, and put your parachutes on!" These South Korean UDT members were perfectly willing and ready to go out of the aircraft with no parachutes, and hang onto the rubber boat as it fell out of the aircraft. Thank God, we stopped them.

Chapter 72

It's Easy, Come On Down!

Patrolling silently at night is hard enough, but when you are patrolling at night through a thick jungle, it can be torture to your mind and body. Some jungles are so thick that you have to be right next to the guy in front of you so that you do not lose sight of each other. On the other hand, patrolling at night through the jungle, in a combat zone, can be a hair-raising experience, because it is not always the two-legged enemy that can be a threat to you. Depending on the country that you are in, you may well be confronted with all kinds of insects, reptiles, and predators that can make you ill or kill you.

Tim was our point man. He was a good man for the job, because we all trusted his instincts. However, that was all about to change one night when we were patrolling through the deep jungle on the way to our target area.

Tim was doing a great job of leading our patrol through the thick jungle at night, and it was raining hard. This was a good thing as it concealed any noise that we were making. Tim halted all of us, so that he could check out a small animal path. A few seconds had passed, and we heard a loud rustling sound. Not hearing from Tim, our officer slowly moved forward to check out what had caused the noise.

When our officer got to the edge of the jungle path where Tim had disappeared, he called out to Tim to see where he was. Tim responded back saying, "I found a quick way down. Tell everyone just to follow the path, and it will be easy."

What Tim left out was the fact that he had fallen down the side of a steep 30-foot muddy cliff. As each one of us got to the edge of the path, and took a step out into space, each one of us slid 30 feet down to the bottom of the muddy cliff.

We were all pissed off at Tim, but Tim said, "Well, there was no way for me to come back up to you guys, so I thought to myself, screw it, I will make you guys come down to me." Luckily, the only thing that was injured was our pride.

As we patrolled deeper into the jungle, we finally came to a large open area where we decided to rest. John told Tim to take out the night-vision goggles and scout the area for any bad guys. It was not long before Tim came back and said that he had spotted hundreds of guys walking around with Cylume lights (chemical lights that light up when you break and shake the internal contents. Kind of like the stuff that kids wear to glow at night).

At this point, we all knew that Tim had lost his mind, and we told him to quit screwing around. Tim was adamant that he had seen hundreds of guys walking around with Cylume lights, and if we did not believe him, we should come and check it out for ourselves. So, to humor Tim, we did just that, we all crept up to the clearing where Tim saw the hundreds of guys walking around with Cylume lights, and lo and behold, there they all were.

I took Tim's night vision goggles off his head, and slapped him on the side of his head. Tim looked at me and said, "What the hell was that for?"

I said, "You are a stupid moron, those are fireflies out there!"

Tim said, "Fireflies? Well, son-of-a-bitch! But hey, when you wear these night-vision goggles, they looked like guys with Cylume lights to me!"

It took a long time for Tim to regain our trust after that night.

Chapter 73

Underwater Search and Capture

One of the many good things about the old days in the SEAL teams, was how you could check out operational equipment and use it (within reason) whenever you wanted to. What was even better was when you were in a SEAL platoon, and you could make plans for a night reconnaissance dive to search and capture an enemy.

You might think that capturing an enemy underwater is an easy operation, but it is not. First, you must plan for every contingency, and searching for an enemy underwater is not to be taken lightly. In the daytime, the enemy may hide inside crevasses or outcroppings underwater, and reaching inside to pull them out can be risky. Should there be a moray eel resting inside, he will look at your arm or hand as food, and take a chunk out of you.

In addition, the enemy has support boats that patrol the surface of the water as the Luftwaffe would patrol the skies over Germany. These support boats are to be feared, because should they catch you outside of your operational area, attempting to capture the enemy, you will be hit with a hefty fine, with the possibility of being taken to jail.

When we planned our night reconnaissance mission, our platoon cleared the operational target area with all the local officials where we were going to be conducting the night reconnaissance diving operation to capture as many of the enemy as possible. We had our mission briefing, and everyone was clear on all the threats within our operational target area, above and below the water.

We checked out our reconnaissance equipment — underwater compasses, underwater lights, catch bags, and gloves. Before starting the dive, we assigned two team members to attack the enemy surface support boat. Their mission was to secure a steel cable around the propeller and the rudder so that when the propeller was engaged it would pull the rudder into the prop and seize the propeller shaft.

With the enemy support craft out of commission, we were all set for our search and capture mission of the enemy. We all had one hour of air in our tanks, and we loaded up our boat to head out to the operational target area. Once in the water, we took a bearing to the jetty (a rocky peninsula known to harbor the enemy), and we all submerged and headed for the bottom.

Turning on our underwater lights was almost laughable, as we would never use them on a real mission. Diving for the enemy — lobsters — with spotlights is the same as hunting a deer with a spotlight: out in the open, they freeze when you shine the light on them. So, one guy puts the spotlight on them, and the other comes in from behind, and he easily grabs the enemy lobster and puts it into the captured prisoner/catch bag.

We had six divers on this mission, and our total capture was 338 enemy lobsters. Frank and I took 60 enemy lobsters that failed interrogation to a nearby restaurant for a prisoner exchange. We traded the enemy lobsters for a week of free beer! To this day, no one is sure who got the better deal, but I feel that we did, as the enemy lobsters were put to death in boiling water, and our beers were always fresh and cold. Besides, there were always more enemy lobsters to be captured and traded.

Chapter 74

A Friendly Hotel in Italy

When it came to deploying for a SEAL mission, Walter and I were always volunteering. So when we heard about an operation in Italy that needed field radio communicators, we both jumped at the chance to go there. Having been accepted, we were both sent on the deployment to Italy for the purpose of establishing a clandestine radio communication relay site for a larger operation that was going to involve several SEAL platoons. Both of us had a background in clandestine communications, and we selected a mountain site that had some old ruins on top of it. This mountain location would afford us a good tactical position to set up our communications equipment, and the ruins would conceal our equipment and radio antennas from view by ground or air units. At the base of this mountain was a small town named San Felice. The town was small, and it had only one hotel. Nevertheless, the hotel was near our communications operating area, so we both thought it would be a great place to stay, as opposed to driving 23 miles to a different hotel that was located in another town.

When my partner and I went to the hotel to ask for a room, we were greeted by some strange stares. I asked if there was a problem, and the owner of the small hotel said that he did not rent rooms to gay men. This should have my first clue as to what kind of a place this was where we were trying to get a room, but we were both tired and suffering from jet lag, and a hotel room with a bed for each of us was our top priority. After reassuring the owner that we were indeed straight, we told him that we needed two rooms for three weeks.

Oddly enough, this statement really caused a lot of confusion; it seems that they only rented rooms by the half hour or full hour, and because of this, the owner was not sure how to charge us. I looked at my teammate and said, "Who the hell rents a room by the hour?"

My teammate just shrugged his shoulders and said, "I guess they do."

I said, "Well, there are 24 hours in a day, how much could it be?" I told the owner that when we were in Rome, we paid 150.00 US per night, which included breakfast. He said that he would charge us the same rate, and he would have breakfast brought to us each morning. The rooms were very basic as hotel rooms go. There was a bed and a bathroom, no other furniture, and no TV or mini bar. However, there was entertainment in the form of moans, groans, screams, and beds banging against the walls all through the night.

As sleep was out of the question, my teammate Walter and I walked down to the nearby bar to consume a few liquid sleeping pills. It was at this bar and after a few drinks with the locals that we found out about the type of hotel that we were staying at: it was a bordello.

The locals all thought that it was amusing that we would try to sleep at a hotel filled with whores and people having one-night stands. After the first week, we both started to look like zombies, so we asked the local bartender if it was possible to rent a room from someone in town. He said that he would ask around for us, and let us know.

The next day, after working all day in the rain at the communications site, Walter and I went to the local bar. The bartender said that he had great news for us. It seems that a local farmer was willing to let us sleep in his barn, free of charge, if we did not mind doing a little work for him. Later that same night we both met the local farmer. He was a pleasant elderly gentleman, and he said that he would be happy to have us stay in his barn, and in return all we needed to do was to keep it clean for him. He also wanted us to do a little minor work for him like chopping wood for fire, and to feed his horses.

Now, maybe shoveling crap sounds like a bad deal to some of you people reading this book, but let me tell you that our lack of sleep in that whorehouse made the barn sound like a penthouse suite! We took the farmer's generous offer. We were dry, it was warm, free, peaceful, and the air (when the horses did not flagellate) was fresh, and for breakfast, the farmer gave us great-tasting strong coffee with a huge chunk of bread, and a brick of cheese.

Now that barn was a great bed and breakfast hotel!

Chapter 75

Swimming in Circles Underwater and at Night

Night training dives in the SEAL teams can be a rather boring event. You slide into the cold water from a boat several miles offshore, take a bearing with your compass to your intended target and submerge. You swim with your dive buddy to your intended target on a designated compass bearing with your rebreathing rigs, attach your explosives to various key points on the vessel, and after you have attacked your target, you take a reverse bearing and swim back out to sea, where hopefully you will get picked up. As always, it is dark, wet, and cold.

Occasionally (if you are not the guy concentrating on the compass and depth gauge), you might get to see something that created a huge phosphorescent glow go right past you, and you think to yourself, "That was big; hope it doesn't come back. However, if it does, I will grab my swim buddy and put him between me and whatever that big glowing thing is!" Hey, when danger comes to you at night and underwater, it sucks to be the compass diver.

Anyway, while on one of these, many boring training diving missions (as I have said before, boredom is the mother of all inventions, and practical jokes), I got the idea to mess around with my dive buddy. I brought along a powerful magnet and a bunch of extra lead dive weights. When we launched from the boat, my dive buddy (Doug), took a compass bearing to our target, and we submerged for the long underwater swim to our designated target.

After about 30 minutes into our dive, I carefully took out one of my 4-pound lead weights and placed it gently on his back. As we were wearing wetsuits, he did not feel the added weight. I heard him add air from his pure oxygen bottle to adjust for the increased weight on his body. I took out another 4-pound lead weight and carefully placed it on his back; again I heard him adjust for the added weight by adding more air into his rebreathing bags so that he could maintain the proper diving depth.

When my diving buddy had adjusted himself to the added weight, I quickly took both weights off his back. When I did this, he started to shoot towards the surface because of all the extra air that he put in his breathing bags to compensate for the extra weight, which was now gone. I pulled on our buddy line (this was about a 4 or 5 foot line that is attached between two divers) to keep him from breaking the surface of the water, which would have given away our position. I squeezed his arm once to ask if he was ok, and he squeezed my arm back to say yes. It was funny because Doug prided himself on being so professional on night compass swims.

After another 30 minutes had passed, I felt that it was now time for my powerful magnet. I took out my magnet, and I slowly moved it next to the compass. As the compass needle turned towards the force of the magnet, so did we underwater. I knew that we were going to be swimming way off course, but what the hell — this was fun. We swam for about an hour, and then we surfaced for a quick peek, only to find that we were nowhere near our target, and as a matter –of fact, we were swimming out to sea!

The safety boat from which we had started our mission came over to us and asked if we were all right. I removed my regulator from my mouth and said, "Hell no, this guy is swimming in circles!"

Doug replied, "I don't know what the hell is wrong, this never happens to me. Maybe this compass is messed up." The guys in the safety boat checked the compass and of course, it was fine.

I looked at Doug and said, "You are like a new guy underwater! You had a hard time maintaining your depth, I had to pull you down to keep you from breaking the surface of the water, and look, we are not even anywhere near our target. Next time I will do the driving, because you suck!"

Doug was clearly upset with himself as we failed to hit our target. After the training mission, we all went to the bar that same night just to have a few brews before going home, As I was sitting there with Doug, he was feeling really bad. So I told Doug what I had done to him. Doug looked at me and said, "You are an asshole!"

Yup, that's me, Doug.

Chapter 76

Monkey See Monkey Do

During the war in South East Asia, one of the team guys had a pet monkey. This monkey was a real pain in everyone's ass, because it would steal the food from everyone's care packages and eat it. Dave loved M&Ms, and whenever Dave got a care package from home with M&Ms in it, Dave was one happy guy.

One night while most of the guys were playing cards, Dave got up from the card table to get his bag of M&Ms. When Dave got to the end of the bed where his footlocker was, he found that his M&Ms were missing. Immediately, Dave was pissed off and yelled out, "Where is that f--king monkey?" Dave did not have to look far because there, crouching in the corner of the barracks, was the monkey and the empty bag of M&Ms, which the monkey had stolen from Dave's footlocker.

Dave picked up the monkey and put him on his bed. He took out one of his concussion grenades (used to kill enemy swimmers underwater). Dave held the concussion grenade in his hand, and while holding on to the safety lever, he would repeatedly pull the pin out of the concussion grenade while the monkey watched.

When the monkey started reaching for the grenade, and became upset when Dave would not give it to him, Dave realized that it was time to follow through on the final phase of his plan.

Dave picked up the monkey, and placed the monkey inside an old heavy safe, with the concussion grenade and a flashlight that Dave turned on so that the monkey could see inside the safe.

Dave closed the door to the safe, locking the monkey inside. Dave then returned to the card table. A period of time had passed without any further event, and while everyone was playing cards, they all had forgotten about the monkey inside the safe until they were all startled by the sound of a muffled explosion, "Whump!"

Dave smiled and said, "That's the end of that monkey's thieving days!"

Chapter 77

Dance of the Flaming Asshole

I have conducted intensive research on this subject, and I can conclusively say that the significance and origin of the "dance of the flaming asshole" is widely unknown.

Once in a great while SEAL team guys will get together for a wake or to just to raise some hell, and to release a few demons. There are times when things might appear, to the average person, to be getting out of hand. Let me assure you that among all the SEAL team guys present, everything appears perfectly normal.

One day/night at a team bar in Coronado, Calif. (it is called a team bar because it is a place most of the SEALs frequent) drinks were flowing after we had all received word that five of our brother SEALs were killed when the helicopter that they were flying in was shot down by enemy fire. It was the first time that so many SEALs were killed at one time, and sadly, it would not be the last.

For the average person that might be present at one of these SEAL team wake parties, you might be in for a shock, or two, or three. SEAL team wake parties are for the guys in the SEAL teams to celebrate the lives of their lost brothers and tell funny stories about them. Given the atmosphere, anything could happen with the mass quantities of booze being consumed at the bar or on the floor.

Things were getting rowdy as we were all slamming down our beers and whiskey, sharing our funny memories about our fallen SEAL brothers, and toasting to them. It was then that one of the SEAL team guys came out of the bathroom. He was naked, and he had a long strand of toilet paper stuck up his ass, and the far end of the toilet paper was on fire. Everyone was cheering the dancer as he danced around the entire bar naked, with the toilet paper stuck up his ass and on fire — that is except for a couple of non-SEAL types and their dates, who were seated in a booth at the end of the bar.

I guess they were offended, because they had called for the police. When the police arrived, they told our dancer to put out his toilet paper fire, and put his clothes back on. As he did, one of the SEALs lit the last bit of the toilet paper hanging out of the dancer's butt, and burned the dancer's ass. It was nice to see the cop laugh, and say that we were all insane. You don't call it the dance of the flaming asshole for nothing. We explained to the police officers that this was a wake for our fallen team-mates who had been killed in battle.

It turned out to be a great night, as we were all ordered to leave the bar by the police. As we left the bar, we decided to take refuge on the small grassy center median, and we started to sing SEAL team songs, as once again, the flaming asshole danced around for us to see.

Again, the police arrived, and they ordered our "dancer" to put his clothes back on or we would all be arrested. Fortunately, our dancer complied, and while he was putting his clothes back on, one of the police officers was overheard saying to his partner, "These guys face death way too often to take anything like being arrested seriously, so let them have their fun, as long as they don't hurt anybody!"

Upon hearing this, we all yelled out, "Hooya Police Officers!"

It is so sad that those days are long gone.

Chapter 78

The Environmentalist Killer

On an island out in the Pacific Ocean where we conduct some of our basic and advanced training, there is a large population of goats, which from time to time threatens the existence of a rare fox that lives on this island. Because of this situation between the goats and the foxes, once in awhile we (the military killers who are much hated by the environmentalists) are called upon to do their dirty work for them by thinning out a herd of goats, while under the direct supervision of an assigned environmentalist.

As it would happen one day, while our platoon was conducting some training on the island, we got word to meet an environmentalist that had arrived on the island, and he was waiting at the airport for us to pick him up. This environmentalist informed us that we were tasked to kill off some goats that threatened the rare fox's environment. So, we went down to the armory and checked out two M14 rifles, and an M60 machine gun with a few hundred rounds of ammunition. We loaded up our truck with all our weapons, ammo, and gear to include the snobbish environmentalist, and we all headed out to where the goats were doing their grazing on the sides of the cliffs.

It was a beautiful day to slaughter ugly enemy goats that are a threat to the cute friendly foxes; just like any geo-political war, we were directed by someone else to do their killing for them. I always felt that if you ever wanted to see an end to any war, let world leaders fight world leaders or those in political office fight others in political office. However, it seems like it is always those pompous asses who sit at their desks in their air-conditioned offices, who are the ones who direct people like us to do their killing for them. To me, killing these goats was not unlike genocide, but I guess the führer of the environmentalists knows what is best for the goats and the foxes, although I doubted that all of the goats that we were going to kill shared the environmentalist's point of view.

Killing goats is not a real challenge for any Navy SEAL, so we would try to shoot at their feet to make them jump on the sides of the cliffs, lose their footing and fall to their deaths on the rocks below. (Come on, anyone can kill a goat. The real challenge is to make the goat kill himself).

As we were helping these goats to kill themselves, the environmentalist was keeping a count of our kills and filming us as we did his killing for him. This whole situation started to piss me off, because who knows where this film would end up, or if it would be used to make the military look bad in some BS environmentalist propaganda film that this asshole created.

I walked over to the environmentalist, and I asked him if he had ever fired a weapon before, and he said, "No." I asked him if he would like to fire our machinegun. He said, "Sure, if you don't mind." No, not at all, I said. I gave him a quick briefing about the safety of the weapon, I also instructed him on how to load and fire the machine gun. I gave him an area to shoot at that was away from the goats.

Like anyone who fires the M60 machine gun, he was impressed with the ease and accuracy of the weapon, and that feeling of power that it gives you. I told him to take aim on one of the goats. He said, "No, I can't do that."

"Sure, you can," I said, "just think of the goats as members of the US military, aim and pull the trigger. Besides, we won't say anything." He looked at one of the goats for a long time and said, "Well maybe just this once."

When the environmentalist fired the machine gun and killed one of the goats, we all cheered, saying, "Great shot, you are a natural!" A look came over his face, as if he was somehow possessed, and he started firing the M60 machine gun, and killing more goats.

The way the environmentalist was firing that M60, you would have thought that all those enemy goats were overrunning our position. One of our guys picked up the environmentalist's video camera, and without the environmentalist knowing it, our teammate started filming the environmentalist killing all the goats.

After the environmentalist left, we all had a good laugh thinking about that environmentalist going back to his headquarters and showing the film to the rest of those bleeding-heart environmentalists, with him at the end of the film starring as the primary killer!

Chapter 79

Pulled Over by a State Trooper for Flying

While completing two months of advanced training in the California desert, a few of us decided to go to a city called Brawley to do a little celebrating (well, maybe a lot of celebrating). Making the eighteen-mile trip into Brawley always required a quick stop at the local store for a few beers (a case) to assist us on our long journey. Heading down the highway in a military pickup truck, the four of us (two in the front and two of us in the open bed of the truck) were enjoying our beers as we sped down the empty 111 Highway into Brawley.

Once we pulled up to our favorite bar, we got out and went inside. Cori's Place was a great spot to unwind, drink, and have fun with all the locals. We would always bring a few Cyalume lights to throw around and impress the girls (I know, but remember this was over 30 years ago). Once we drank our fill, it was time to make the long trip back to our base out in the desert. We purchased a case of beer for the trip back, and Walt and I climbed into the open bed of the pickup truck while Doug and Berry got into the front.

Doug was driving his usual 100 miles per hour down Highway 111, making it difficult at times for any of us to drink a beer. As we were drinking, I noticed some red lights flashing up ahead of us, and when we got alongside the vehicle with the pretty flashing red lights, I saw that it was a California State Trooper. I guess the state trooper was in a hurry, but he could not have been in that much of a hurry, because we passed him. I could just imagine the look on this state trooper's face as we passed him doing over 100 mph. Of course, the trooper chased after us, and with his loudspeaker, he was yelling at Doug to pull over. To my amazement, Doug pulled over on the side of the deserted desert road.

As the State Trooper got out of his vehicle and started walking towards us, Walter said, "Evening officer, nice night for a desert drive, isn't it?" He paid no attention to Walter or me drinking our beers in the back of the pickup truck, and continued up to the driver's side to where Doug was sitting behind the steering wheel. The trooper asked Doug if he was in the military (as we were driving a military truck). Doug said that we all were in the military, and the trooper asked Doug for his driver's license.

Doug handed the State Trooper his pilot's license, and the trooper responded, "Yes, this is why I pulled you over, for flying! Step out of the vehicle, please."

Doug got out of the pickup, and the trooper asked Doug if he had a driver's license, to which Doug said no. The trooper asked if we had been drinking to which I replied, "Does a bear shit in the woods?"

Walter said, "A Polar bear doesn't." Again the trooper was not amused, and started to tell Doug that he was going to be subjected to a sobriety test. Walter said, "That's not fair, Troop, Doug didn't have time to study!"

As the trooper was explaining the rules of the test, he was interrupted by Berry. Berry was standing next to the Trooper, and peeing on the ground next to the trooper, and laughing his slow hearty laugh as his pee splashed onto the trooper's shoes. By this time, we were all standing around the trooper with our beers. The trooper asked Doug, "Who the hell are you guys?"

Doug told the trooper, "We are all Navy SEALs."

The officer said, "Don't you know that you could all get killed, drinking and driving?"

Doug said, "What's the difference, trooper? Die here; die over there; sooner or later we all die!"

The trooper looked at all of us and said, "I want you all to give me your word that you all will get back into your pickup truck and follow me back to your base, and if you don't, I will take all of you straight to jail!" We gave the state trooper our word, and we all got back into the pickup truck and followed the trooper back to our base camp.

When we got back to the base, the trooper asked to see our officer in charge, so we went and woke him up. The trooper explained everything to our officer, and said that if he had not lost his brother in the war, he would have taken all of us to jail.

Our officer passed on his regrets for the trooper's loss and said that he would not allow us to leave the camp. We all thanked the trooper, and he left, saying that next time our asses would belong to him. Thanks again, trooper!

Chapter 80

A Navy SEAL's Wife... "Help, I'm Going to be Arrested!"

When you are in the SEAL teams, it is hard to keep any secrets from the other SEAL team members whom you know. One day while I was standing duty on the quarterdeck, I got a telephone call from Joe's hysterical wife. It seems that there were a couple of police officers in her home that were going to take her into custody for an apparent hit and run on a vehicle that was parked at a 7-11 store. She told me that her husband left four days ago for guard duty out at one of our remote training areas, she does not have her husband's van, and could I please hurry to get in contact with her husband, as she did not want to go to jail.

I asked her to put one of the police officers on the telephone, which she did. When the police officer answered, I asked the officer to explain the situation to me, and he said that a woman fitting her description was driving a van. The van backed into a parked vehicle at one of the 7-11 stores and sped away, but not before the owner of the damaged vehicle caught a glimpse of the driver and wrote down the license plate number. "The owner of the damaged vehicle called our station, and when we ran the plate, it came back to this residence, and this woman fits the description of the driver of the van, so we are going to arrest her for felony hit and run."

I asked the officer if he could please hold off arresting her for about 5 minutes while I call her husband who is out at one of our remote training areas, and I would try to get to the bottom of this. I told the officer that I would call him right back. He said that he would, but only for about five minutes, and whether I called back or not, she was going to be arrested.

I got on the radio telephone and contacted her husband, Joe, who was the camp guard out at the training camp, and explained to him about the two officers at his house that were going to arrest his wife for felony hit and run with his van. Joe told me that he loaned his van to one of the prostitutes that he frequented, and he said that she could use his van as a form of payment. It was the prostitute who was driving his van, and not his wife.

I called the officer back and explained the story to him; he told me that he needed to speak to the husband. I said sure, I would put him on a conference call as it was going through a radio relay to a telephone, and we could all listen in (except Joe's wife).

When Joe got on the telephone, he pleaded with the officer not to arrest his wife, or tell her about the prostitute. After all, the prostitute was driving his van and not his wife. The officer asked if he knew where his van was, and Joe gave the officer the prostitute's address. The officer assured Joe that he would not arrest his wife or say anything as long as his story checked out. If it was true, then his van was going to be impounded as part of their investigation. Joe thanked the officer and said goodbye. When Joe's wife came on the line, she asked me what I had said. I told her that it was just a simple case of mistaken identity, and a misread on the license plate.

She thanked me several times for helping her out. I told her that I would call her husband and let him know about her misfortune. She said that she was sure he would get a good laugh about the whole thing. Oh yeah, I am sure that she is laughing now. Because Joe filled his marriage with improprieties, it was only a matter of time before Joe's wife would catch on to his foul lifestyle.

While Joe was on a deployment, Joe's wife sent him a porn tape to watch. On the tape was a title, "For your entire Platoon's enjoyment." Joe ran the movie for his entire platoon; there were two guys and a woman wearing a full mask with fancy feathers. If you were thinking it, you were right... at the end of the tape, she took off her feathered mask and said, "Hope you enjoyed it, it is the last time you will ever see me until we get to court!" As everyone was aware of Joe's evil lifestyle, Joe's platoon was laughing about the tape and the payback that he got from his wife. However, Joe was not laughing and as of this writing, they have been divorced for many years.

Hey Joe... Aren't paybacks sweet? Well... Perhaps not for you, but you did earn it.

Chapter 81

You're on the News

When you serve in the SEAL teams as a SEAL, you always want to stay away from the NEWS people as much as possible. The reason is that the NEWS people, for the most part, have their own self-serving agenda, and they could really care less about the real truth of what matters in their stories, or the events that "they" are reporting about, because it is their network ratings that rule, and not the real truth. After all, there is nothing like the sight of blood, guts, and gore to get the attention of the viewing audiences. The truth about what happened doesn't really matter; what matters is that everyone tunes in to their network to see all that carnage, and anyone that was a part of or responsible for it.

When I was deployed overseas as an advisor/trainer, I was returning from one of our many all-day training evaluations at the rifle range with a group of commandos. I was stunned as I watched this female reporter and her cameraman running up to confront me. I guess she thought that she had the scoop of the year, when she looked at me and said into her microphone, "Here we have it, positive proof that US troops are engaged in combat operations in this country! What do you have to say about it, solider?"

First off, I was thinking, I am not a soldier, and I was also thinking that I would like to take that microphone and shove it up her arrogant ass. I looked at her, and in a calm voice I said, "If you would please shut off the camera, and the tape recorder, I would like to make a statement first, and then I would be glad to give you an interview with me." She looked at the cameraman and told him to shut it off. I asked that he place the video camera on the hood of their vehicle with her recorder and microphone.

Once they both had done what I had asked, I turned to my men and said, "Arrest them, and put them in the holding area for prisoners of war." My men did what I asked, and they escorted this NEWS team away. The NEWS people were screaming and yelling obscenities at me as they were pushed into the back of the troop truck, and were transported to the enemy prisoner holding area.

I knew that these NEWS people were not authorized to be in our training area, because I had not received any contact from our military group commander about NEWS personnel visiting my location. So

I picked up their video camera, and I took out the videotape and ripped the tape to pieces. I took out my 9mm pistol and shot a hole through the lens of the video camera; I then shot several more holes in the body of the camera itself. I picked up the reporter's audio recorder and tore out all the audiotape, and I smashed her tape recorder to pieces (it felt so good).

I was so pissed off at these NEWS people and their preconceived opinions, and their willingness to distort the truth in order to discredit US military personnel without first obtaining any facts. I thought about just leaving them in the prisoner holding area for a few weeks without notifying anyone in my chain of command about them.

As I was in a generous mood (and they were Americans — although, in my opinion, of the lowest form), I called the US embassy military group commander to report that I had two NEWS personnel in custody, and that I was holding them in our prisoner holding area. I also wanted to find out who these people were, and if they were given any special permission to be in my operational training area without first notifying me.

I was informed by my contact within the US embassy, that they did not have any permission or clearance papers to be in my operational area, and that a helicopter was going to be sent down to pick them up. I was further informed that once they were back at the US embassy, they were going to be processed out of the country for violations of their agreement with the US embassy.

I asked my contact if he could please delay the helicopter until nightfall, as I had them both inside an enemy prisoner holding area, and it would be a shame to release them so quickly. It was agreed that the helicopter would arrive just before nightfall.

I went to the enemy prisoner holding area where the reporter and cameraman were. I informed them that their video and audio equipment was being examined by the host country, and that they were both in violation of the armed force's agreement act with the host nation (whatever that was, but to me, it sounded good).

They both started yelling at me about the freedom of the press. I looked at them both and said, "This is not America, and your freedoms do not apply here. For your information, you are both going to be brought before a military tribunal and put on trial for propaganda crimes against this government. The supreme military commander of this base is preparing confession statements for the both of you to sign. Should either of you choose not sign these papers, the commander advised me that the both of you will be taken by helicopter to a remote area where you will both be shot for sympathizing with the enemy, which in this country, just like in America, is treason."

The reporter said that I was full of shit, and that I was the one who was going to be in a lot of trouble for imprisoning them. I left them and went to see the base commander. When I arrived at the base commander's office, I told him what I had said to both of his unauthorized guests, and what I had planned for them about the helicopter. We both had a good laugh about it, and the commander could not resist going over to the enemy prisoner holding area to see them.

When the commander arrived at their cells, he started yelling and cussing at the both of them, and accusing them both of being enemy sympathizers, and that they had both committed high treason against his government and the people of his country. The commander told them that they were going to be flown to a remote area by helicopter where his execution squad would be waiting for them, and that after they were executed their bodies were to be left there to rot as a warning to all other enemy sympathizers. The base commander cursed at both of them again, and told his guards if they tried to escape, shoot them!

You should have seen their faces as the reality of the situation began to sink in. They had a complete change of attitude. They were now pleading with me to help them and to call the US embassy to let the embassy know where they were. I said, "You belong to the commander of this base now, and not the US embassy. You have no clearance papers to be here, you have been convicted of high treason against this government, and there is nothing that I can do for either you." When I turned to leave them both, they were in tears begging me, as a fellow American, to please help them.

After about three hours, I got a radio call informing me that the helicopter for the journalists was inbound; I went back to the enemy prisoner holding area with four armed guards. I opened up their cells and told them that I would escort them to the helicopter pad and take any last statements that they might want to give to their families.

They climbed into the back of the covered truck with the four armed guards and when we got to the helicopter pad, they climbed out of the truck, and stood there with their faces full of fear. I asked if they had any last words before they were to get onto the helicopter, and flown to their execution point. They were both crying and pleading with me to please save them. The guards motioned for them to get moving towards the helicopter.

The reporter and the cameraman were both begging me to please help them, and that they would do anything for me if I would just help them (what a difference it makes, I thought, when THEY are the ones who need the help of the US military). I said, "I have done everything that I can for the both of you. Now get on that damn helicopter, and try to die with some dignity."

The guards escorted them to the military helicopter, and as the helicopter crew was strapping them in with their safety harnesses, they saw that the helicopter crew were members of the US military. They both looked at me and started yelling. I could not hear what they were saying because of the loud sounds that were coming from the helicopter's engines.

I did, however; completely understand both of their middle fingers that they were waving at me. I thought, Ahhh, it is so nice to be appreciated, and good riddance to a couple of complete losers!

Chapter 82

West Coast SEALs vs. East Coast SEALs

No humorous stories about the SEAL teams would ever be complete without a little light-hearted slamming between each coast. Awhile back, I made a statement about how training (back in the day) was harder on the East Coast than it was on the West Coast. Mainly because of how cold it could get on the East Coast. I mean, how could anyone ever compare three-mile ocean swims in the winter on the East Coast to three-mile ocean swims in winter on the West Coast of sunny southern California?

First off, on the East Coast, during the wintertime, you have to break the ice along the shoreline just so you can get out into the deep water to swim. On the West Coast, they have to decide on what sun block to wear with their cool designer sunglasses that are built into their diving masks.

On the East Coast, a 5-mile run consists of running five miles through the deep forest, and then out onto the soft sand. On the West Coast, a five-mile run consists of running to the Starbucks for a double latte grande, and then running over to the Hotel Del Coronado to talk with the babes sitting around the swimming pool.

On the East Coast, the Pentagon wakes up at the same time as the SEALs at Little Creek, VA. On the West Coast, the Hollywood SEALs get to sleep in for three more hours to get ready for their SEAL calendar photo shoot. That is ok with the SEALs on the East Coast because when Pentagon needs SEALs for a mission, they call the East Coast first, because the Pentagon knows that the SEALs on the East Coast are always up and ready to deploy for any tactical mission, and the only photo shoot that East Coast SEALs do are the ones to confirm the enemy terrorists that they have killed.

The beer is always colder on the East Coast than it is on the West Coast, and both coasts can all agree here that the only thing that is colder on the West Coast, are the hearts of all the single or married women who have ended their relationship with a U.S. Navy SEAL.

Chapter 83

Finding Spies in All the Right Places

After returning from a long mission, while deployed to an Island in the Pacific Ocean, the guys in our platoon decided to have a great time by going up to the officers' club. Now granted, we were not officers, but the enlisted club was a complete waste of time when it came to "hunting for talent." The reason for this was because, on the weekend on this tiny island, there were about 150 guys inside the enlisted club, and about 20 females. (Why is it never the other way around?)

However, at the officers' club the odds were a lot better, because there were only about 30 officers for 20 females, and the ladies who visited this particular club were on the hunt for fly boys (pilots). As military uniforms were optional at the officers' club, and no one asked for our identification, we got in easily.

We all saw enough combat pilot movies to BS our way around any conversation that we were engaged in with the ladies. Robert was going on and on about his low level flying at night over the jungle, and coming back with parts of trees stuck in his fuselage.

"Oooh weren't you scared that you would crash?" one of the ladies said.

Robert replied, "Nah, I had a parachute!"

We were all having a great time drinking with the ladies and telling BS stories when a guy joined us that none of us knew. This guy Oscar asked if he could join us, and we all shrugged our shoulders, "Sure." Not feeling comfortable, Oscar said that he was an A-6 pilot. As I was an A-6 jet engine mechanic before I became a Navy SEAL, I took the lead on keeping this guy on the defense. To my surprise, he did not know much about the mechanics of an A-6 jet. I mean, he did not even know what kind of engines it had, because when I made a statement that the J59 engines were fantastic (in fact, they were J52s), he agreed with me!

As the night wore on, we all became even drunker, and more suspicious of whom Oscar really was. I guess Dave could not take it anymore, so Dave challenged Oscar to produce his military ID. Oscar declined, and he tried to excuse himself from our table. Paul looked at Oscar and said that if he tried to get up and leave that he would break both of Oscar's legs.

It was at this point that the ladies got up and left our table. Now, it was only us, and our newfound friend Oscar, who oddly enough was not displaying any fear at all. I looked at Oscar and asked him directly, "Who are you and what are you doing here?" Oscar just smiled, sitting there saying nothing.

Robert found the officers' club mascot (a cat), and was holding the cat by the scruff of its neck. Robert then produced his KA-Bar knife, and while standing next to Oscar, Robert started to shave the hair off the cats' belly, saying, "This is what we are going to do to you if you don't start talking, pal."

Oscar just folded his arms in front of him and continued to smile. It was all Robert and Dave could take. Robert grabbed Oscar's hair, and shoved the cat in Oscar's face. The cat clawed the crap out of Oscar, and Dave came around behind Oscar and pulled out Oscar's chair, and then threw Oscar on the floor.

All the officers came running over to our table, but they stopped when they saw Robert and his KA-Bar knife. Dave was kicking the crap out of Oscar on the floor saying, "Smile you asshole! Keep smiling!" Oscar was bleeding from the cat, and he was beyond smiling at this point, as were we all. The base SPs (Shore Patrol – Military Police), came running into the officers' club, and tried to break up our pounding of Oscar. When they saw Roberts' knife, they all pulled out their pistols and instructed Robert to drop his weapon.

Robert dropped the knife as requested, and the shaved cat, which took off like a bat out of hell with all of its fur flying — what was left, anyway. Dave kicked Oscar one more time before looking up at a pistol aimed at him. Feeling that this was all about to go bad for us, I told the military police that Oscar was trying to obtain classified information from us, when a cat, which Robert tried to pull off Oscar's face, had attacked Oscar. The only reason that Robert had the knife was to protect himself from the cat, and Dave was trying to kick that crazy cat off Oscar's face just when they came in.

At the time, I thought that it sounded good (must have been the beer). However, we were all arrested, and taken to the military stockade (jail). In the wee hours of the morning, our platoon officers came into the jail area to see us, and after exchanging a few custody papers we were released into their custody. We were later informed that the person named "Oscar," was indeed a spy who had been under surveillance, and that we had just blown eight months of undercover work.

The good thing was that we were not going to be charged with impersonating officers (not that we would want to, other than to impress the babes). We were all to be fined 500.00 for disturbing the peace (something that we were good at), and carrying concealed weapons (KA-Bar knives). Overall, it was not a bad night, except for our poor officers, who once again had to stand on the carpet of a high-ranking officer to explain why they cannot control a few loose cannons in their platoon! Yes, we were to be punished for our sins.

Our next deployment was to Australia, and we were confined to the barracks. We were told by our officers that because they got their butts chewed out for our actions, our punishment was going to be no drinking, no bars, and no women. It sucked to be us, but we earned it!

Chapter 84

The Harder It Is, the More Painful It Gets

Sometimes, when a SEAL member is wounded, depending on the location of his wound and how he got it, it can be a lot of fun for the rest of his SEAL teammates. As it would happen, during a combat patrol mission in a far-away contested area of the world, Bob had to stop and answer one of nature's calls. It was while Bob was taking a crap that an enemy solider shot Bob in the ass. You have to admit that this particular enemy solider has the same warped sense of humor that almost all SEALs have.

After the firefight was over, and all of the SEALs had been extracted by boat, Bob was treated for his gunshot wound by the platoon corpsman. When Bob arrived at the field medical hospital, he was to learn the true extent of his injuries. The bullet had entered his right butt cheek, striking his pelvis bone, and continued on its path, exiting out through the side of his penis.

In order to save his penis, the doctors decided to send Bob back to the United States where a specialist would be able to treat the severity of this kind of wound. Before Bob arrived at the hospital in the States, the rumor was that an enemy sniper had shot off his penis. When Bob had finally arrived stateside, a friend informed him that his girlfriend had left him for another guy because he no longer had a penis. (Heck, it might not have been big, but I am sure it made Bob happy).

After the surgery on Bob's penis was declared a success by the doctors, those of us that were in the States went to the hospital to see him. Bob told us that the doctors had to stitch up the entire length of his penis with 132 stitches. Of course, we all asked to see it, but it was all wrapped up with bandages that Bob did not want to remove just for us. We were all laughing and having a great time making comments about Bob's penis until the nurse came in and told us that Bob had to rest, and we would all have to leave.

The next day a few of us went back to the hospital to visit Bob. Bob asked the nurse how long he would have to wait before having sex. The nurse said that it would be several more weeks, because if his penis were to get hard, it would tear the stitches and possibly reopen his wound. After hearing what the nurse said, we told Bob that we had some other places that we had to go to, and that we would see him again much later.

When we got down to the first floor, we all started laughing about an idea that we had: we would all go to downtown San Diego and pick up a prostitute for Bob (oh yeah). When we arrived at our destination, we picked up a prostitute, and we asked her if she was willing to indulge us in a practical joke. She said yes, and it would cost us 100.00 dollars for one hour. We asked her if she had a nurse's uniform, and she said, "Of course." So, we took her to her apartment where she changed into the nurse's outfit, and we all went over the plan as to what we wanted her to do.

When we got back to the hospital, we escorted our nurse up to Bob's room, and we told her that we would wait just outside his door while she went into Bob's room to do her "performance." Surprisingly, we did not have to wait long before we heard the loud screams of pain coming from inside Bob's room. Hearing Bob screaming, we all went inside and there was our nurse totally naked, and sensually playing with her body right next to Bob. Bob's penis was erected and oozing blood from his stitches, and of course, he was in a lot of pain from all the stitches tearing at the skin of his penis, as the harder it got, the more painful it got.

Bob's screams, however, did not go unnoticed by the real nurses who were working on the hospital floor. When the real nurses came running into Bob's room to see why he was screaming, they were astonished to find a totally naked woman next to Bob's bed, and not so astonished at seeing all of us standing there laughing.

The real nurses were extremely pissed off at us, and they started yelling at our "nurse" to put her clothes back on, and for all of us to get the hell out of Bob's room before they called the Shore Patrol (military police).

We told Bob that we would see him tomorrow, and that we were glad to see that his pecker was still in good working order. Bob did not respond to us as he had more pressing matters, laying there on his back moaning in pain, while the real nurses tended to his wounded, bleeding penis.

Chapter 85

Old SEAL Team Guys vs, Young SEAL Team Guys

In the SEAL teams, the old SEALs always love how the young SEALs strut their stuff without any thought as to where the older SEALs might have been or what they might have done. Take a squad of seven men, two old SEAL team guys with five young SEAL pups/new guys, and sooner or later the young SEAL pups will try to flex their muscles around the old guys to impress them.

Out in the desert, our squad was formed to evaluate how long it would take a seven man SEAL squad to patrol to a target, which in this case was a surface-to-air missile launching site, conduct a reconnaissance of the target, and then blow it up. After this, we would all patrol out to our designated pickup point. We were given five days to complete the mission. The one stipulation to this mission was that we were to start the mission with all of our water canteens empty. Any water that we needed, we were to "find" along the way if we wanted anything to drink.

We were to commence our mission after we all drank as much water as possible, and our urine was clear of any color. To start our mission, we were inserted thirty miles away from our target area, with food, our combat equipment, radios, and no water. At 5 pm, we were dropped off at our insertion point, and we patrolled fast for about two hours before we took a short break.

It was during this break that the young SEAL pups let their alligator mouths overload their tadpole asses by saying to Bucky and me, "Do you think you two old guys will be able to keep up with us?"

"Yeah, we don't see any walkers out here that you two old guys can use."

"Hey, if you two old guys get tired, we can carry you the rest of the way."

Bucky and I looked at each other and nodded. We looked at the young SEAL pups and said, "Wait here, we are going to scout around for any signs of water." When Bucky and I got far enough away, we sat down and discussed a plan to put these young SEAL pups in their place. It was a simple plan really: we were going to patrol non-stop to our target in one night. We both knew that we would also be hurting, but in the end, it was going to be worth it.

We arrived back at the location where we had left the young SEAL pups and said, "We didn't find any signs of water, so let's go." We were all patrolling at a fast pace, and we were not (according to our plan) going to take any breaks to look for water, eat food, or rest. It was not long before we heard one of the young SEAL pups say, "Are we going to stop and search for water?"

"No, keep moving," Bucky replied.

A short time passed, and yet again, another young pup said, "Can we stop for a short break?"

"No, we are going to keep moving," I said.

We were covering a lot of ground and if this had been a real mission, we would not be this careless, but as we were not in a foreign country and there were no real "bad guys," we stuck to our plan to punish these young smart asses. A couple of hours had passed, and one of the young pups said, "I need a break, can we stop?"

Bucky circled up our squad and said, "If you guys don't shut up and quit your damn crying, you can patrol back to the camp and quit. We are going to reach our target by morning, and we are not going to stop for anything or anyone." Bucky looked at me and said out loud, "I don't know what the f--k is coming out of BUD/S these days, but it isn't SEALs!"

We reached our target area just before dawn. We found an area that provided us all with cover and concealment, and I told the young SEAL pups to get some rest at this concealed area (lay up point), while Bucky and I went out and scouted around the area for any signs of water or the bad guys.

When Bucky and I were out of sight of the young SEAL pups, we found another spot that offered some concealment from any would-be bad guys. We took off our boots and aired out our feet, moaning and groaning from the pain we were in. We both rested there for a couple of hours and then we patrolled out to find some water. As luck would have it, we found a small crevasse that had a little water in it. It also had a live rattlesnake, and a dead and rotting jackrabbit covered with maggots.

Bucky killed the rattlesnake, and we decided to bring the jackrabbit as food for the young SEAL pups, so we scooped it out of the crevasse and put it inside one of our plastic bags. Bucky started to laugh as he cut off the head and tail of the rattlesnake and skinned it. Looking at me, Bucky smiled and said, "We're not done with those poor bastards yet." I watched as Bucky replaced the jackrabbit's intestines with the skinned rattlesnake. Bucky looked at me and said, "You and I are going to eat the snake, and nothing else." It was going to get hot out in the desert sun, and the smell from this rotting jackrabbit was going to be a bit overpowering for those young studs.

When we patrolled back to where we had left the young SEAL pups, all but one of them was asleep. Bucky threw the jackrabbit in the center where they all were and said, "This is everyone's lunch." We also told them that we had found some water, and that we would patrol back to it with everyone's canteens after we ate the jackrabbit. The young SEAL pups looked at the jackrabbit inside the plastic bag, and when one of them opened it, he gagged, saying that it was rotten and covered with maggots.

Bucky put on his disgusted face and said, "Is there no end to the whining of you new guys? Billy and I will eat the intestines from this jackrabbit, and the rest of the jackrabbit, you spoiled little new guys can have!"

One of the new guys said, "If you eat the intestines from of that rotting rabbit, then we will eat the rest of that rabbit!"

"OK, you're on!" said Bucky.

Buck ripped out the intestines (rattlesnake meat), from the rabbit and said, "I will cook it up right now, and Billy and I will eat it." When Bucky was finished cooking the intestines/snake meat, the young SEAL pups stared at us in disbelief as we both ate all of it. When we finished our meal, Bucky said, "Give us your canteens, we are going to go fill them up, and while we are gone, you guys eat that rabbit!" We left them to their lunch and headed out to the spot where we found the water.

When we got back with everyone's water, we saw that they had burned the rabbit to a crisp before they ate it (hey, at least they ate some of it). Bucky looked at all of them and said, "One day, we 'old guys' won't be around to care for you young SEAL pups. So you might want to start thinking about listening to us, getting tough, or getting out!"

It was funny to see so many humble heads hanging low. If only they knew the truth! Well, now they do!

Chapter 86

SEAL Team Wives Do Not Sit on the Sidelines

It is not often that you get to enjoy a few drinks with your wife while out on the town, mostly because guys in the SEAL teams are gone so much. One night while my wife and I were drinking at a local pub, a few rude rugby players from the bar next door, which served only beer, kept coming into the bar where my wife and I were, whooping it up and interrupting us with crude remarks.

The rugby players were drinking shots of tequila and running back to the beer bar to watch their game on the television. They repeated this process until one of them became belligerent, and pushed an old man sitting next to me off his bar stool. I helped the gentlemen back up onto his chair, and told the rugby player to apologize to the man whom he pushed off the chair.

The rugby player looked at me and said, "f--k off!"

So, I went back over to my wife and said, "Please just sit here. I will only be a moment; just sit here, ok." I walked up behind the rugby player who had pushed the elderly gentlemen on the floor, and I punched his kidney as hard as I could; when he went down, I was facing the other four rugby players.

As all of them jumped me, they were all trying to get a piece of me. They knocked me down and kicked me in the head. I grabbed the leg of the guy who was kicking me, and I bit a huge chunk of flesh out of his leg and spit it out. He screamed in pain and held his bloody leg where I had bitten him.

When I got up off the floor, I heard the screams of a familiar woman. When I turned around, I saw my wife on the back of one of the rugby players. She was like a wild woman, scratching and punching the rugby player's head (I was truly impressed).

I kicked that guy in the nuts as hard as I could, and he went down. As my wife climbed off his back, I told my wife to go back to the bar and stay out of the way. She looked at me and said, "Are you crazy? There are three left!"

I said, "I cannot fight them if I am concerned for you! Now go!" (Team wives do not like to sit on the sidelines.)

The guy that I bit came at me again, so I choked him until he gave up. Having had enough, they picked up their friends and left the pub.

My wife said, "Oh look, honey, a gold chain necklace! It must have come off one of them during the fight." My wife handed it to me as a souvenir.

The next day, my wife and I were again sitting inside the same pub. We both watched as two of the same rugby players came in and were asking about a missing gold necklace. I turned to them (with the necklace displayed around my neck) and said, "What did it look like?"

He stood there with his bandaged leg, looking at me, and said, "Forget it; it's not worth that much." They both turned and left the pub.

Chapter 87

Enlisted SEAL Pranks vs. Officer SEAL Pranks

There was a time at SEAL Team 1 when most of the enlisted men were pulling all kinds of pranks around the cities of Coronado and Imperial Beach. In Coronado, the enlisted guys would go into the town and remove several Stop signs. They would then place them at the top of the Coronado bridge (both ways); they spray painted a thick white line on the road with the word STOP AHEAD. They also mounted several STOP signs about every 50 yards on a stretch of highway from the hotel Del Coronado, to the entrance of SEAL Team 1.

There were a bunch of enlisted SEALs that got together and spray painted signs which read, "Beach closed due to nuclear submarine radiation leak." They mounted these signs every 50 feet along the silver strand beach in Coronado. This got the attention of the local authorities who went on the local NEWS network to announce that there was no such radiation leak, and that this was a hoax perpetrated by some juveniles.

One day, when we were all coming into work at SEAL Team 1, we looked up to see a huge billboard of a gorilla climbing the Empire State Building. This billboard was once on top of the movie theatre in Imperial Beach. This billboard was 50 feet high and 100 feet long!

Now, this was a major feat because not only did "they" have to get it down from the movie theatre without getting caught, but also they had to transport it all the way to SEAL Team 1 from Imperial Beach, and mount it on top of the SEAL Team 1 building, without getting seen or caught!

I looked at Jim and said, "Whoever did this is better than any of us!"

It was then that Lieutenant Holler asked me, "What did you say Billy?"

I said, "Whoever did this is better than any of us, sir!"

Lieutenant Holler smiled and said, "Billy that is the difference between a high school education, and a college education!"

As we were all smiling and conceding to the fact that the officers had truly outdone our enlisted pranks, our commanding officer looked up at the billboard and said, "Whoever did that has 30 minutes to remove it!"

It was nice to see the guilty officers disappear, and the other officers cover for them by having an "all hands" run down the beach. The billboard was removed while everyone went for a run, and the guilty parties were never caught. Hooya Officers!

Chapter 88

Tampons Inside Your Canteens

Some SEALs can be lazy when it comes to carrying their own weight in the field. They will try to mooch off the other SEAL platoon members because they do not want to carry the extra weight of water or food for themselves. In a SEAL platoon that is going on a training or combat mission, every SEAL is loaded down with all kinds of special equipment, their individual primary and secondary weapons, bullets, explosives, grenades, flares, individual medical supplies, food and water.

So, when I saw Mike sneaking a drink of water from another platoon member's canteen while we were sitting around on a break, I got pissed off and told Mike to drink his own damn water and don't steal from his teammate. As we were all going to be patrolling in the desert for the next five days, you would have thought that everyone would have brought enough water for the time that we were all going to be out in the desert.

It was not long before I saw Mike asking one of his teammates for a drink of water, and that was it for me. I walked over to Mike, and I asked him, "What the f--k is wrong with you? I told you to drink your own water and not your teammates'."

Mike looked at me and said, "Chief, I did not bring any water with me."

I was astonished at this statement. I looked at Mike as if he was speaking Greek, and I said, "Why would you not bring any water with you on a five-day operation in the desert?"

Mike looked at me and said, "Well chief, I thought that we would find water along the way."

I could not believe his response. I said, "Where were we going to find water, Mike? The wells have been poisoned; I don't see any drinking fountains out here or any 7-11s. I'll tell you why you did not bring any water; it is because you did not want to carry all that extra weight, so you decided to sponge off your teammates instead. Well let me tell you what is going to happen now. You are going to die because no one in this platoon is going to give your sorry ass any water, and I had better not catch any of you giving Mike water, you guys all got that? I want him to die!"

My reasoning for denying Mike water was simple enough. Mike was shorting his teammates of the vital water supplies that they would need to live and stay operational. As Mike thought nothing of this, and he was only thinking of himself, it sufficed that he and everyone in the platoon knew that I wanted him to die for his lack of compassion for his fellow teammates, and his shameful irresponsibility.

The days were hot and the nights were long as we patrolled to our target area. Mike was starting to show signs of dehydration, but I couldn't care less. During one of our breaks, my platoon officer asked me, "How long are you going to allow Mike to suffer chief?"

I said, "Sir, before we departed on this mission, I checked all of the men's gear. I knew that Mike did not have water in his canteens. So I put extra canteens of water in my backpack just for this occasion. When I see him get to the point where he realizes that he put his teammate's lives in danger, I will give him the canteens of water that I have been carrying for him."

My officer smiled and whispered, "You're getting soft, chief."

The next day, Mike approached me and said, "I am really sorry chief. I know that I screwed up, and by drinking my teammates' water it puts their lives in danger. Please chief; I got to have some water."

I looked at Mike, and I said, "I will give you some water, but the next time that you do something like this, I will just shoot your sorry ass." I took off my backpack and took out the extra canteens of water that I was carrying for him, and I said, "Here, keep these, they are especially for you." Mike took the canteens and thanked me.

When Mike opened one of the canteens and tried to drink the water, nothing came out of it. Mike said, "Hey chief, the water inside this canteen will not come out."

I said, "That's because I put tampons inside both canteens before I filled them with water. If you want to drink, you have to pull on the string, you pussy!"

Everyone laughed, and my officer said, "I take back what I said about you going soft, chief."

It was a learning experience for everyone, especially for Mike, as he got a silent reminder that he was a pussy for not carrying his own water every time he pulled that tampon string and drank from his canteen.

I do not know how women walk around with those things inside of them without looking like they are dried-up mummies! Those things sure do absorb a lot of water!

Chapter 89

Freeze to Death

There was a time, in the late 70s, when a SEAL platoon was near the end of their deployment, all the members of that platoon would be placed in isolation and given a briefing on a threat that they were going to have to deal with. As our platoon was near the end of our seven-month deployment in the Philippines, we were placed in isolation and given a briefing on the current threat to the US. It would seem that those insidious shits, the Kabulize, were going to attack a facility in the USA, and it was our mission to stop them. We were told that we would receive sealed orders onboard a C-130 aircraft, and once airborne, our officers would open the sealed orders, and we would all know our target area and our mission.

Once we were at 30,000 feet, our officer opened the package that was marked "Top Secret." He started to read the orders, and from the look on his face, we all saw that we were going to be screwed. It would seem that these Kabulize were going to attack an airfield in Alaska, and our mission was to parachute into Alaska, about 300 miles north of Nome, and take out a platoon of the enemy Kabulize before they reached their designated target.

We all read the orders and could not believe the stupidity of our mission. A platoon of SEALs that had spent seven months in the jungles of the Philippines, where the daily temperatures were in the 90s, was going to jump into Alaska in the dead of winter and in an area where the temperatures were in the minus 60s! After cursing the higher-ups for their obvious stupidity, we all opened up the containers that were placed onboard the aircraft for us. We found that we were each supplied with olive-drab overcoats (so much for camouflage) that had sheepskin linings, wool socks, ball caps, leather gloves with wool inserts, metal thermal canteens, pup tents, down sleeping bags, rubber boots, and C-rations ("C" means canned, and there was enough food for 16 days in the field for each of us to carry). Of course there were our usual mission supplies like our parachutes, communications equipment, batteries, night-vision scopes, compasses, maps (that were just about useless), weapons, ammo, flares and smoke grenades that we would need to carry with us.

After our officers and platoon chief formulated a plan of attack on the Kabulize, we all sat around preparing the equipment for our mission and tried to figure out exactly who the idiot officer was that thought up this training exercise. The pilot onboard the C-130 gave us a weather update for the location into which we were all going to parachute. It was reported to us that there was a storm front moving in and the temperature on the ground was minus 67 degrees. When we were 30 minutes away from our drop zone, it was time for us to suit up. We put on all of our cold-weather gear and then our parachutes. Each of us attached our combat equipment bags that contained all of our food, water, medical supplies, batteries, electronic equipment, ammo, smoke grenades, tents and sleeping bags, etc. As I was the radioman, I had all the extra radio batteries, antennas, the platoon radio, plus all the other common equipment. Everyone's backpack (contained inside a combat equipment bag) weighed about 120 pounds; mine was the heaviest at 175 pounds.

The good thing about being the heaviest member in the platoon was that you got to jump out of the aircraft first. When it came time for all of us to jump out, we all lined up on the back ramp, and the jumpmaster yelled, "GO!" I took two steps and slipped on some hydraulic fluid that was on the ramp, and I fell over on my back and then rolled out of the back of the aircraft. The harness from my parachute wrapped around my leg and when my parachute opened, I thought that my parachute harness had ripped my leg off. I was slowly falling to the earth under a nicely opened parachute; however, I was upside down. My platoon members were yelling out very supportive words of encouragement to me like, "You are SO screwed Billy!"

"You are going to DIE Billy!"

"Hey Billy, why can't you jump like a normal person?"

As the ground came closer, I knew that I was going to hit hard. I could not let down my combat equipment bag because the lines were now wrapped around my neck. So if I did lower my combat equipment bag, I would have hung myself. I watched as the ground came closer and closer, I tucked my chin into my chest and waited for the impact.

When I came to, our platoon corpsman was asking me if I knew where I was, and I replied, "On the ground." I slowly got up and surprisingly, the only thing sore was my neck from the impact. We buried our parachutes, and after we moved away from our drop zone, we all sat down to try to figure out where we were. We all took out our maps, because we were in a hilly area that was all white and snowy, and when we looked at our military maps, except for the vertical and horizontal lines, it looked the same. We tried to get a compass bearing, but we were so far north that there was a 26-degree variation in our compasses (this meant that if you had to walk on a bearing/direction of 90 degrees, your line of error would be either 116 degrees or 64 degrees. As there was no such thing as GPS at that time, it was also somewhat amusing).

The snow was powdery and only about two feet deep, so walking was not very difficult. We patrolled for about three hours before taking a break. It was funny when we took off our hats and we could create a steam cloud over our heads, and when we were sweating, our sweat would freeze and we would flick it off our faces at each other. Those of you that went through cold-weather training (we did not) are shaking your heads, because you know things are very wrong here. Well, just wait, because the story of this mission gets a lot better/worse!

We found that we could not rest in one spot very long because it was too cold. This was also due to the fact that our clothes were wet from sweating and walking in the snow; our clothes would freeze like cardboard, and the only way to stay warm was to keep moving. The steel thermal canteens that they gave us for this mission were useless, because all the water inside our canteens was frozen solid. So, whenever we got thirsty, we ate the snow.

As this was a combat training mission, there were no fires to be started to melt the snow because we did not want the evil Kabulize to see or smell any fires. When we finally got hungry, we opened our canned rations of food. We ate the frozen food inside their metal containers by chiseling it out of the cans with our K-bar knives. After patrolling for sixteen hours, we found a secure area to set up our tents. This was hard to do with those leather gloves, so we took them off and used our hands in the minus 67 degrees temperature. After our fifth day in the field, things were getting bad for us. We did not know where we were, our communications were wiped out every time we had our scheduled communications contact because of the Aurora Borealis (this is an ion storm the makes communications on high-frequency radios extremely difficult because it affects the ionosphere).

We were all starting to get leg cramps from exhaustion, lack of food, water, sleep, and we were all urinating dark brown. To make matters worse, we were now in a full-blown blizzard. I got out my HF radio and tried to call our base, but all I got was some radio station in Ohio that was playing "You Make Me Feel Like Dancing" by Leo Sayer. None of us felt much like dancing, so we kept moving hour after hour, and exactly where we were patrolling would be anyone's guess. I felt that we were all in bad shape, so I suggested to our officers that I turn on our emergency radio that had a homing beacon in it. Our officers agreed, as this was no longer a training combat mission, and it had turned into a very real mission of survival.

The snow was falling hard, and we were now pushing our way through waist-deep snow. It was difficult to see, but stopping to pitch our tents was out of the question, as we all had a fear of falling asleep and freezing to death. We all took turns leading the way through the deep snow, when suddenly I saw two trucks in front of me. I yelled out, "Ok guys, load up the trucks!"

I was later informed that I took off my backpack and fell on top of it as I tried to load it on the trucks that were not there. I had also stopped breathing, and our corpsman was giving me mouth to mouth resuscitation. When I came to, I heard the sounds of a helicopter. God bless the US Coast Guard! They had picked up our emergency radio beacon and followed it until they found us.

We were all checked into the hospital in Anchorage, Alaska for dehydration, minor frostbite injuries, and stupidity. As my frostbite was a bit more severe, and as I had stopped breathing and was knocked out from my parachute landing, they wanted to keep me for a few days for observation.

It was at this hospital and after a few X-rays that I was informed that I had fractured my neck on that parachute landing. It was a hairline fracture, but my stay at the hospital just got extended.

Because the hospital was overcrowded, I was placed in a ward with patients who suffered from severe cold injuries and who had a few mental problems. When you are in a military hospital, the nurses would conduct roll call every night. As the head nurse was calling out names and waiting for a response, she called one guy's name several times, but he did not answer. She walked over to his bed and yelled at him, "Why don't you answer when I call your name?"

He snapped back at her saying, "Just where the hell do you think I am going to go?"

When she had turned and left the ward, I got up and walked over to this guy that yelled at the nurse. I saw that he was an elderly gentleman and said, "Hey pal, why did you give the nurse a hard time?"

He looked at me and said, "See this tent over my legs? They put this stupid thing over my legs because I don't have any f--king legs! So, if I don't have any legs, just where the f--k do they think I am going to go?"

I started to laugh at his logic, and I said, "My name is Billy."

He started to smile and said, "My name is Rusty." As we were both staring in silence at his tent for a few moments, Rusty said, "You know, I wish I had a beer!"

"Well," I said, "I think that can be arranged. I'll be back in a few." I left the ward in my medical PJs and went across the street to the enlisted club. As I had no money or clothes, for that matter, I asked one of the soldiers sitting at the bar to buy a couple of beers for my friend and me over in the hospital.

He looked at me and asked if I was from the Psycho ward. I looked at him and said, "What's the difference between getting medicated in the Psycho ward or in this bar?"

The gentleman slowly nodded his head, and he said, "Good point."

I brought the beers back over to my ward and toasted my new legless friend. Rusty asked me how I came to be in the hospital, and I told him my story. Rusty laughed and said "God, you guys are a bunch of dumb asses!"

Laughing at his remark, I said, "You have an eye for the obvious, Rusty!"

I asked him how he lost his legs, and he said, "I didn't lose them, you stupid twit, they cut them off." As I was laughing at his retort, he explained that he had lost his legs while climbing Mount McKinley. They were frozen so badly that they had to cut them off.

I looked at him and said, "You're a dumb ass! I would have waited for summer to make that climb, or better yet, not at all!" He just smiled and said, "Everyone has 20/20 hind sight after a mission, but if an old Marine wants to feel alive, he needs to be challenged, and that mountain was my challenge."

I smiled at him and said, "I can understand that. I guess now you've got the biggest challenge of your life."

He laughed out load and said, "You got that right! Everyday is a f--king challenge!" We finished our beers, and we departed company, smiling.

I was to find out later from an old Marine friend of Rusty's that came to visit him in the hospital, that Rusty was awarded the Navy Cross for his acts of heroism during the Korean War. I wasn't surprised. Semper Fi, Rusty!

Chapter 90

Leave Your Ass Behind

As a testament to the volunteer spirit and nature of the SEALs, many years ago there was a SEAL that I knew, who not surprisingly volunteered to be picked up by the Fulton surface-to-air recovery system out in the Salton Sea area in California.

Those of you who are unfamiliar with the Fulton surface-to-air recovery system, allow me to summarize. The Fulton surface-to-air recovery system is an extraction method. The person to be extracted wears a special harness; a take-up line is attached to your harness and to a balloon that is filled with helium floating about 500 feet above you. A specially designed C130 aircraft flies in to grab the line between you and the balloon.

When this happens, you are catapulted straight up about 100 feet before you start to move forward with the aircraft. It is at that time that you are slowly reeled inside the aircraft. You should also know that the person who is being reeled into the aircraft cannot wear a parachute, because if the parachute was deployed while attached to the take-up line, the person being reeled into the aircraft would be torn apart by the force of the aircraft pulling one way, and the parachute pulling the other way.

Sammy would volunteer for anything that he had never tried before. So, when our SEAL command put out the word asking for a volunteer to be picked up by the Fulton surface-to-air recovery system, Sammy jumped at it.

The operation was to take place out in the Salton Sea area of California. When Sammy arrived at the El Centro air base, he received an in-depth briefing on the Fulton surface-to-air recovery system. After his briefing, Sammy asked if his bowels had any possibility of flying out of his ass when the C130 aircraft picked him up. The air operations officer said, "No worries there, as there has never been any reported cases of that ever happening, but if it ever did happen, it would make for great film."

The night before Sammy was to patrol out to his pick-up point with a few of us, Sammy called his wife and spoke with his two little girls to tell them that their daddy was going to catch an airplane with a rope and fly up to it, and then climb inside. Sammy's daughters were so excited and said, "WOW Daddy, are you going to be like Superman?"

Sammy replied, "No, Daddy is just going to be a SEAL, I will see you all tomorrow night ok? Be good girls for Mommy, and Daddy will bring you both something nice."

When Sammy hung up the phone, we all looked at Sammy and said, "Awww, such a good daddy you are."

Sammy looked at us and said, "Screw you guys, now let's get some sleep. I got a plane to catch tomorrow."

The next day we patrolled with Sammy out to the pickup point and when we arrived at the designated position, Sammy put on the safety harness and inflated the balloon. Sammy let the balloon go, which was attached to the take-up line. Sammy sat down on the ground and waited for the C-130 aircraft to fly in and snatch him up. While Sammy and the rest of us were waiting to see if his bowels would indeed fly out of his ass, we all decided to sit on the ground next to him and play a game of cards.

As we were all sitting there enjoying our card game with Sammy and he was losing, off in the distance, we heard the familiar sound of the C130's aircraft engines. Tom looked at Sammy and said, "Hear that Sammy? That's the sound of the Grim Reaper coming to get your ass!"

Sammy smiled and said, "I will open a case of whoop-ass on Mr. Grim if he messes with me."

Tom laughed and said, "Oh yeah? Hard to give what in about one minute you aren't going to have. But don't worry Sammy; we will be here to scoop up your intestines for you!" As we were all having a good time teasing Sammy, the field technicians started the cameras rolling to record the event as the C-130 was going to fly in a racetrack pattern over the Salton Sea area while it reeled Sammy inside the aircraft. We all started to laugh, and we waved goodbye to Sammy when we saw the aircraft snag Sammy's take-up line.

It was really cool to watch Sammy take off like a bat out of hell straight up in the air. On board the C-130 aircraft, the cameras were also rolling. Sammy looked cool flying on the take-up line outside of the aircraft at about 180 mph as he was being reeled into the back of the C-130 aircraft.

Just before he was brought inside the C-130, the main support line attached to Sammy's safety harness came loose, and as Sammy started to fall away from the aircraft, he was filmed flipping off the air crewmen with both middle fingers as he fell towards the earth at 150 miles an hour.

As we were watching from the ground, we all watched in disbelief as Sammy fell to his death in the Salton Sea. The impact was both swift and horrific. Sammy hit the water at about 150 mph a good half-mile away from us. As we watched Sammy hit the water, the sound, when it reached us, just like Sammy, will never be forgotten.

It is times such as this that all officers hate to be in command, as it was the duty of the commanding officer to go see Sammy's wife and two daughters, to inform them that their father and loving husband, had been killed.

Epilogue

The men who perpetrated the events in this book in their time, as they are now, are all true professionals in every sense of the word. It amuses me that this group of men known as the U.S. Navy SEALs can be so cold-blooded when the need arises, and at the same time find humor and compassion in the face of extreme adversity.

I would venture to say that most of the SEALs my age were trained differently than the SEALs of today. Not that we were trained any better, but we were certainly subjected to harsher training methods both in the physical and verbal sense. I think this would explain why there are stark differences between how SEALs of today pull off their practical jokes. It would be extremely difficult for a SEAL of today to get away with what we got away with back in my day.

Today's SEALs are held to a higher standard of professionalism, and they are under the microscope way too much to get away with all the crap that we did back in my day, not that they won't or don't try.

Several former SEAL team members in this book have passed on due to some sort of illness from God knows what or where. A few have lost their lives because they carried their swords into battle a few more times than they should have (it is true that the body on the inside will always feel younger than the body on the outside), as they were killed by some roadside bomb built by a cowardly terrorist.

As an old WWII veteran once told me "No one needs door gunners after the war, so what do you expect warriors to do? The only thing that warriors know how to do... look for another war." It comes with the territory of being a SEAL, and after all, being a SEAL is the only profession that most of us cared to know.

In Retrospect

I know lots of SEALs that, when asked, would tell you that they have had a full life (and they are in their 30s and 40s!) They did their job because they loved/love their country, their families, and their teammates. They did not join the SEAL teams to earn medals; most of the SEAL team guys whom I know rarely wore them, let alone talked about them. They are men of honor with a deep sense of loyalty and duty.

After all is said and done, most SEALs have seen, felt, and done things that few people on this planet will ever dream of. I believe that SEALs live more in one lifetime than most people would if they were given two lives to live. That old saying that, "Most people pass through life, but few people truly live life," applies to the guys of the U.S. Navy SEAL teams that have lived/are living their lives. As most SEALs burn the candle of life at both ends, perhaps this too explains why a good number of SEALs die in their late 60s. They are like shining stars in the night, burning ever so brightly, and then they are gone.

For some of you, you may think that being a U.S. Navy SEAL is cool, and you may want to seek that profession. If you do, you will NOT find it an easy life or path to follow. Knowing the serious nature of a SEAL's job, and all the realities that come with it, I can tell you that being a U.S. Navy SEAL is far from being cool. It has always been easier to destroy than it is to create. Your life, and the lives of your brother SEALs, will be in jeopardy almost on a daily basis. You should aspire to be the best at whatever your chosen field/career is, but more importantly, you should aspire to be a noble person with honor.

It may be true what Thetis said to her son, "If you marry and live an ordinary life, you will be remembered by your sons and daughters, and their sons and daughters. However, in time, you will be forgotten. Such is the fate of all ordinary men."

However, and thankfully, there are thousands of "ordinary" men and women out there, and they are the unsung heroes, who on a daily basis, help people, save lives, care for a special child when others would not, fight the good fight for others who cannot, keep their word when they give it, and tell the truth, even if it means their demise.

To those Heroes... I will always lift my glass in respect.

Closing Remarks

Now that you have read the many stories within this book (and God knows how many there are left untold), I hope that you have gained some small measure of appreciation, and gained some insight as to why SEALs pull pranks, tell funny stories about those who have been injured or killed, and why SEALs, in general, look to find humor in tragedy. I have no deep philosophical explanation what it means to be a Navy SEAL. However, after reading all of these stories, one can assume that it is a life filled with sacrifice, honor, and brotherhood. For most of us who are/were Navy SEALs, it means serving with honor and with the greatest guys on earth.

There may be a diversity of reasons as to why SEALs find humor in tragedy. However, the majority of the reasons might just be that for those of us who have served/serving in the SEAL teams, death has become all too familiar. We do not hate or fear death, because we all know that one day death will come for us, and take us home to see all our brothers that have gone before us.

Those of us who have served/are serving in the SEAL teams keep our brothers alive within others and within ourselves through the stories that we all share about each other. I (like other SEALs) do not want our brothers to feel sorrow for us should we be personally wounded killed, or die of natural causes. We just want to be remembered for what we did together, and the fun times that we all shared as brothers in the SEAL Teams.

As members of any U.S. Navy SEAL team, we all know that it is/was an honor, and a privilege, to serve our country. We also know that fighting for freedom leaves a taste in the mouth that the protected will never appreciate.

There are a few who will even ridicule us for our service to our country. Those who ridicule our chosen career will never know how much was sacrificed, or all the footprints that we left behind on countless accomplished missions on their behalf, so that we ALL may keep our rights to voice our opinions, and to live free.

Acknowledgements

To ALL the Frogmen and SEALs that have gone to the other side ahead of us, let us never forget them, and let us honor them by telling their funny stories as often as we can, and to all who will listen.

To all those whom I have come to know and call my brothers or friends (very few that you are), to those of you who have dedicated your time and efforts to encourage me to write this book.

To those of you who assisted me in the structuring of this book, and kept me focused on what it was that I was trying to achieve with my writing, I thank you for your blunt honesty.

I give a very special thank you to:

NavySEALs.com for their version of "History of the UDT and SEAL teams."

The SEAL Foundation - nswfoundation.org

The Navy SEAL Museum - navysealmuseum.com

The UDT SEAL Association - udt-seal-association.org

Lida E. Quillen, for her faith in the publishing of this book - twilighttimesbooks.com

To Enio Rigolin, for his insight about writing and the type of business this is, and to Stan and Dorothy Cheslock for their insight and support.

To all of you who have read or purchased this book, I thank you. If this book made you smile, cry, or reflect on what a life of a U.S. Navy SEAL is like, and to open your eyes to the fact that those who are or have been U.S. Navy SEALs are not just professional killers, then I have achieved my purpose in writing this book.

About the author

William Allmon is a retired Navy SEAL and honorably served his country from 1969 to 1993. He retired as a chief petty officer, and is a combat veteran of three wars. While in the SEALs, Mr. Allmon participated in numerous covert and overt missions around the world in support of US and foreign governments, militaries, and other official agencies.

Order Form

If not available from your local bookstore or favorite online bookstore, send this coupon and a check or money order for the retail price plus $3.50 s&h to Twilight Times Books, Dept. LS112a POB 3340 Kingsport TN 37664. Delivery may take up to two weeks.

Name: _____

Address: _____

_____

Email: _____

I have enclosed a check or money order in the amount of

$_____

for _____ .

If you enjoyed this book, please post a review
at your favorite online bookstore.

Twilight Times Books
P O Box 3340
Kingsport, TN 37664
Phone/Fax: 423-323-0183
www.twilighttimesbooks.com/

CPSIA information can be obtained at www.ICGtesting.com
Printed in the USA
LVOW100134041012

301299LV00001B/4/P